Yuengling

Yuengling

A History of America's Oldest Brewery

MARK A. NOON

McFarland & Company, Inc., Publishers

Jefferson, North Carolina, and London

The present work is a reprint of the illustrated case bound edition of Yuengling: A History of America's Oldest Brewery, *first published in 2005 by McFarland.*

LIBRARY OF CONGRESS CATALOGUING-IN-PUBLICATION DATA

Noon, Mark A., 1958–
Yuengling : a history of America's oldest brewery / Mark A. Noon.
p.   cm.
Includes bibliographical references and index.

ISBN-13: 978-0-7864-3758-0
softcover : 50# alkaline paper ∞

1. Yuengling (Firm)   2. Microbreweries — Pennsylvania — Pottsville — History.
3. Yuengling, D. G. (David Gottlieb), 1806–1877.   4. Breweries — United States — History.
5. Brewing industry — United States — History.   I. Title.
TP573.5.Y84N66   2008   338.7'6633'09748 — dc22   2004028966

British Library cataloguing data are available

Cover photograph ©2005 Index Stock

Manufactured in the United States of America

*McFarland & Company, Inc., Publishers
Box 611, Jefferson, North Carolina 28640
www.mcfarlandpub.com*

Contents

A Note on Sources

At one time, writing about beer and other alcoholic beverages was considered taboo. If the subject was tackled, it was usually from the perspective of temperance advocates who addressed the "liquor problem" in order to spread anti-drink propaganda. America's beer makers have suffered from a degree of neglect as well, particularly when one considers the importance the brewing industry has played in the country's economy. Fortunately, that is no longer the case. The social history of alcohol has received more attention from historians in recent years, and more and more articles and books about brewing, drinking and barrooms are being produced. This history of the Yuengling Brewery has taken advantage of recent, outstanding work by researchers into the brewing industry, prohibition and the social history of alcohol consumption in the United States. Particularly helpful studies included those by Will Anderson, Stanley Baron, Leland Bell, Lew Bryson, Eric Burns, Carl Childs, Timothy Holihan, Earl Kaylor, Carl Miller, Madelon Powers, and Gregg Smith.

A great deal has been written about the Yuengling Brewery, but some periods in the brewery's history were harder to document than others. Understandably, the earliest decades of the brewery's development were the most difficult to resurrect. Very few company records from the era of David Gottlieb Yuengling survive. Most of the nineteenth-century information had to be garnered from indirect sources. Early books focused on the brewing industry, such as *One Hundred Years of Brewing* (1903), and newspaper reports in the Pottsville *Miners' Journal,* Pottsville *Republican,* and New York *Times* were helpful. An important study of the company's history was written in the late 1950s by a family member, Edith Yuengling. Her article, "The Story of the Yuengling Brewery," was published by the Schuylkill County Historical Society and documents several important points about the early history of the family business. Researchers note that books and articles produced by temperance organizations and groups favoring prohibition are often biased. The same can be said of commemorative publications, brochures and press releases put out by most companies. Still, such documents in Yuengling's archives yielded important information and interesting details.

Yuengling's recent history is very well documented. The company's success has attracted coverage from a notable variety of newspapers and magazines. In addition to local and regional papers, feature articles about the brewery have appeared in major publications like the *Wall Street Journal,* Philadelphia *Inquirer,* Pittsburgh *Post-Gazette, Forbes,* and *Money.* Industry magazines like *Malt Advocate* and *Modern Brewery Age* have noticed the progress that the Pottsville brewer has made. The Yuengling Brewery has also proved popular on the Internet — and not only on eBay. Beer lovers and Yuengling fans have posted valuable information and photographs online for those surfing between brews.

Acknowledgments

I am very grateful to many individuals who helped make this book possible. The Yuengling Brewery was growing rapidly even as I was conducting research. Still, Dick Yuengling Jr. shared valuable time to answer questions at the brewery or over the phone. Some interviews were quite lengthy, but the company president was always available to assist. In fact, I am indebted to several members of the Yuengling family for lending a hand in a variety of ways, whether responding to e-mails, answering letters, or providing photographs.

I was fortunate to have full access to the historical records on file at the brewery. Several Yuengling employees helped tremendously during my visits to Mahantongo Street and the new brewery at Mill Creek. A special note of thanks to Cleo Logothetides, the curator of the brewery's museum, who shared a tremendous amount of material from the company archives and helped solve several riddles in the brewery's early history. The museum manager, Christine Logothetides, also provided help with illustrations for the book. Important clues to Yuengling's history were turned up in conversations with another person captivated by the subject — David Casinelli, Yuengling's vice president and sales manager. I also benefited from an early morning tour of the old storage caves behind the brewery with brewmaster James Buehler.

I also received tremendous support from the library staff at Pennsylvania State University's Hazleton campus. Michael Kattner, who handled interlibrary loan requests, deserves special thanks for ably locating hard-to-find books and articles and offering suggestions about sources. Also cordial and helpful were staff members Shannon Richie, Ronald Harman, and Lisa Whitish, who not only helped provide research materials, but also dealt with my numerous requests for book renewals. The research was also facilitated by the skill and effort of staffs at the Historical Society of Schuylkill County, the Pennsylvania Historical and Museum Commission, the Library Company of Philadelphia, the Historical Society of Pennsylvania in Philadelphia, and the National Canal Museum, Easton, Pennsylvania. Editors at the Pottsville *Republican* also provided important assistance.

Many others offered very important suggestions and ideas as the book was in its various stages. Among those who answered my inquiries or provided feedback were Dwight Ackerman, Lew Bryson, Thomas Dublin, Chuck Hogan, Jean Harvan, Tim Holsopple, Robert Janosov, Al Kogoy, Garrett Kurtek, John Lieberman, Carl Miller, David Noon, Irene Goldman-Price, Peter Reid, Ray Reu, Ed Schreppel, Leo Ward, Peter Yasenchak, and Edith Yuengling.

My entire family provided continual support and encouragement. The heaviest debt of gratitude is owed to my wife, Helen, who, from the first time I mentioned it, thought a history of the Yuengling Brewery was a good idea. She remained behind the project the entire time. Finally, the book would not have been possible without the inspiration of my mother, Rosemarie (Keller) Noon. Over the years, she has made so many sacrifices, not only for her family, but also for the people of her community. And she always had a way of reminding me that there was a German side to the story.

Introduction

When opening a bottle or can of Yuengling beer, the hand covers an image of an intimidating American eagle, its wings spread wide and powerful beak open. One set of talons is braced on solid rock as the other defiantly clutches a keg of brew marked "Y & S." The magnificent bird of prey — appropriately a symbol of longevity — takes the Yuengling drinker back to the brewery's origins. Brewer David Gottlieb Yuengling came to Pottsville in 1829 and established the Eagle Brewery. Since that time, thousands of American beer producers have closed and faded into obscurity, but D. G. Yuengling and Son, Inc., now marks its 175th anniversary. The milestone raises a significant question: How has this small family-owned business managed to endure to become the nation's oldest brewery?

This book had its origins more than fifteen years ago when I was a reporter for the Shenandoah (Pa.) *Evening Herald*. My editor asked me to write a story about the installation of a new cereal cooker at the brewery, a delicate operation that required the removal of a brick wall from the upper floor of the plant. I still recall lying in the middle of Mahantongo Street trying to get the right angle as I took a picture of a huge crane beginning the process of lifting pieces of the enormous pot into place. Later, I returned to the business to cover the unveiling of a new product, Yuengling Light. As I was catching my breath at the top of the steep staircase leading to the company office, I was welcomed past the old paymaster's window to the large, cluttered desk of Dick Yuengling Jr. The new company president shared with me details about the development of the new brew, in a setting that was a Pennsylvania history buff's dream. I was distracted from Dick's comments by the wood-paneled décor, the antique advertising signs, and (staring down at me) the oil portraits of the four other Yuenglings who had headed the brewery since its beginning. I seemed to have stepped back into the nineteenth century.

Actually, though, the beginnings of this book could go back even further — to my first tour. The Yuengling Brewery is noted for its tours and my first came in the early 1980s. The bartender at the company pub following the tour that day was the previous company president, Dick Yuengling Sr. He was obviously a history lover himself, as he took the time to share entertaining stories about the brewery to a gathering that was clearly enjoying the free samples. The company president could draw on a long history.

Over five generations of family ownership, the company has found itself in some serious battles for survival. The following chapters cast the company as a player in the highly competitive brewing industry, emphasizing two major, ongoing struggles. Yuengling's first major opponent was Prohibition — a word that prompts images of speakeasies, hip-flasks, and tommy-gun-toting gangsters of the "Roaring Twenties." But organized efforts to stop or limit the use of alcohol — and shut down the nation's breweries — reach back to the early nineteenth century. In Pennsylvania, Prohibition forces were forming and launching crusades at about the same time D. G. Yuengling came to the anthracite coal region. That threat to the brewery lingered with varying intensity until the Yuengling Brewery could celebrate the repeal of the Eighteenth Amendment in 1933. The celebration, however, would not last long. In the decades following national Prohibition, the other serious threat to Yuengling's survival gained strength. The threat this time came from the national brewers, who took full advantage of advances in brewing technology and transportation in the late nineteenth and early twentieth centuries. Corporations like Anheuser-Busch, Miller, and Coors grew larger. Hundreds of small, independent regional breweries like Yuengling closed.

The Pottsville brewery did have advantages in its business skirmishes. A part of Pennsylvania history that has faded into obscurity is the commonwealth's prominence in the brewing industry. For many decades, the Keystone State, and most notably the anthracite coal region, led the nation with many successful and widely respected beer-making operations. The Yuengling story cannot be fully told without calling attention to some of the other brands that were enjoyed for decades by the area's beer lovers: Kaier's, Stegmaier, Fuhrmann and Schmidt, Columbia, Gibbons, and Mount Carbon. The list could go on. These breweries were competitors of the Pottsville company, but Yuengling ultimately benefited from the rich brewing heritage evident at both the local and state levels. In the beginning, the Eagle Brewery focused on its home base in Pottsville. It has since, of course, spread its wings to other parts of the country but, as the final chapter of this book illustrates, it always come home to nest with its local populace. In many surprising ways Yuengling mirrors the social conditions of Schuylkill County and the entire anthracite region.

A major focus of the early chapters of this book is the patterns of immigration to northeastern Pennsylvania and the use of alcohol among the German, Irish, and Slavic groups. Drinking is also placed in the context of the occupation that helped lure many immigrants to the region: coal mining. Theories about the origins of the Prohibition movement in America abound. One intriguing theory suggests that efforts to curb alcohol stemmed from class conflicts. The drinking customs of some immigrant groups, brought to the United States from their homeland, were deemed immoral by sober, native-born, largely Protestant Americans. The newcomers needed to be reformed. As one researcher put it, "Temperance was a crusade directed against immigrants and workingpeople, and the strongest opposition came from immigrant workingpeople."[1] An examination of alcohol use in the ethnically diverse anthracite region provides the opportunity to explore this issue. As will be seen, immigrants—principally coal miners—stood in opposition to forces in favor of temperance and prohibition. As a result, they indirectly played a role in the success and longevity of the Yuengling Brewery.

Immigrants also provided a large, steady market for beer. This point, in fact, leads to consideration of one of the most intriguing pieces of anthracite region lore. Usually, after quaffing a couple of beers, some imbibers in coal region taverns will fondly evoke an earlier time, proudly pointing out to their drinking buddies that the area was once a leader in the number of bars that were open for business. Is the claim just barroom bluster? Was Schuylkill County indeed the "wettest" in the nation? Did some anthracite coal communities have more bars per capita than any other place in the United States? An examination of the local market for Yuengling beer invites consideration of these questions.

The Yuengling Brewery's ties to the heritage and culture of the anthracite region could partly explain customer loyalty to the brand—an important issue in the beer industry. Significantly, Yuengling places itself on the side of the people in its home region by emphasizing its family ownership. It distances itself from "corporate" America. And while recent trends point toward a shrinking "blue-collar" market for beer, the beverage continues to be the choice of Joe Six-Pack. "With all of beer's obvious success in all social strata," one social commentator recently noted, "it carries overtones of nose-thumbing at class pretension and high culture.... If wine was about class aspiration, and cocktails were connected with compulsive striving for success, beer ... was about accepting who you are and trying to get by."[2] If beer is indeed the drink of choice among workers just "trying to get by," no wonder Yuengling has been able to maintain a loyal customer base through the generations. Faithful fans of the old brewery look for the local brand when they enter a crowded bar or move among the tall stacks of cases at the beer distributor. Nothing else will do.

The name isn't heard as frequently now, but the people in Yuengling's core market at one time took pride in being labeled "coal crackers." Raised against a backdrop of a difficult, dangerous occupation, labor struggles, ethnic conflict and a depressed economy, "coal crackers" are often noted for their capacity for hard work and resiliency. Difficulties only strengthen their determination to press forward and succeed. The story of the Yuengling Brewery provides the opportunity to consider the work ethic of the region and the response of its people to sharp changes in economic conditions. The Yuengling Brewery stood witness to it all, from the earliest days of the coal boom, when D. G. Yuengling arrived in Pottsville, to the decades when coal was king and the elegant days of the "anthracite aristocracy" at places like Mahantongo Street, to the decline and death of the industry and the resulting economic devastation. On one level, as many of the photographs in this book show, Yuengling employees share the work ethic of the region. Many Yuengling employees stay with the company for decades, some as long as 40 or 50 years. Younger employees are often the sons or daughters of former workers. Through the generations, Yuengling beer has been made through the efforts of many hard-working, dedicated workers who run the clanking bottle line, cork the kegs, give the tours and run the office, or who load and drive the delivery trucks.

This strong, hands-on work ethic has been passed from generation to generation by the descendents of David Gottlieb Yuengling. Perhaps more than anything else, it is a family bond that has kept the brewery going. In the difficult times, those running the company could turn to family members for support. There is a bond that extends to the community, too. The Yuenglings remain one of the leading families in Pottsville and have traditionally played an important role in the development of the city and many of its organizations. Despite their prominence, those who guided the company over the years rarely distanced themselves from the day-to-day operations of the brewery or avoided some of the difficult decisions that came with the making and marketing of beer. In the mid-nineteenth century, one commentary on the life of the brewery's founder described him as a "worker rather than a talker." Is it a coincidence that, several generations later, journalists make the exact same point about the current president of the family business?

When taking that last sip from a bottle or can of Yuengling beer, the hand covers a simple phrase near the script "Yuengling" and the American eagle surmounting a beer barrel. It says, "Since 1829." That's quite a record. But that's only part of a remarkable story.

One

The Pioneer Brewer

"The brewery, brewing, the malt, the vats, everything that is done by brewers...."
— Walt Whitman, "A Song for Occupations,"
from *Leaves of Grass* (1855)

Early in the afternoon of Saturday, September 29, 1877, a melancholy mood slowly descended upon the people of Pottsville, Pennsylvania. Even a visitor would have sensed that many of the city's residents had been touched by something, something beyond the rich, colorful changing leaves on Sharp Mountain and the surrounding hills. In the more affluent sections, prominent citizens noticed a slight chill in the air as they respectfully boarded their horse-drawn coaches. In the working-class neighborhoods, immigrant laborers also noted the hint of autumn as they interrupted their daily chores and solemnly stepped onto the sidewalk in front of their simple dwellings. They all knew the funeral of David Gottlieb Yuengling would be held at three o'clock at his home neighboring the brewery at Fifth and Mahantongo streets. The brewer and community leader had died at the age of 70. Despite enduring the pain and stiffness of rheumatism in his later years, a common ailment among nineteenth-century brewers, he continued to oversee the making of his popular beer. Earlier in the week, he had left the brewery office at the end of another day of work, and a spell of vertigo had struck the elderly man as he climbed a flight of stairs leading into his residence. He would not recover from the injuries suffered in the fall.

The stature of the deceased dictated that the funeral was not a private affair; rather, a public pageantry of woe, typical of the nineteenth century, unfolded. The Yuengling home was a house of mourning. Inside, rooms overflowed with arrangements of fragrant flowers, mostly tuberoses and lilies, limiting the space for those who wished to pay their respects. Outside, black crape and ribbons darkened the doors and windows. Black also blanketed the streets and sidewalks surrounding the home as hundreds of people — relatives, friends, neighbors — respectfully gathered near the red brick structure where traces of the familiar aromas of grain, hops, and yeast lingered. The imposing business they stood beneath — D. G. Yuengling and Son — now stood oddly silent, a monument to the man whose memory was being honored. And the time had come. When the pronouncements over the

deceased were completed inside the home, eight pallbearers gripped the silver han-
dles of the walnut casket and brought it to the hearse that was waiting next to the
tree-lined sidewalk. The large gathering watched wordlessly as the German immigrant passed within the shadow of his brewery for the final time. Still, the spirit of
the occupation he loved did not surrender easily. It shadowed him to his final rest-
ing place.

Brewery workers—including 40 men from competing breweries in Pottsville
and the surrounding area—were among those in a winding procession of over 50
carriages that made its way through the streets of Pottsville to the Charles Baber
Cemetery on Market Street. D. G. Yuengling's grave was located in an appropriately prominent place near the entrance to the cemetery. Once the mourners had
gathered, the community's leading clergymen conducted religious rites. Then, leaders of Pottsville's Masonic lodge and members of the German benevolent association, the Order of the Harugari, presided over traditional ceremonies, offering
moving tributes for a fallen brother. The service broke with traditional form after
the coffin had been lowered and settled. The Yuengling Brewery employees– malsters, grain handlers, kettlemen, vat men, cellar men, icemen, coopers, racking men,
and deliverymen—made a small break with protocol and brought the ritual to its
conclusion in a final act of respect. "The brewery employees then, one by one, took
a last look into the grave of their kind old employer, many of the stalwart men part-
ing therefrom with moistened eyes," noted a newspaper report of the funeral.[1]

On Monday morning, those same workers made their way back to Fifth and
Mahantongo streets as the brewery's steam-powered whistle again resonated
through the neighborhoods of Pottsville and signaled the beginning of another
work day. The community had suffered a loss, but life returned to normal. Yuengling beer was being brewed once again as it had been since 1829. The tradition continued, and that's just as D. G. Yuengling had hoped—even as a young man in a
place far from Pottsville.

Yuengling was an immigrant, but, surprisingly, he might not have considered
himself a *German* immigrant. The history of the brewery extends back so far that
the political entity known as Germany had not formed yet, and most "Germans"
felt more closely connected to smaller states, regions, or principalities under the
political control of different rulers. Yuengling was a native of Aldingen, a small,
rural village located along the Neckar River in southwest Germany's kingdom of
Württemberg. He was born on March 22, 1806, the son of Johann Friedrich
Juengling (the Anglicized version of Yuengling) (1774–1855) and Anna-Maria (Wil-
dermuth) (1771–1847).[2] What brought Yuengling to northeastern Pennsylvania?
Why did he decide to become a brewer? Unfortunately, very little has been written about the young man's upbringing in the Black Forest region of Germany south
of Stuttgart. The same can be said regarding D. G. Yuengling's early experiences
in America. The limited information in existing sources is conflicting as well.

One of the earliest biographical sketches of D. G. Yuengling—written a few
years before his death—states that his father was a brewer and that as a young man
he learned the brewing trade "in his father's establishment."[3] Other descriptions

of the brewer simply note that he was an immigrant from Württemberg. In fact, a Yuengling company document — provided by a church in Aldingen — states that Yuengling's father was not a brewer but a butcher by trade, as was his father, Peter, before him. The occupation indicates a degree of prominence. Meat vendors were respected in German towns and villages, since they owned land and livestock. Indeed, Yuengling's father was also a leader in the community, serving as a councilman. It is possible that Johann, in addition to working as a butcher, developed skills as a brewer, passed the secrets of the trade along to his son, and encouraged him to pursue the craft. German lads typically learn a variety of occupations, and brewing was a pivotal profession in Germany. More specifically,

David Gottlieb Yuengling (1806–1877), the brewery founder. (D. G. Yuengling and Son, Inc.)

the Yuengling family's home region of Württemberg had developed a solid reputation for its production of lager beer.[4]

While questions surrounding D. G. Yuengling's career decision and the extent of the brewing background of the Yuengling family in the early nineteenth century linger, there is little doubt that he learned the craft in Germany before coming to America. In the early nineteenth century, when a young man became old enough to learn a trade, he customarily gained insight into the craft under an apprentice system, first serving as an assistant to a master craftsman and then working as a laborer.[5] In most cases, apprenticeships in brewing were completed at the age of 21. As a young apprentice, Yuengling had much to learn in order to develop the intuition and skill to produce quality beer. In the earliest step, cereal grain was converted into malt for making beer through the process known as "malting." This process involved steeping the grain in water until it absorbed the proper amount of moisture. The grain then had to be allowed to germinate and was later roasted to a desired darkness and consistency. Other stages included the "mashing" process, in which the sugars from cereal grain were transformed into a syrupy liquid called "wort." Next, the "hopping" stage was ready to begin. A brewer-in-training had to be guided through several other steps before the process was complete. Brew kettles were then used to combine the "wort" with hops and boil the mixture to an exact temperature. The brew was then cooled and yeast was added as part of the fermentation stage. Final measures included the "clarifying" of beer before transferring it to wooden kegs.

Successful brewing was often accomplished through trial and error. Without gauges or panels to guide them, early brewers depended on empirical means. Grain,

D. G. Yuengling was a native of Aldingen, a small village south of Stuggart in southwest Germany's kingdom of Württemberg. (This map shows the German confederation in 1815.)

for example, was tested by placing it between the thumb and forefinger and pinching it. Brewing temperatures were determined through a keen sense of touch and skillful manipulation of the open flame beneath the brew kettle. The entire process was much more physically intense than pinching grain and determining temperature. Unfortunately for Yuengling, little or no mechanical assistance was available in the early nineteenth century for completing other tasks. From beginning to end, the process involved a demanding amount of physical labor, and hours—from fifteen to seventeen a day—were spent hauling, dipping, pumping, stirring, and boiling. Because uniformity in beer-making brought about by science and technology was still decades away, the skills learned as a brewmaster's assistant in the early nineteenth century were unique. The young Württemberger developed his own process and made beer that was distinctively his own. His training was concluded when he was barely in his twenties, in 1826, and in a rudimentary journal dated that year, Yuengling was already sketching plans for a brew-house.[6] Although the notes that accompanied the crude drawings were written in German, the brewery he would build would be far from the farmland of his native Württemberg.

D. G. Yuengling faced the question that confronts most individuals at the end of training in their chosen profession: What next? For many young Germans with a sense of adventure, immigration to America was an attractive option. Germans can be counted among America's earliest and most numerous colonizers, and Pennsylvania welcomed them. Notable German settlements were established in the commonwealth starting in 1683, when Francis Daniel Pastorius led Quakers and Mennonites to Germantown. Sizable annual German migration to the Keystone State began in the 1720s, and the German immigrant trade remained strong throughout the century. Pennsylvania's German population stood at about 225,000 by the first American census of 1790 — about a third of the state's population. Census data also describes a majority of residents of Eastern Pennsylvania's Berks and Northampton counties, not far from D. G. Yuengling's eventual hometown of Pottsville, as German.[7]

The decision to immigrate, of course, is very serious and motives vary. A simple yet helpful way to begin investigating the complexities of immigration is to examine the "push factors" and "pull factors." Living conditions in Germany topped the list of "push factors." Yuengling's home region, in the southwestern section of the country, was consistently a major area of migration to the American colonies, largely due to an outdated feudal political system dominated by bloodlines and class structure. In times of both war and peace, people were forced to finance the often wasteful and arrogant behavior of the king in power. Farmers and tradesmen like Johann Yuengling "carried a disproportionately heavy share of this burden, and consequently they and their children became indebted, impoverished, underemployed."[8] In addition, inheritance laws requiring an equal division of parental property among all children resulted in dismemberment of family farms. In many cases, farms became so small that they could no longer turn a profit large enough to support a family. Increased emigration from southwestern Germany resulted.

The chief "pull factor" was the possibility of better opportunity for prosperity and success in America. Emigrants were widely recruited for settlement projects in the eighteenth and nineteenth century, and promotional literature, emigration guides, and newspapers in Germany featured "glowing account[s] of the geographical features, climate, animals and plants, and other notable characteristics of the colony."[9] An attractive, though often mythical, image of the New World as a land of opportunity prevailed. Letters by migrants to relatives and friends in the homelands tempered propaganda by providing a more realistic description of the difficulties encountered in the journey and the initial years of settlement. As a young man with ambitions of starting his own brewery, what may have been most appealing to Yuengling was America's reputation as a "free country." The unrestricted right to conduct business was virtually nonexistent in Germany, but immigrant letters praised America as a place where one could "buy, settle, and borrow without restrictions" and where "all trades and professions are free."[10] Some correspondence warned that financial success in the United States would only come about through hard work, but for Yuengling any negatives were outweighed by positives. The young man proved to be a hard worker as he developed the skills to become a brewmaster, and he had plenty of perseverance, drive, and ambition. More importantly, he had the finances to make the transatlantic journey and start a new life. If he could establish a brewery in the New World, a promising future was on the horizon.

Despite the optimism, feelings of uncertainty and anxiety must have crept into Yuengling's mind in 1828 as he packed his cabin trunk and prepared to say goodbye to his family.[11] There is the possibility that Yuengling did not immigrate alone. He may have traveled with other family members or with a group from his native region. A primary concern must have been the journey itself. The transatlantic voyage from the Rhine lands to America was long and difficult.[12] Since inland travel in Germany was arduous in the fall and winter, most migrants set off in the spring when rivers were navigable. Yuengling's point of embarkation was Rotterdam, and reaching the port city from Württemberg required a trip northward on the Neckar River and then westward on the Rhine. Depending on river conditions, the journey to Rotterdam alone took anywhere from two weeks to two months. After leaving Germany, the masted vessel made a stopover in England and then set sail for America. The time at sea fluctuated according to route and wind conditions and ranged from six weeks to three months.

Yuengling's ship may have been a little less crowded than a typical immigrant ship, because he made the crossing to America in the 1820s when there was a lull in German immigration. Census figures show that a total of 128,502 people immigrated to America between 1820 and 1829, and Yuengling was among only 5,753 Germans (or just 4.5 percent of the total) who immigrated during that time. Still, conditions during a transatlantic crossing were stressful, testing the endurance of all passengers on board, regardless of social class. Hygiene was rudimentary and sickness common. Generally, food was poor, and water had to be rationed. After weeks at sea, Yuengling was no doubt relieved when his ship's destination—Baltimore—finally came into view. German immigrants formed a substantial percentage of Baltimore's population in the early 1800s, and the brewer must have found some comfort in the familiar sound of the German language echoing through the port. He took his baggage ashore after enduring the landing procedures, and somewhere inside the luggage and provisions were the beer recipes that he hoped would be popular in his new homeland. But the young immigrant was about to learn something that he may not have been totally aware of when he boarded his ship: It was an odd time to enter the beer trade in America.

For German brewers in the United States, the 1820s did not offer optimum business conditions. The young nation had, of course, a significant brewing heritage prior to Yuengling's arrival. Native American Indians are credited as the nation's first brewers and records of brewing also exist among English explorers and the Pilgrim fathers.[13] Women in early American families kept beer available through the practice of homebrewing. Outside the home, thirsty individuals looking for beer followed the dirt path to the local tavern.[14] Drawing on a tradition established in England, early American inns were highly respected. They were often operated by British colonists, often the most distinguished residents of the community. Their main purpose was to serve travelers, and by law innkeepers were required to offer their visitors beer, wine, and liquor. Eventually, town officials recognized that the tavern could function as a meeting place for important social and civil activities.[15]

Busy taverns would normally be a positive sign for a brewer hoping to start a business. However, in the early colonial period innkeepers provided a variety of services, and the title of "brewing specialist" was thrust upon tavern owners as well. The arduous process generally took place in the inn's back rooms, amid tubs, barrels, and pails. Not surprisingly, the quality of the beer was unpredictable and often disappointed the tastebuds. Still, as population increased, so did demand for beer. Innkeepers became more and more willing to rid themselves of the inconvenience of having to brew on site and instead purchased the beverage from the growing number of local commercial brewers.

The first commercial beer maker in British North America was the Dutch West India Company in Lower Manhattan, New York, which opened for business in 1632. In the colonies, seventeenth-century commercial brewers were hampered by a scarcity of barley and other grains, as well as by government regulation of the price of beer.[16] Significantly, the market for the beverage in the colonial period was more British than German. A thirsty colonial traveler ordering a beer would most likely be served a draft brewed in the English tradition — an ale, porter, or stout. Imports from Great Britain also helped satisfy America's thirst for these beers. The success of the American Revolution slowed the flow of England's dark, cloudy beverages to a trickle, but the small number of American breweries lacked the size and skill to meet demand. To address the problem, a national brewery was under consideration by Thomas Jefferson, who made and bottled his own brew, and, as late as 1810, James Madison also considered the idea. The concept never took root, and the brewing industry struggled in the young republic.

Several other factors — in addition to proposals for a national brewery — could create the false impression that beer was the most popular beverage in the country in America in the early nineteenth century. Potable water was often scarce, particularly in urban areas. Many people were wary about the quality of water in lakes, rivers and streams and felt it was only suitable for farm animals. The drink was dangerously dirty, and its consumption led to diphtheria and typhoid. In some communities, the local stream was fouled with garbage and human waste, and people would not even think of drinking from it. Milk was an alternative, but it was costly and not always easy to find. It was too perishable in the days before refrigeration. It often harbored germs and bacteria and, like water, caused serious illnesses. Tea cost too much as well. Beer, however, was still not the libation of choice in the United States, despite the drawbacks of these other drinks.

Americans in the Early Republic generally preferred whiskey, rum, and cider rather than beer. These beverages were cheap, more readily available, and served a variety of purposes.[17] Whiskey, for example, was believed to supply energy for difficult physical labor. In addition, because it warmed the body, it was also considered particularly suitable for those enduring the cold northern winters. Distilled spirits were also used by physicians and nurses as an anesthetic and analgesic, as they worked to ease the pain and soothe the sick and injured. Rum was the most popular drink in America in the seventeenth and eighteenth centuries, due in large measure to its promotion by taverns and retail stores. Later, economic changes wrought by the American Revolution and a boost in Scottish and Irish immigrants caused a decline in rum consumption and a rise in the popularity of whiskey and other distilled spirits. Around the time D. G. Yuengling and his immigrant ship sailed across the Atlantic Ocean, distilled spirit consumption was at an all-time high in the United States, with whiskey being the primary contributor. Economic and agricultural conditions were perfect for whiskey production. It was the nation's favorite drink.

More importantly, distilled spirits were cheaper than beer. Brewers were challenged to increase beer's popularity, but German-style beer makers like Yuengling were handicapped by the spoilage issue. Before the development of stainless steel and aluminum barrels, beer was primarily packaged in wooden kegs that were lined with tar to prevent the brew from contracting a "woody" flavor. The standard barrel held 31 gallons, although coopers (barrel makers) also constructed fifteen gallon half-barrels. Few taverns could sell beer in these large quantities, and, as a result, it would frequently turn sour or flat. In contrast to German-style brews, the English-style, "surface-fermented" beers were more convenient for innkeepers in colonial America because they could remain on tap for weeks without turning stale — a true benefit in the thinly populated regions of a developing nation where a glass of beer was only occasionally sold.

Evidence of the depressed state of America's brewing industry and an intense competition for jobs is found in accounts of experienced brewery employees who were having difficulty finding work. A diary written by a contemporary of D. G. Yuengling provides a detailed example. Unhappy with the political climate in Germany, George Herancourt arrived in America from Bavaria on August 27, 1830. Since the brewing season did not get underway until October, he initially had trouble finding employment, despite offering his services to most of the brewers in Philadelphia and Reading. "I asked at some breweries for a job, but all the places are already promised to others. Five brewers alone are expected from Germany and await a job," Herancourt wrote in his diary on October 1, 1830.[18] The German immigrant eventually found temporary work as a malster, but later abandoned the brewing trade. Herancourt was from a fairly wealthy family, but his first years in Pennsylvania depleted almost all of his income. He eventually went west to Cincinnati and, about a decade later, opened his own successful brewery.

Yuengling faced the same frustrating job market Herancourt endured as he began the difficult process of adjusting to life in a new country. The young brewer probably realized very quickly that Baltimore would not be an ideal location to start his business. The needs of the beer lovers in the port city were already being met. Baltimore had a brewing tradition that extended back to 1744 with the construction of the Globe Brewery. By the 1820s, the city had several established breweries providing beer for the city's populace. As a craftsman with the lofty ambition of brewing his own beer, he needed to find a community that needed a new brewery, an area with a solid base of beer customers. He began to move inland, and, understandably, Pennsylvania was his destination.[19] He would continue, however, to deal with a reality that has since beleaguered the generations of his family: There's always plenty of competition in the beer business.

To place the Yuengling Brewery's longevity in its proper context, one need only consider the number of breweries that have come and gone through the decades in Pennsylvania. The Keystone State has a long, rich brewing history rooted in its high number of German settlers. William Penn, the founding father of the commonwealth, gained the distinction of being Pennsylvania's "first brewer" when he opened breweries in the Philadelphia area in the late seventeenth century. By the middle of the eighteenth century, Philadelphia had developed into a leading brewing center, providing beer for cities as far south as Charleston. Other notable beer-making operations sprung up before and after the Revolutionary War.[20] The late nineteenth century marked a boom period in the state's brewing history. At the time D. G. Yuengling made his way through the Pennsylvania countryside in search of thirsty, beer-loving Germans, about 250 commercial breweries operated in the United States. By the close of the century, the Keystone State *alone* boasted more than 300. Census data from 1860, for example, are striking. Yuengling was among 182 breweries operating in the Keystone State. Pittsburgh could boast 30. Philadelphia had 65. In fact, a section of the City of Brotherly Love between Broad Street and the Delaware River would be nicknamed "Brewerytown" for its large number of breweries, its beer gardens, and its vast beer-drinking population.[21] As Yuengling considered his prospects in Pennsylvania, he may have realized that population centers like Philadelphia already had several established breweries. But the young brewer was mistaken if thought he would easily find a profitable location for a brewery in the central counties of the state.

Yuengling and Pottsville are virtually synonymous, so it is surprising to learn that the future Schuylkill County seat was not the first location Yuengling considered for his beer-making business. He traveled first to Lancaster, a significant site of German settlement that would eventually earn a reputation as the "Munich of the United States." A major problem loomed, however. Lancaster was already awash with plenty of beer and ale. In the late eighteenth century, it was an important beer producer, accounting for seven percent of all the beer brewed in the early republic.[22] After an apparently brief stay in Lancaster, the young brewer journeyed to Reading in Berks County, another area with a large German population. But similar business conditions prevailed. Reading was one of America's earliest brewing centers and already had several productive breweries. One of the most celebrated breweries in Reading was also established before Yuengling emigrated — Frederick Lauer's Park Brewery, which opened in 1826.[23] Like many others, Yuengling could

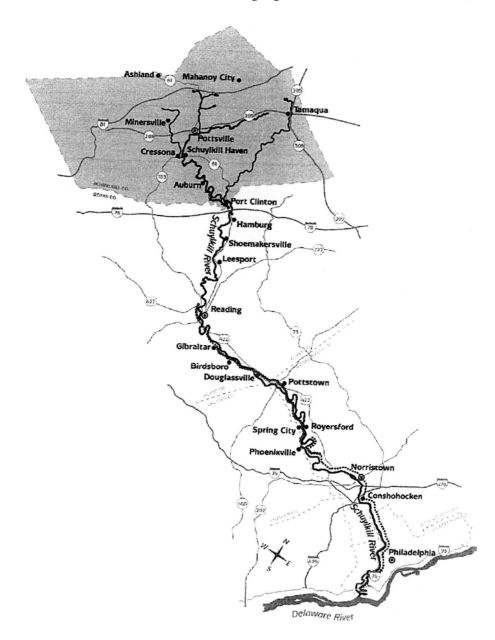

D. G. Yuengling established his brewery in Pottsville in 1829 at the height of the anthracite coal boom. Schuylkill County is Yuengling's primary market. Pottsville's access to the Schuylkill River and its canal system was a key to the community's development in the midnineteenth century. (Courtesy of Schuylkill River Greenway Association.)

have been frustrated to the point of seeking another trade. But his personality was marked by a heavy dose of German perseverance. Soon, a ray of hope broke through the gloom, approximately thirty miles away in the heart of Schuylkill County, Berks County's relatively new neighbor to the north.

Accessibility is a primary concern for anyone hoping to start a successful business. Can raw materials be obtained easily and can the products be transported to markets economically? Still in its infancy, Schuylkill County was beginning to meet these criteria. With the construction of a few cabins around 1800, the county had its first permanent inhabitants. It was officially incorporated on March 1, 1811, from parts of Berks, Columbia, and Luzerne counties. Its most substantial community was Pottsville, which was first settled in 1806 and planned as a town by John Pott in 1816. A horse trail already ran from Philadelphia to Pottsville's neighbor to the south, Schuylkill Haven. Another route, known as the "King's Highway," started at this point. Surveyed in 1770, the road ran through Pottsville to Sunbury in Northumberland County (known then as Fort Augusta). In addition to these roads, travelers on foot or on horseback were eventually afforded another way to reach the lower anthracite region.

From its source in the hills embracing Pottsville until it merges with the Delaware River, the Schuylkill River is relatively short—128 miles long. The waterway's impact on the history of eastern Pennsylvania, however, was substantial. In 1815, the Schuylkill Navigation Company incorporated with the aim of developing a canal system on the river that would link the Pottsville area to Reading and, most importantly, Philadelphia. The canal would not have become a reality without the financial and physical participation of the Pennsylvania Dutch.[24] In what could be considered a promising omen for Yuengling, the initial proposal for the transportation system took place, in all probability, over a few tankards of ale. A group of German settlers, meeting at Reifsnyder's Tavern in Orwigsburg in 1813, came up with the novel idea to petition the state to develop the navigation system so the market for their agricultural products would include the City of Brotherly Love. When completed, the canal started at the mouth of Mill Creek, just above Pottsville. The canal gave Yuengling the accessibility he needed, but to establish a successful trade he also needed a healthy business climate that would attract and retain customers.

Yuengling had ample reason to feel very positive about Pottsville's commercial outlook, thanks to the unearthing of a valuable commodity in the nearby hills several decades earlier. According to legend, that discovery occurred in 1790, when Yankee trapper Necho Allen lit a campfire at the base of Broad Mountain and woke the next day to discover that he had inadvertently ignited an outcrop of anthracite coal.[25] At about the same time, German settlers in parts of what would become Schuylkill County were finding outcroppings of coal when they turned up the soil for their farms.[26] Anthracite coal sparked America's industrial age and kept it burning. In the mid-1820s, word spread about the benefits of the fuel. Homeowners, particularly those in major cities on the eastern seaboard, learned that the clean, long-burning coal was a cheaper fuel for home heating and cooking than wood, charcoal, or bituminous coal.[27] Similarly, metal manufacturers recognized that anthracite was a less expensive, superior fuel for furnaces and foundries. Other companies dependent upon heat-using processes soon fell in line with the trend and adopted anthracite. Even brewers like Yuengling, who needed heat for the production of beer, used it.[28]

The planners of the Schuylkill Canal thought that the transportation system would primarily move general merchandise, but by the time of its completion in 1825, black diamonds were the system's dominant freight. In that year, Pottsville was more like a frontier outpost, with "only fifteen houses, three taverns, three stores, a printer's shop, a post office, and the shops of a few craftsmen."[29] These figures shifted dramatically over the next decade as Schuylkill County's great coal rush ensued:

> Towns and villages appeared virtually overnight. Port Carbon had a single family in 1829; a year later it claimed 912 residents.... Between 1826 and 1829 the number of buildings in Pottsville increased sixfold; its population twenty-seven times. And between 1829 and 1844, the number of inhabitants doubled again. As a transportation center and county seat Pottsville became a prosperous boomtown, its economy bolstered by the canal and railroads, coal mining, iron manufacturing, brewing, banking, and a host of other commercial and mercantile activities.[30]

Remarkably, in a few short years, Pottsville emerged as one of the state's most important cities. Its population stood at 2,464 in 1830, surpassing older communities like Bethlehem, Doylestown, Chester, and Norristown, and approaching the population of cities like Lebanon, Harrisburg, and York. A year later, 4,000 people called Pottsville home.

Any frustration Yuengling experienced in Lancaster or Reading as he tried to start his brewery was forgotten when he learned fortune hunters were flocking to Schuylkill County. The boomtown attracted entrepreneurs from all over the world—including many young capitalists from Philadelphia—who explored the territory with the aid of civil engineers and geologists. The number of people heading north stunned the inhabitants of Reading as they "looked with wonder upon the groaning stagecoaches, the hundreds of horsemen, and thousands of footmen."[31] In 1829, when coal speculation reached its pinnacle, Yuengling loaded his brewery kettle and other belongings onto his horse-drawn wagon (or into his canal boat) and joined the great exodus.

More log cabins may have been the first sign that Yuengling was getting closer to Pottsville, but as he came upon the community's southern outskirts, another reason to be optimistic greeted his ears. The sound of hammers driving nails echoed in the hills as builders worked to meet the demand for housing. The coal rush put the developing community in the midst of a sustained and remarkable building boom. Wholesale lots with as many as twenty homes sprung up. To speed construction projects, builders in Philadelphia framed houses and used canal boats to send the precut structures to Schuylkill County's boomtown. The shipment of the houses created the spectacle of a town floating up the Schuylkill River. Pottsville had several hundred houses by the time Yuengling arrived, many of them quite large. Other encouraging signs included a weekly paper, the *Miners' Journal and Schuylkill Coal and Navigation Register*, and a new bank, Miners National, which had just opened the year before. Of course, as coal speculation continued to grow, so did business. Dry goods, grocery, and hardware stores sold materials for speculators digging area coal mines and also offered supplies to residential customers. Conditions certainly favored a new brewery finding its place among Pottsville's growing list of successful businesses. Getting started, however, would not be cheap. One consequence of Pottsville's rapid growth and lucrative business conditions was skyrocketing real estate costs. Rents became exorbitant. Leasing a two-story building on Centre Street could cost as much as $25 a month, a sizeable sum in 1829. Nonetheless, Yuengling had the resources to set up his business at North Centre Street, a particularly expensive section of town and the site of the present-day Pottsville City Hall.

D. G. Yuengling named his business the Eagle Brewery. The choice is not surprising considering the popularity of the image at the time. Evidence strongly suggests that the eagle image, like the image of the "goddess Columbia," was one of the most important symbols in the early republic. Its use was a phenomenon.[32] The German immigrant probably became familiar with the eagle image as he made his way through Pennsylvania, where the stately bird was growing in popularity. Proprietors of inns and taverns painted the bird of prey on their signs, and many volunteer fire companies adopted the eagle as their emblem. When D. G. Yuengling arrived in Pottsville, he would have been able to find temporary lodging in the Eagle Hotel, located at the corner of Centre and Minersville streets. The two-story frame building was built by Samuel Heffner in 1827, and a brick addition was added in 1830.[33] German-American newspapers in both Reading and Pottsville were titled, *Adler* (Eagle). In Pottsville's neighboring community of Saint Clair, coal operators John and William Johns started opening tunnels for coal in the late 1840s and later named the large mine the Eagle Colliery.

The Pottsville brewer was not the first to adopt the name Eagle Brewery, nor the last. The name "eagle" and the image have been closely linked throughout much of American brewing history. At least 62 "eagle" breweries have been documented, including ten in Pennsylvania alone.[34] Why so many? The most probable reason is that immigrant brewers selected the name in an effort to convey their allegiance to America. Anheuser-Busch offers an example. Brewer Adolphus Busch decided to use the company's familiar A and Eagle logo around 1872 and, in one of the earliest examples of trademark registration, obtained a certificate of trademark for the logo in 1877 from the United States Patent Office. Even company historians have been unable to document the exact reason Busch opted for the image; however, there has been speculation that the eagle was selected "as a mark of respect for America, the adopted country of the brewery's founder."[35] The first brewery named after the stately bird was probably James Vasser's, which operated in Poughkeepsie, New York, in the opening decade of the nineteenth century. Notable nineteenth-century Pennsylvania breweries bearing the name include Joseph A. Lieberman's,

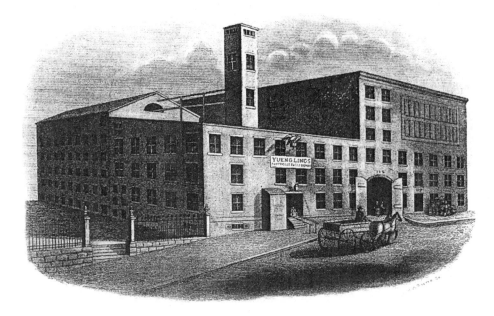

One of the earliest portraits of D. G. Yuengling's Eagle Brewery—possibly from the 1830s. The brewery founder's pride in the name Eagle Brewery is illustrated by the carving of the bird of prey over one of the entrances to the beer-making operation. (D. G. Yuengling and Son, Inc.)

which began operating in Allentown in 1864, and Conrad Eberhardt's, which began operating in Pittsburgh in 1849. D. G. Yuengling's pride in the image is evident in the earliest illustrations and photographs of the brewery. An architectural carving of an American eagle can be easily spotted over one of the entrances to the building.[36] The brewery founder retained the name Eagle Brewery until 1873, when a partnership with his son prompted the name change to D. G. Yuengling and Son. Customers, however, continued to refer to the business as the Eagle Brewery until at least the 1890s. In addition, the company retained the eagle image despite the name change, as it appeared on keg labels, business stationery, letterheads, and advertising. Over the decades, the keg-clutching eagle has remained essentially the same, with only the wings and body changing positions occasionally.

Limited technology dictated that early American breweries were small operations, turning out beer on not much more than a household scale. In Pottsville, D. G. Yuengling managed to roll about five barrels out his brewery door each business day. Limited production, however, does not translate into a life of leisure. The existing early portraits and photographs of the brewer create the false impression that he spent more time behind a desk crunching numbers than among his beer barrels. He is usually formally dressed in a suit and cravat, sometimes standing proudly with his hat and walking stick at Fifth and Mahantongo streets. The tasks Yuengling performed, however, were very strenuous. This was particularly true before 1850, when the use of steam power began to transform American brewing.

Yuengling, just as he had as an apprentice in Germany, spent long hours carefully monitoring the brewing process and inspecting open tanks, kettles, and vats. He did all the arduous work by hand—the hoisting of grain, the stirring of mash, the pumping of water. One description of a typical nineteenth-century beer-maker, published in 1909, accurately reflects what beer lovers arriving at D. G. Yuengling's Eagle Brewery might have seen:

> The German artisan who founded the American beer industry was a kind of special cook with a trade recipe he learned in Germany. He began by boiling beer in small quantities in family kettles or wash-boilers, and often, with his wife, retailed it to a German trade in a small saloon. The man and wife were typical Germans of the working-class—industrious, frugal, honest, and rather unsophisticated.... The old-time brewmaster worked in necessarily uncleanly underground cellars, full of the drip of great ice-houses overhead, and of quantities of carbonic acid gas, sufficient to smother small animals, below; with floors saturated with the organic matter of former brews, and slippery with the molds that grow under such conditions. In this place he tramped—a heavy figure in a slouch hat, course workmen's clothes and high leather boots.[37]

In the first brewing season, about 600 barrels of the beverage were produced. By standards of the period, this could be considered a promising beginning, but there was room for improvement. In 1822, the largest brewery in the United States produced about 250 barrels a day. Even though Yuengling's output was relatively low, it produced a variety of beers and offered a portfolio similar to the company's current lineup: a pale ale similar to the Lord Chesterfield brand, a "strong beer" (a colonial beer with high alcohol content), a "Dunkel-like" (dark) lager, and a dark porter.

Once beer is brewed, it needs to be marketed. Fortunately for D. G. Yuengling, a market for his product was already in place and growing in 1829. More and more German-American immigrants made Pottsville their home. They loved their beer and viewed the local brewery as a vital part of the community. Breweries could be accurately described as "neighborhood" businesses, in which the exact confines of the markets were known and respected. Pottsville's beer drinkers appreciated Yuengling's skills, and, as word about the product spread, a loyal local customer base evolved. This foundation of customers would play an important role in the company's longevity and would be sustained by subsequent generations of the brewing family.

In the initial years following the opening of his business, D. G. Yuengling may have performed the important duty of delivering the beer. Other major brewers performed the task when they opened their own breweries. Adolph Coors, for example, reportedly was seen using a wheelbarrow on Larimer Street in Golden, Colorado, as he worked to cut the transportation cost of his brew during the early years of his beer-making operation. Similarly, Charles Stegmaier, in the opening years of his business, used a wagon drawn by a husky goat to personally deliver each barrel of his beer to customers in Wilkes-Barre, Pennsylvania. Later, once their brewing businesses were financially stable, these pioneer brewers were able to hire help to deliver their finished beer, allowing them to devote more time to overseeing the intricacies of the brewing process. Because the spoilage problem still hovered over the brewing business, deliveries had to be made frequently and regularly. Horse-drawn wagons or pushcarts were the primary method of transporting kegs. The brewer loaded a barrel or two in the morning and made his rounds through the rapidly growing coal town. Local taverns and inns, of course, would have been the first stops. If any beer was left when the delivery route was finished, he had the option of selling his product on the streets of Pottsville. Nineteenth-century neighborhood brewers customarily sold beer by the mug in the center of town to thirsty passersby, tapping the brew from a keg on the back of a small cart. Some also bartered excess brew in the marketplace to obtain necessities for their families.

Improvements in transportation eventually provided Yuengling with a growing number of outlets and customers for his product. Following the Revolutionary War, the horse trail known as the King's Highway improved and became suitable for stagecoach travel. The road became known as Centre Turnpike. By 1829, three daily stagecoaches passed through Schuylkill County, and most communities had at least one "stage tavern" where coaches of stage lines were scheduled to change horses. In addition to offering temporary, overnight lodging to travelers on stagecoaches and Pennsylvania Dutch Conestoga wagons, proprietors of these inns in the early republic also served as stage company agents, posting the latest information on stagecoach and canal schedules. The taverns, as transportation hubs, also became major sites for getting news about events outside the area. These busy, crowded inns and taverns also offered plenty of food, hospitality, and, to Yuengling's good fortune, beer. One probable stop on D. G. Yuengling's delivery route was the White Horse Tavern, which was established in 1818. This hostelry played an important role in Pottsville's early history and was located at the intersection of what is now the busiest intersection of the city, Centre and Mahantongo streets.

In all probability, the number of taverns disappointed Yuengling when he arrived in his new hometown. In 1829, there were only two inns besides the White Horse Tavern, but Pottsville's young businessman must have been pleased as he watched the number of inns and taverns grow with astonishing rapidity. The lure of inns, taverns, and hotels deepened as more mines opened in the region. In a key indication of the area's boomtown status, the number of saloons increased to twenty-five by 1832, and all were doing brisk business. By 1847, Schuylkill County had close to 200 businesses with liquor licenses. Pottsville could claim one-fifth of all the liquor licenses in the county, with at least 32 businesses legally dispensing alcohol.[38] The numbers would continue to grow.

Some were substantial buildings similar to the stage taverns of the colonial period. On the ground floor they featured a large hall or meeting room, a dining area, and a bar with tables and chairs. The larger places could be considered boardinghouses, with rooms for visitors or permanent residents on the upper floors. Eventually, more places that did not offer shelter and sleeping accommodations served beer and liquor. People regularly gathered at the local drinking "club," barroom, or saloon. Rather than travelers, these establishments served a regular clientele from the surrounding neighborhood. Finally, drinks were served in the late hours at the houses of prostitution in the region. These "disorderly houses" were "invariably kept by a woman … and at late hours provided 'nice young men' with drinks and the social services of a small bevy of female boarders."[39]

The anthracite coal boom also led to an impressive number of hotels in Pottsville prior to the Civil War. Some establishments geared their accommodations and services to meet the needs of coal speculators coming to the region. Others could more accurately be described as taverns, since they offered very limited lodgings for weary travelers and their horses. Notable hotels in the early history of Pottsville that were possibly early retail outlets for Yuengling beer included Pennsylvania Hall, William Penn Hotel, Park Hotel, National House and Exchange Hotel, Rising Sun Hotel, and the American House. At least one facility, the Northeast Hotel at 400 North Centre St., catered to a German clientele. In the 1830s, a German immigrant, Peter Woll, transformed a bakery at the site into a tavern noted for its German food and an important gathering place for German immigrants. Clearly, Pottsville's business environment allowed Yuengling to develop a decent local trade in his initial years in the community. Not long after he started his business, however, the young man was confronted with his first serious setback.

Fires were a common problem for early brewers, largely due to the open burning of wood or coal in the beer-making process. One early method of roasting malt, for example, required the brewmaster to place the grains inside drums and then pass the drums over hot coals. In addition, wort was boiled in a large brew kettle over an open flame. The Yuengling Brewery survived a series of fires in the nineteenth century, but many of the company's business records did not.[40] Nevertheless, thanks to newspaper reports, the accidents provide some insight into the brewery's early history. One fire struck in January, 1833, and readers of the *Miners' Journal* found themselves caught up in the dramatic details of efforts to fight the blaze:

> Fire—Yesterday morning some hours before day, a two-story frame building in Mahantongo Street, occupied as a Brewery, the property of David G. Yuengling, took fire and before the flames could be extinguished the greater part of the main body of the building was burnt to the ground. By the well directed rigorous and enterprising exertions of a numerous concourse of citizens who were present, the adjoining part of the manufactory in front was rescued from the devouring element. The loss is not indeed very considerable, exclusive of the building. We understood that about 100 bushels of malt were damaged and destroyed. The only information we can gather respecting the origins of the fire is that it broke out in the upper story. Wood was used as a fuel in this manufactory. We noticed with pleasure the alacrity and promptitude of our firemen in repairing to the spot with their engines and fire apparatus. Their efficient services have elicited the gratitude and approbation of their fellow-citizens, which we trust they will long continue to merit.

The fact that firefighters were joined by "a numerous concourse of citizens" in the effort to save the brewery indicates a developing bond between the people of Pottsville and the relatively new business. In all probability, many of those helping to haul water to extinguish the blaze were German immigrants who wanted to save the source of the beer they enjoyed.

A blaze of less significance (about $800 damage) occurred in 1855 when a worker fell asleep and let the water in the brewery's large copper kettle get too low, but another fire in 1888 serves as a reminder of the hazards of working in a nineteenth century brewery. The account of this conflagration in the *New York Times* also provides an indication of the growing fame of the Yuengling Brewery as the century progressed:

> Pottsville, Penn., Sept. 7. – Fire broke out in the great Yuengling brewery at Fifth and Mahantongo streets this morning. The fire was occasioned by the overflow of a cauldron of boiling pitch in the cooper's shop. John Aller, a workmen [sic], was terribly burned about the head and body. The firemen succeeded in confining the flames to the cooper's department. The loss is not yet estimated, but covered by insurance.[41]

The insurance coverage is not surprising because Pottsville was the region's leader in the insurance trade. In fact, D. G. Yuengling is among those listed in the application to the Schuylkill County Court of Common Pleas for the charter of the Pottsville Mutual Fire Insurance Company of Pennsylvania. In all probability, Yuengling's interest in fire insurance was motivated by his memories of the fires at his brewery. But of all the fires in the Yuengling Brewery's early history, the most extensive and most significant was undoubtedly the first.

In 1831, while still operating at its North Centre Street location, D. G. Yuengling's Eagle Brewery was destroyed by a blaze.[42] Such a loss within two years of opening must have been very discouraging; in fact, many brewers never recovered after their businesses went up in flames. By the next brewing season, however, Yuengling's Eagle Brewery, like the mythological phoenix, rose from the ashes, and relocated to its present site on the side of Sharp Mountain at Fifth and Mahantongo streets. The location is extremely significant. Before prominent families of the Pottsville area began developing impressive properties along the street, the largely undeveloped lane was simply known as Mahantongo Road. The importance of the thoroughfare in Pottsville's history was elevated in 1827 when the founder of Pottsville, John Pott, donated a corner lot at Fourth Street to Irish immigrants seeking to construct the community's first building to be used exclusively as a place of worship. Builders completed a small framed structure — Saint Patrick's Church — in 1828 at a cost of $1,000.[43] In an intriguing twist, Yuengling, a devout Protestant, donated $10,000 to construct Pottsville's first German Lutheran Church.[44] He saw, however, several advantages in the parcel of land next to the recently constructed Catholic church. Above all, Yuengling gained access to a more plentiful source of water, a paramount concern for any brewer.

When a bartender sets down a mug of cold beer at the local taproom, nine tenths of what the thirsty customer is reaching for is water. It is essential to good beer, giving the brew its sparkle and clarity. Mahantongo Street had long been recognized as a source for quality water. The purest water that could be found at this

Yuengling's Private Mountain Spring Reservoir. Located approximately five blocks from the brewery at Tenth and Mahantongo streets, the spring was an important source of pure water for production of beer for much of the brewery's history. (D. G. Yuengling and Son, Inc.)

time came from springs, and anthropological evidence suggests that an everlasting spring of water was located at Mahantongo near Twentieth Street. The location was a regular stopping point for Native Americans traveling through the region. Indeed, like the names of many places in Schuylkill County, the word Mahantongo is Native American in origin, meaning "where we had plenty of meat" or "plenty of venison." What would develop into a key spring-water source for the brewery is located approximately five blocks from the brewery, at Tenth and Mahantongo streets. The spring, Pottsville's first municipal water supply, was first known as the Potts-Patterson spring, named for the community's founder and another prominent leader, Burd Patterson. Through Patterson's efforts, a park and reservoir were built there. Two buildings are located at the spring, dating to the 1830s. One is a large, stone, square building that houses the reservoir that collects the spring water. Up the slope is a smaller structure that provides access to a tunnel that allows the spring water to flow to the reservoir.

The City of Pottsville stopped using the spring in 1854. Yuengling eventually purchased the land around the water supply and it became known as "Yuengling's Private Mountain Reservoir" or "Yuengling Park." The park, the size of a city block, was the key source of water for Yuengling beer for most of the company's history. As late as 1954, in a booklet to mark the 125th anniversary of the brewery, it was noted that "a special feature of the early brew was the pure mountain spring water used in combination with a brewer's formula from his native Germany.... And now, after generations, that same crystal clear mountain spring supplies all the water needed for the brewery's production of its beer, ale, and porter."[45] Beer labels in the 1950s also emphasized the water used to make the brew: "Only Sparkling Mountain Spring Water Used."

In addition to the water supply, D. G. Yuengling gained another benefit at the Mahantongo Street location, one which provides an indication that he had strong instincts about the future of brewing in his new homeland. He may have been among the first brewers to realize that a new style of beer would become popular in America — lager. When Yuengling was looking for a place to rebuild after the fire of 1831, all beer was fermented with yeast that rose to the top. In other words, using the vernacular of today's beer connoisseurs, beer was *ale*. As early as the thirteenth century, however, Bavarian monks in the vicinity of Munich had produced a different type of beer called lager, a clearer, lighter-tasting brew made with bottom-fermentation yeast. Lager eventually made it to the United States under uncertain circumstances that continue to be debated by brewing historians. One of the most significant issues in the debate is this: Why did it take until the mid-nineteenth century for lager to come to the United States? According to one of the most popular theories, lager beer yeast could not survive a long trip across the Atlantic, but in the 1840s speedier clipper ships were developed that brought the yeast safely to America's shores. Most scholars agree that Johann Wagner, a Bavarian brewer, first brought the bottom-fermenting yeast to Philadelphia. He then used an eight-barrel kettle to make the lighter brew behind his home on Saint John Street.[46] Wagner sold some of the yeast to local brewer George Manger, who established the first commercial lager brewery.

Production of lager on a significant scale started in the United States around 1840. In 1842, Prussian brothers Frederick and Maximilian Schaefer successfully experimented with lager in New York City and established the first large-scale lager brewing enterprise. The drink spread quickly to other urban areas, most notably to eventual brewing centers like Saint Louis and Milwaukee. Originally available only in local German communities, lager's popularity spread to the general population. Soon most beer drinkers wanted lager. The light, crisp beverage fit well with the country's climate. Innovations in glassmaking also enhanced its popularity, as inexpensive glass could highlight its clarity. The use of old pewter, wood, clay, or leather tankards, which were intended for darker ales, diminished. One indication of lager's increasing popularity is found as early as 1857, when sales figures from Philadelphia show it was outselling ale and porter. True, lager was the last major style of beers to make it to America's shores. It proved, however, to be the most important beverage, eventually catapulting the United States past Germany as the world's leading beer producer.

Brewers faced some special problems if they intended to produce lager, and Yuengling apparently recognized them. As part of one of the earliest projects at the new brewery on Mahantongo Street, the brewer directed laborers to cut two tunnels into the steep hill behind the brewery. Workers wielded the same tools used by coal miners to complete two wide caves which ran parallel into the mountain for several hundred feet. Lager requires a longer aging period than ale, so a place to store the beverage is crucial (the term lager comes from the German word

Brewery workers pose for a photograph at the entrance to the Yuengling caves. The caves, dug several hundred feet into Sharp Mountain, proved to be perfect for the production of lager beer, which began in the United States around 1840. (D. G. Yuengling and Son, Inc.)

"lagern," meaning "to store"). The caves dug behind the Yuengling Brewery were perfect for the production of this style of brew, providing plenty of dark, secluded storage space for barrels of beer. The man-made caverns also provide chilly temperatures conducive to brewing lager. The light brew's yeast performs better in lower temperatures. Inside the caves, the temperature is still 42 degrees year round. This consistently cool temperature aids the brewing process, but the caves were not quite cold enough to prevent the spoilage of beer. Ice was still needed in the storage area to keep the beer cold.[47] Only with the development of ice-making machinery decades later did brewers have the cool temperatures necessary to produce lager year round. Another advantage of the caves was water. At the end of one of the caves, water flowed continuously from a cistern.

D. G. Yuengling's decision to relocate his brewery next to Sharp Mountain and his early resolve to excavate caves at the location provide convincing evidence that he was among the earliest lager producers in the country. True, other breweries around the country used tunnels, caves, and caverns to keep their beer cold. But in the early 1830s Yuengling appeared to have the foresight to realize that the lager that he was very familiar with in his native Württemberg would *eventually* make it to his new homeland and become popular. When lager's bottom-fermenting yeast finally came to America around 1840, Yuengling had a facility that was perfectly equipped to brew this type of beer.[48]

One of the most significant factors in lager's eventual success is the large market that developed for the beverage. The groups that comprised the "old immigration" prior to the Civil War — the British, French, Germans, and Irish — presented the opportunity for tremendous and sustained growth in the brewing industry. The editor of a brewer's journal in the nineteenth century enthusiastically expressed confidence that organizations fighting for temperance or prohibition in America would be defeated because there was a growing market for beer among the nation's new arrivals: "The future is ours! The enormous influx of immigrants will in a few years overreach the puritanical element in every state in the Union."[49] Immigrants from D. G. Yuengling's native Germany gave the nation's brewers one of the biggest reasons to be optimistic. A major wave of immigrants from Deutchland ensued in the 1840s, giving the nation an additional 1.33 million Germans. They composed the largest number of immigrants, known was the "Forty-Eighters," who came to the United States for political reasons after the democratic revolutions of 1848 failed. Germans arriving after 1840 were more fortunate than earlier generations of immigrants. In addition to ales and porters, they could relax and escape the pressures of American life by enjoying steins of lager — a taste that reminded them of life in their homeland.

Beer was indeed essential in the daily life of German immigrants. They felt that the beverage was necessary to their well being, and they drank it with daily meals and in beer gardens. Nineteenth-century German immigrants also shocked many of their contemporaries by drinking beer on Sundays — a day that many felt was inappropriate for intoxicating drink. One noteworthy effort to curb the German tradition of drinking beer on Sunday afternoons occurred in 1855 when the mayor of Chicago increased liquor license fees and attempted to bring back an old law which prohibited alcohol and beer sales on the Lord's Day. After approximately 200 Germans were arrested on the first day of enforcement, the Chicago Lager Beer Riots broke out. Violent confrontations eventually forced Chicago officials to reconsider their campaign, and the German practice of Sunday afternoon beer parties returned.

In northeastern Pennsylvania, new arrivals also carried on a love affair with beer that kept regional brewers busy. To Yuengling's benefit, the earliest settlers of Schuylkill County and, more specifically, Pottsville, were Germanic. "They are descended from sturdy German stock, principally," one history of Schuylkill County notes in its description of Pottsville's citizens.[50] The area's ties to the Pennsylvania Dutch region are reflected in the description of Schuylkill County as "the daughter of Old Berks." Indeed, the mountainous area was originally comprised of communities of Pennsylvania German farmers who migrated not only from Berks County, but also from Dauphin, Montgomery, and Northampton counties.[51] Early in the county's history, the primary occupations among Germans were farming and timbering, but they also mined coal before the English, Welsh, and Irish came to dominate the trade.[52]

Foreign-born German immigrants brought even greater depth to the German community in the region. Early foreign-born community leaders in Pottsville were

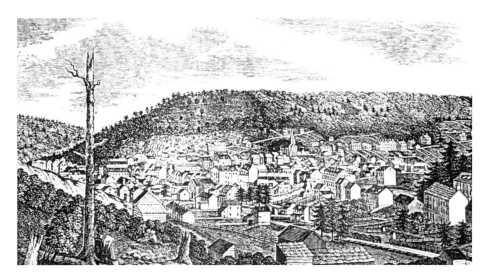

A view of Pottsville facing south in the 1850s. The Yuengling Brewery benefited from its location at the base of Sharp Mountain, next to Saint Patrick's Cathedral. (From the collections of the Historical Society of Schuylkill County.)

generally Catholic or Lutheran Germans from provinces like Hanover, Hesse, and Rhenish Palatinate. Yuengling's native state of Württemberg was also a significant source of Pottsville's German immigrants, including several successful businessmen. For example, Jacob Ulmer, D. G. Yuengling's friend and a pallbearer at his funeral, arrived in Pottsville from Württemberg in 1854 and established a very large and successful meatpacking house in the 1870s in the city's Jalappa section. Like Yuengling, Ulmer prospered financially through a number of business enterprises and was among Pottsville's most important community leaders. More concrete evidence of a vibrant German community in the region is evidenced by a strong German-language press. Schuylkill County had several German newspapers, including the *Stimme des Volks* (Voice of the People), which began publishing in 1828, the Schuylkill County *Bauer* (Farmer), founded in 1832, and the *Demokratische Freiheits Presse* (Democratic Liberty Press). The beer-loving German-American community in the region would be overshadowed by another immigrant group, and in the region's inns and taverns these newcomers quickly proved that they too, had a considerable thirst for malted beverages.

In the 1840s and 1850s, the anthracite coal region was the destination for thousands of immigrants from Ireland, particularly those from Sligo, Roscommon, Kilkenny, Mayo, and Donegal counties.[53] On the eve of the Civil War, people of Irish ancestry comprised 25 percent of Schuylkill County's population. New arrivals from the Emerald Isle fueled the continuing rise in the number of drinking establishments in the hard coal region. The tavern emerged as a central institution for the area's Irish population. Indeed, some Irish immigrants viewed the alcohol trade as a means of escape from the hard labor and danger of the mines. A key example of the growth of saloonkeeping in the region is found in the notorious Molly

Maguire episodes. The Molly Maguires were members of a secret society of Irish immigrants who were accused of a wave of violence and killings in the anthracite region in the late 1870s. Historians have noted that a striking number of the accused Molly Maguires were self-employed tavern owners. One Molly Maguire ran a wholesale liquor business and another operated an illegal still.[54]

It has been argued that opponents of the Mollies viewed the drinking habits of alleged members of the secret society as a weakness and used the tavern as a weapon against them. Pinkerton detective James McParlan gathered incriminating evidence against the Irish immigrants through his "jovial talk and liberal spending at the bar," which led to "unguarded saloon talk."[55] Certainly, the detective's earliest exploits led him to small mining towns and patches in southern Schuylkill County, where he made acquaintances by free spending in bars and sheebeens (illegal, private bars). His investigation soon led him to Pottsville and the Sheridan House — a saloon considered a gathering place for Molly Maguires in the area. Because he could always be depended upon to buy a round of drinks in the saloon, McParlan was popular and accepted at the Sheridan House. Here he talked, gambled, fought, and drank his way into the confidence of Patrick Dormer, a reputed Molly leader. He obtained important information that prompted him to focus his investigation on the communities in northern Schuylkill County and, particularly, on John Kehoe, a saloonkeeper in Girardville. Kehoe was among twenty Irishmen hanged, due in large measure to information gathered at area saloons by the Pinkerton detective.

The drunken Irishman was certainly a major stereotype of the nineteenth century, but the label was at least partially rooted in reality, as "the Irish apparently did suffer from a much higher rate of inebriety than did other groups."[56] The severity of problems related to alcohol among the Irish is indicated in a plea delivered in a speech in 1872 at the organizational meeting of the Catholic State Temperance Union of Pennsylvania. The speaker called special attention to the problem of intemperance among "our Irish co-religionists" and called on them "to cast off forever the chain of evil habits, and enlist at once under our glorious banner."[57] In comparison with Irish immigrants, Germans won some respect for their moderate use of alcohol, largely through their overwhelming preference for beer over hard liquor. More intoxicating, traditional Irish whiskey was the drink of choice among most of the Irish, but the regulars lining the bar also called for lager when it was on tap. While Irish immigrants often faced discrimination and prejudice, regional brewers who were looking to expand their markets welcomed them.

Pottsville's Irish immigrant community might have been pleased to know that a Saint Patrick's Brewery once operated on Mahantongo Street not far from the Yuengling Brewery.[58] Constructed by several German immigrants, the substantial stone building was located at Seventh and Mahantongo streets in the vicinity of the current First Baptist Church. Originally, there was a retail saloon at this location with a small brewery connected to it. The saloon was later torn down, and, in the closing decades of the nineteenth century, Yuengling bought the business, closed it, and offered jobs to its German workers. Later, Saint Patrick's parish utilized part of the old structure that housed the brewery when it needed to construct a convent. What year did it open? When did it close? These dates are undetermined despite the efforts of researchers. Indeed, winning an old, nineteenth-century beer sign, tumbler, or tray on eBay might be possible today, but obtaining written documentation about specific breweries that have gone out of business is challenging detective work. Ownership, names, and addresses frequently changed. If records are found, they are often sketchy. Physical evidence of most early nineteenth century operations is very difficult to find or no longer exists.

One of the most extensive listings of breweries from the beginnings of the industry to 1995, *American Breweries II*, offers help to those investigating regional brewing history. The book is the result of painstaking work by brewery historians and local researchers, who spent "mind numbing hours going through local records to come up with the most accurate information available."[59] The existence of Pottsville's old Saint Patrick's Brewery, for example, might have gone undocumented were it not for the effort of local researchers and historians. The small operation is one of several beer producers founded in Pottsville. The *Schuylkill County Chronicles*, dated January 21, 1830, puts the number of Pottsville breweries at four, brewmasters, eight. In fact, despite Yuengling's record as the oldest American brewery in operation, it may not have been the first brewery to open in the city. D. G. Yuengling faced competition either when he arrived or shortly after he opened the Eagle Brewery. Two significant brewing competitors of the Yuengling Brewery survived in the Pottsville area for a considerable period of time.

A noteworthy example of an early challenger to D. G. Yuengling's Eagle Brewery is the Orchard Brewery, named for the Orchard section of Pottsville where it was originally located. This business proved to be one of Yuengling's most serious competitors through the years. Its ownership shifted several times, providing both a contrast to the consistent family ownership at the Yuengling Brewery and an indication of the volatile nature of the brewing industry. As early as 1831, the Orchard Brewery was in "full operation" and allowed Pottsville to boast that it had a beer "equal to that of Philadelphia."[60] The Orchard Brewery later moved to River Road in Port Carbon and was owned by A.S. Moore. Just as the Yuengling Brewery suffered through a blaze in its early history, so did the Orchard Brewery. Fire destroyed the plant in 1835. The successful Lauer brewing family in Reading recognized the growing market to the north, restarted the business around 1845, and continued to operate the Port Carbon facility until 1877.[61]

Another Pottsville beer maker — the Rettig Brewery — opened in 1865. Originally named the (John) Liebner and (Charles) Rettig Brewery, the business was first located at the southwest corner of East Norwegian and Railroad streets. Early breweries often operated a tavern near their facilities, reminiscent of the modern brewpub. In the decade following the Civil War, the Rettig Brewery also operated under the names Blue Brewery and Saloon and Blue Tavern and Brewery. The Rettig Brewery did well in its initial years, requiring a more spacious location. In 1869 the brewery relocated to the northwest corner of Market and 9th streets, later becoming known as the Market Street Brewery. The beer maker survived until the onset of Prohibition. The demanding nature of the business is demonstrated in two Pottsville breweries that produced beer very briefly. In 1860, Franz C. Kuentzler operated a brewery at 37 Centre Street. Ludwig Raeder made beer in Pottsville from 1882 to 1884. The expanding coal industry led to the growth and incorporation of more boroughs and villages in the Pottsville area — Schuylkill Haven (1841), Minersville (1842), Saint Clair (1850) and Tamaqua. As quickly as communities sprung up, breweries were opened to supply beer for residents.[62]

Breweries were a significant source of more and more jobs, particularly for German immigrants. Barrels of beer are not light, and the physical labor at the local brewery was demanding. Before the close of the nineteenth century, most brewery workers eventually secured a ten-hour workday; however, 16-hour workdays were typical in the decades leading up to the improved labor conditions. Workers sometimes boarded right on the brewery premises under a curfew set by the brewery owner. Herman Schluter's pro-labor book, *The Brewing Industry and the Brewery Workers' Movement in America,* places brewery work among the most unpleasant in the country. However, other accounts emphasize the important role the brewery played in the local community and indicate that working there was considered a great privilege. Many brewery owners were concerned about the welfare of their employees and treated them very well. One perk, of course, was the beer that employees were permitted to drink throughout the workday. In the Early Republic, the brewery wasn't the only place where the amber fluid was enjoyed on the job.

Certain jobs lead to great thirst, and physically strenuous tasks can be eased by a drink. Significantly, a finer line between work and alcohol existed prior to America's industrial transformation. Clearing a wilderness was an enormous undertaking, and the laborers taking part were encouraged to take official booze breaks. Taking a nip every now and then eased the strain and helped toilers continue their tasks. The slower pace of craft occupations allowed workers to enjoy a variety of alcoholic beverages on informal breaks. If a blacksmith, saddler, farmer, builder or seamstress wanted to keep a jug, bottle, or glass close at hand during the workday, few eyebrows were raised under the powdered wig. In fact, in colonial America, what has been labeled "dram" drinking was common. Under this drinking pattern, people ritualistically drank small amounts of alcohol throughout the day. Drinking by "drams" accompanied actions like getting out of bed in the morning, eating meals, completing a task at work or at home, or going to bed at night.[63] In this context, it is not surprising that alcoholic beverages were accepted as a form of currency in many states.

This liberal attitude toward alcohol in pre-industrial America briefly spilled over to the factory setting of the Industrial Revolution, and job-site drinking was common even after the Civil War. In contrast to distilled liquors, beer was not viewed as an intoxicant in the nineteenth century. Urban breweries supplied factory workers with beer throughout the workday. Even in the early twentieth century, morning beer deliveries were made to German factories. At lunchtime, large quantities of beer were enjoyed by workers at places like the Great Standard Oil

A "lager bier wagon" providing refreshments to soldiers during the Civil War. Similar wagons also made their way through communities in northeastern Pennsylvania and searched for customers at surrounding coal mines. (D. G. Yuengling and Son, Inc.)

Works in Bayonne, New Jersey, or in the Chicago stockyards.[64] To get the beer to the job-site, factory workers usually arranged for someone, usually the youngest workers, to "rush the growler." A growler was a relatively small tin bucket for carrying beer, but it could also be any bucket, can, or pitcher that could carry the beverage. The term supposedly had its origins in the sound the can made as it slid along the top of a bar.[65] As breaktime or the lunch hour neared, bartenders in saloons near factories frantically filled the growlers for as little as a nickel. The ritual formed a significant part of a saloonkeepers business.

Work and alcohol were also interdependent in northeastern Pennsylvania. The hard work in the mines was a significant factor in the unusually high number of breweries in the region as well as their longevity. Initially, anthracite coal miners felt free to imbibe, and alcohol use was largely unrestricted. Some employers even paid miners, in part, with a weekly or daily allowance of alcohol. Early anthracite mines were small operations in which miners worked as independent contractors. They were paid by the ton of coal produced and, in comparison with other industrial workers, they had an unusually high level of independence in the workplace and completed their tasks under very little, if any, supervision. As long as quotas were being met, the foreman gave the miners plenty of freedom. Significantly, the tons of coal mined determined the length of the workday. If the quota of coal was mined in six hours, it was time to stop for the day. "We quit when we're through," was a popular saying among miners.[66]

The tradition of quitting after meeting the coal quota gave miners incentive to act responsibly and avoid excessive workplace drinking. Still, younger workers in the mines also followed the practice common in other industries. At breaktime, they gathered the "growlers" brought to the mines by the older workers and fetched beer from the tavern that was usually not far from the shadow of the coal breaker. Horse-drawn wagons with plenty of beer and alcohol frequently stopped at the mines in search of customers. Of course, these beer wagons were busiest at quitting time and on paydays. On special occasions like birthdays, miners would celebrate with a pail or barrel of beer when they exited the mineshafts. Even these restrained traditions would come under attack, however.

As industrialization increased, owners of mines, mills and factories concluded that sobriety increased productivity. Workers who drank were considered sluggish, unreliable, as well as more prone to illness and absenteeism. Sobriety also became equated with safety as workers who used alcohol were viewed as a danger to other workers. The anthracite coal industry provides an example of the shift in attitude. As mining operations expanded and technology advanced (such as the invention and patent of the coal breaker in the 1840s), perceptions of alcohol use around the mines changed. As the miners worked to blast coal from the face of the mineshaft, it just didn't seem wise to trust the black powder kegs and detonators to the fellow miner who had been nipping at a flask of whiskey all morning. An editorial in the *Miners' Journal* expressed delight when a few collieries near Pottsville prohibited liquor:

> No liquor is allowed to be used on the premises. It is stipulated with every man who engages at these collieries, that he must remain sober or lose his situation. The consequence is a different state of affair exists here from that about those collieries where the use of alcohol is unrestricted. The workmen attend punctually to their business, they do more labor, save their pay and render their families comfortable and happy, by judiciously expending it for their benefit, instead of squandering it foolishly in dissipation. Their houses are neat and clean — their furniture though scanty, nevertheless in good order, and everybody exhibits the wonderful difference between the condition of the collieries where rum is and where it is not.[67]

Pennsylvania legislators also picked up the issue and approved some early examples of laws aimed at limiting or prohibiting the use of alcohol. In an effort to keep miners from bringing smaller quantities of alcohol to the mines, lawmakers responded to requests from employers and passed "a series of laws between 1846 and 1860 forbidding the sale of intoxicating liquor in quantities of less than thirty gallons to any individual within three miles of certain iron and coal mines in Armstrong, Clarion, Luzerne, and Carbon Counties."[68]

If miners were being discouraged from using alcoholic beverages inside the mines and around the colliery, there was little to stop them from drinking during their time off. The typical image of the beer-loving miner is found behind a bar. An organizer for the United Mine Workers of America (UMWA) once pointed out, "These men, these coal miners, have always taken a little drink, and it has always been a good thing for them."[69] Just as bars and tavern were located near urban factories in order to attract a working-class clientele, saloons in the anthracite region were often conveniently located in places that miners needed to pass on their way to work—sometimes within walking distance of the colliery. Most bars in the region were influenced by the entire work schedules in the mines. Some opened as early as five o'clock in the morning to allow workers a quick bracer before the start of a shift. At the bar in the early morning hours, a "Miner's Breakfast" could be ordered: two raw eggs dropped into a glass of beer after being cracked on the rim. The miner would first gulp a shot of whiskey and then sooth his burning throat by chugging the raw egg and beer concoction. Then, it was off to the mines, perhaps planning to return to the bar on the way home.

What drew coal miners to the local bar? Their occupation provides a partial explanation. It has been argued that an individual's occupation shapes his leisure time, because "work is always in the back of our minds. When work is dull, tiresome, or stressful people are sometimes unable to do anything satisfying in their leisure."[70] A study conducted early in the twentieth century concluded that "workers with the most menial and lowest-paid jobs spent the greatest amount of time in saloons washing the workday away with beer."[71] In this context, it is easy to understand why miners drank. Conditions in the mines were notoriously brutal. Danger was ever-present in the darkness, a fact confirmed by a high incidence of injury and death. Explosions, dangerous gases, floods, and roof falls were incidents that led to a heavy toll of lives. In the nineteenth century, when mining regulations were weak, three miners were killed every two days. Miners who escaped death in an incident were often seriously maimed. In most cases, accidents killed one or two miners, but there were larger disasters in which scores were killed. A major example is the Avondale mine disaster on September 6, 1869, in which 108 men and boys died when a mineshaft caught fire.

When he emerged into the sunlight after a shift underground, the miner's face, hands, and clothes were blackened with a mixture of coal dust and sweat. He was exhausted but at the same time relieved that he made it through another day without being trapped or buried below. The dangers of the colliery were what he had faced since he was very young. The cycle of the miner's life in the nineteenth century began as early as the age of eight or nine, when he started work as a breaker boy picking slate from the crushed and screened coal. The oppressive conditions often resulted in a "devil-may-care attitude" among miners that extended to life on the surface:

> They felt that the dangers of their mining allowed them to "raise hell" off the job and be "the boss" at home. Generally, they were more extroverted, spontaneous, and independent than the average industrial worker. They were often criticized for their swearing, drinking, gambling, and seeming unconcern with how they spent their money. They excused themselves by claiming that they worked hard at a dangerous job and earned the right to enjoy themselves.[72]

Drinking dulled the senses and eased the aches and pains, helping the miners forget their burdens and the tragedies they may have witnessed on the job.

So, after work they crowded around hand-carved mahogany bars, smoked cigars, and took a long pull on a cool beer to "wash down the coal dust" as they swapped stories with their comrades. Many miners felt at home in the local saloon, and a description of the establishment written in 1901 helps explain why:

> The saloon is the most democratic of institutions. It appeals at once to the common humanity of man. There is nothing to repel. No questions are asked. Respectability is not a countersign. The door swings before any man who chooses to enter. Once within he finds the atmosphere one in which he can allow his social nature to freely expand. The welcome from the keeper is a personal one. The environment is congenial. It may be that the appeal is what is base in him. He may find satisfaction because he can give vent to those lower desires which seek expression. The place may be attractive just because it is so elevating. Man is taken as he is, and is given what he wants, be that good or bad. The only standard is the demand.[73]

Miners could be found at the saloon any day of the week. Paydays—which usually came once a month and on Saturday—were, of course, the busiest times.

The fact that the lager revolution and the rise of the anthracite coal industry virtually coincided is also important as one considers the popularity of beer among anthracite coal miners. In contrast to porters or ales, lager is particularly thirst-quenching and proved particularly popular after (or during) a hard day's work. And its price was right. Referred to as the "new nickel drink," lager was cheap and easily the most affordable beverage for laborers. Its low cost propelled beer ahead of whiskey as the most popular beverage among a growing segment of industrial workers. Finally, a lack of work could lead to alcohol consumption as well. While the work in the mines was difficult and dangerous, it was irregular, too, particularly in the antebellum period. Those coming to the region were often itinerant workers who were on their own; unemployment and loneliness contributed to the heavy use of alcohol in northeastern Pennsylvania. Eventually, some coal operators recognized alcohol abuse and moved beyond banning alcohol at the mines in the interest of safety and production.

While miners spent time in the bars, many of their wives patronized the local churches. They petitioned the Lord for two things. First, they prayed that their husbands would not be killed in the mines. They then prayed that, if he wasn't killed at work, he wouldn't spend all his pay on drinking. If they felt their prayers weren't being answered, miners' wives turned to the owners of the coal mines to address the problem. Some operators wielded considerable control over their mining village and responded to the pressure from the miners' wives by working to eliminate alcohol entirely. They locked tavern doors and prohibited beer wagons. But old habits are hard to break. Miners resisted efforts to change their behavior, and some enjoyed their alcoholic beverages so much that they took the extraordinary measure of walking "several miles from a 'dry' patch to a 'wet' one for a drink."[74] Futile attempts to prohibit or temper alcohol consumption when coal was king were, of course, a precursor to America's Prohibition era in the twentieth century.

The road leading to the passage of the Eighteenth Amendment to the Constitution in 1919 is long. In colonial America, very few laws prohibited the sale and manufacture of alcohol; however, drinking to excess was recognized as a problem, and laws against drunkenness were passed as early as the opening decades of the seventeenth century. Excessive drinking around the Christmas season, for example, prompted the Puritans to ban the celebration of the holiday. An early and significant figure who advocated the moderate use of alcohol was a Pennsylvanian. Doctor Benjamin Rush, known as the "Hippocrates of Pennsylvania," campaigned vigorously to curb America's high liquor consumption in the late eighteenth and early nineteenth centuries. He addressed the effects of liquor from a medical perspective in a 1772 pamphlet, *Sermon to Gentlemen Upon Temperance and Exercise.* Over a decade later, he published another document based on his studies, *An Inquiry into the Effects of Spiritous Liquors on the Human Body.* This study is considered "perhaps the first American temperance treatise to stimulate serious debate."[75] Rush's main focus was on the negative effects of "strong" alcoholic beverages, and he believed serious crime in the new nation would be greatly reduced through total abstinence from "demon rum." Significantly, the noted physician, who was also a signer of the Declaration of Independence, had no objection to beer drinking. In fact, he suggested beer as an alternative drink for imbibers trying to break free from their addiction to distilled spirits. Not surprisingly, Rush's pleas for reform were largely ignored. A few decades later, however, the temperance movement was born as other reformers successfully organized to encourage people to reduce their use of beer, liquor, and wine.

National organizations that sprang up in the name of temperance in D. G. Yuengling's lifetime included the American Temperance Society in 1826. To temperance groups, drink was a weapon of Satan, and it harmed women and children. Many members of these organizations were quite dedicated to their cause, and they believed fervently that alcohol was the primary cause of a host of social ills, including crime, poverty, domestic violence, pauperism, and insanity. They also claimed that alcohol use resulted in economic problems and placed a greater burden on the government. Those favoring temperance or prohibition frequently quoted statistics to support their cause.

Pennsylvania, as one of the nation's leading brewers and distillers, was a perennial battleground state on the alcohol question.[76] Even before Yuengling emigrated from Germany, temperance forces were organizing in Pennsylvania. The state's Quaker communities pressed for moderation. Early examples of temperance societies include the Darby Association for Discouraging the Unnecessary Use of Spiritous Liquors, which organized in Delaware County in 1819. In 1828, the Susquehanna Temperance Society formed in Montrose. This group was particularly dedicated, as members were required to take a pledge to abstain from liquor and actively work to control its use in the area. In 1827, the Pennsylvania Society for Discouraging the Use of Ardent Spirits formed in Philadelphia as an anti-whiskey organization. In less than a decade, the organization changed its name to the Pennsylvania Temperance Society, and total prohibition became one of its goals. The Sons of Temperance came to Pennsylvania in the 1840s and produced some striking results, establishing 385 local divisions and attracting 27,241 members. The juvenile adjunct of the society, The Cadets of Temperance, could boast 125 locals in Pennsylvania and membership in the thousands. The organizations encouraged people to take "the pledge," established temperance inns, and planned dry holiday celebrations in communities from Philadelphia to Erie. More and more similar organizations formed, and by 1843, Pennsylvania had 51 organizations, representing about 35,000 members, working to promote temperance across the state.

Prior to the 1850s, most legislation in Pennsylvania regarding the use of alcohol was minor. In 1752, for example, the state's Provincial Assembly passed bills aimed at preventing the use of alcohol to influence voters. Apparently, office seekers attempted to sway voters by supplying them with strong drink. Other laws dealt with the sale of alcohol to women and Native Americans. Temperance forces gained more political clout in the mid-nineteenth century and progressively scored more legislative victories that limited the availability of alcohol to the general public. Giving alcohol to "minors, intemperate persons, and insane persons" became illegal. It also became a misdemeanor to be involved in "the performances of marriages when either of the parties was drunk."[77] Opposition to liquor on religious and moral grounds continued to grow. Just as abstinence from all alcohol was a fundamental rule in many evangelical churches, so the goal of some groups was no longer simply to *temper* the use of alcohol. The objective was *prohibition*, and Pennsylvania came perilously close to outlawing beer.

The timing of temperance activities could not have been worse for D. G. Yuengling. It came after two decades of hard work to develop his business. In the 1850s, his brew was not only growing in popularity locally but developing a national reputation for its quality. In addition, the movement against alcohol was not simply a business matter. Yuengling was probably more concerned about a major impetus behind the threat of Prohibition, a reason he could take personally. For while many temperance organizers genuinely felt that society would be improved through limits on the use of alcohol, some used temperance as a springboard to vent anti-immigrant anger.

Pennsylvania's Germans immigrants were not spared from the nativist sentiment of the period. In the 1850s, the state demonstrated considerable support for the Know-Nothing or American Party, "which openly professed its disdain for foreigners and pursued a political agenda that, among other goals, would stifle immigration and stiffen naturalization laws.... Germans in the state were probably more conscious of nativist prejudice there than [immigrants] in most other states in the union."[78] The abuse of alcohol was a chief criticism hurled at immigrants, and beer consumption by German immigrants was viewed as a cause for concern among those seeking to limit the number of foreign-born coming to America's shores. Native-born Americans looked with disdain at German traditions like beer halls and drinking on Sunday. The German language was a major problem. Many felt the language was strange and un-American, and they were threatened by the formation of German-language societies among immigrants. The public generally felt that German immigrants needed to be brought under control for the greater good. Mayors of major American cities, even one as close to Pottsville as Philadelphia, introduced "draconian liquor license laws to drive small German beer gardens out of business."[79]

All this spelled trouble for D. G. Yuengling, who took tremendous pride in his German background. His membership in the German secret society, the Order of the Harugari, is a clear sign that he was aware of the nativist mood in the country and occasionally felt the bigotry and intolerance associated with it. The fraternal order was founded in 1847 in reaction to prejudice directed against German immigrants. Despite the widespread nativist sentiments in the nation, Yuengling was undaunted and worked to preserve Pottsville's German heritage. There are several examples. In 1839, a Pottsville Lyceum was formed to offer the opportunity to hear lecturers on a variety of topics and exchange ideas. German immigrants appeared to have been excluded from the lyceum because, in that same year, a German Lyceum was formed in the city, and Yuengling was elected president of the club. He also assisted the German Lutheran Church in the community, providing monetary contributions that led to the church's construction. As part of his leadership position in the German Lutheran Church, he helped develop a Sunday school for the city's Lutheran congregation in the 1850s. A description of the school indicates that Yuengling believed strongly in preserving his German heritage. The only language that was taught or spoken at the school was German. The rule was so strictly enforced that two members of the church council were assigned to attend classes to make sure that it wasn't violated by teachers or students. Those caught using another language during classes were penalized under "the strictest discipline."[80] Yuengling's efforts to preserve Pottsville's German heritage probably drew the ire of those opposed to the growing number of "foreigners" in the region.

While the struggles between the native- and foreign-born largely took place in "ethnically" diverse major cities, the anthracite region, with its large influx of German and Irish immigrants, was not immune to anti-immigrant thought during the antebellum period. Nothing illustrates this point more than the career of a journalist who D. G. Yuengling was probably well aware of—the fiery Benjamin Bannan (1807–1875), editor of one of the region's most significant newspapers. Born on a Berks County farm, Bannan was trained as a stereotype printer following the death of his father. He moved to Pottsville the same year as D. G. Yuengling, and in April of that year he bought the failing *Miners' Journal*. Through his ownership over the next thirty-seven years, he transformed the newspaper into one of the principal political journals in the state. Bannan earned a reputation as one of the leading coal statisticians in the country and for his extensive knowledge of the anthracite coal trade. Like most publishers of the period, Bannan expanded his business ventures. He ran a stationary store where Pottsville residents could also purchase a wide variety of merchandise, including tickets, sheet music and patent medicine.

The *Miners' Journal* carried Bannan's conservative political views. Significantly, he was a Whig, a party that crusaded for social and moral reform and supported issues such as sabbatarianism and temperance. Not surprisingly, Bannan was the treasurer of the local temperance organization and was a leading figure at its meetings. In Bannan's view, sobriety, along with self-discipline and punctuality, was the key to success in a capitalist society. On the surface, the newspaper editor's major

Benjamin Bannan (1807–1875), editor of the
Miners' Journal, one of the major political jour-
nals in the state. Bannan waged a vigorous
campaign to bring statewide Prohibition to
Pennsylvania and shut down its breweries.
(From the collections of the Historical Society of
Schuylkill County.)

concern was that intemperance was
hurting the regional economy. He
estimated that "one-quarter of the
work force spent more time in the
beer shops than in the mine breasts,
costing the coal trade one thousand
tons and one thousand dollars a
day.... Instead of mining more coal
and doubling their pay, as right-
thinking miners should, intemperate
miners worked fewer hours, spending
the remainder 'at [rum] establishments.'"[81]

Bannan made the *Miners' Journal* a platform for temperance reform,
posting statistics on the growth of
saloons and "beer houses" in the
region. In June of 1853, for example,
Bannan counted 636 taverns in
Schuylkill County — or one for every
nine voters.[82] The tone and approach
to the issue indicate that Bannan was
motivated less by concern for the
regional economy and more by
nativism and anti-Catholicism. He
made it a point to emphasize "foreigners" as both the supplier and major consumer
of alcohol in the region. In his columns, he blamed Irish Catholics for the region's
problems with intemperance. This immigrant group was the main focus of Bannan's attacks; however, even immigrant Germans involved in the alcohol trade —
men like D. G. Yuengling — were implicated in the pages of Bannan's paper. The
criticism of immigrants in the *Miners' Journal* was so strong that Bannan was labeled
as a member of the Know-Nothing Party by his enemies — a charge that has never
been proven. Still, when Bannan's printing office and bookstore on North Centre
Street went up in flames on October 10, 1854, it was assumed that Bannan's foes
were responsible. The fire only stopped the newspaper for a short time. He started
work on a brick building less than a week after the setback, and, about a month
after the blaze, the *Miners' Journal* was being printed once again in the basement
of a new structure. The temperance campaign in Schuylkill County could continue.

Bannan was pleased when some local collieries banned alcohol and the state
legislature passed laws prohibiting the use of alcohol near the coal mines. But these
measures were not enough to satisfy him and other temperance advocates in
Schuylkill County. They saw an opportunity when Maine passed a prohibition bill
in 1851. In the aftermath of this important moment in the Prohibition movement,

Bannan penned editorials encouraging statewide prohibition in Pennsylvania. D. G. Yuengling was probably greatly concerned when he read the following comment in an editorial in the *Miners' Journal* that argued for a "Prohibitory Liquor Law": "We are daily becoming more and more persuaded that nothing short of a prohibitory law can reach the root of the evil, or effectively cure this moral leprosy in Schuylkill County." In 1852 Bannan's idea was applied to one day of the week. The Pennsylvania legislature banned the sale of alcohol on Sundays. In the October 1, 1853, edition of the *Miners' Journal*, the editor celebrated successful efforts by temperance groups to "close up all the Bars and the Taverns and Beer Houses in Schuylkill County on Sunday." But the day of rest was not enough. Bannan urged readers to vote for temperance candidates in the upcoming election, adding, "Now boys, we have a Maine Law for one day in seven — let's go for the six other days."

The campaign to place Pennsylvania in the same category as the "dry" state of Maine would be decided by the voters. State lawmakers, in response to pressure from temperance organizers, passed legislation to make the prohibition question a referendum. The Prohibitory Liquor Law was on the ballot in 1854. If passed, it would "entirely prohibit by proper and constitutional regulations and penalties the manufacture and sale of intoxicating liquors, except for medicinal, sacramental, mechanical, and artistical purposes." What followed was "one of the most bitterly contested elections in the history of the state."[83] In the end the "wet" factions were victorious by a narrow margin. Statewide Prohibition was defeated by only 5,139 votes. Eastern Pennsylvania's Germans proved to be the most vocal among those who opposed it. Schuylkill County, with its largely German immigrant population, did its share to defeat prohibition, with 2,762 votes cast for Prohibition and 5,658 against — undoubtedly Yuengling drinkers among them. The numbers from the "Pennsylvania Dutch" county of Berks are even more telling: 2,612 for prohibition and 10,599 against. Pennsylvania's temperance leaders clearly had a formidable foe among the Germans.

Following the failed attempt at statewide Prohibition in 1854, the temperance issue was pushed aside by the anti-slavery debate leading up to the Civil War. Prohibition forces would rise again, but with a difference. In an odd twist, the idea proposed by Benjamin Rush in the 1780s — that beer was a healthy alternative to stronger spirits — resurfaced with the growing popularity of lager beer in the 1840s and 1850s. More temperance organizers subscribed to a philosophy that actually benefited D. G. Yuengling: Because lager contains less alcohol than ale and much less than hard liquor, it could aid in the war against intemperance and serve as a milder alternative to the more potent spirits. The brewer on Mahantongo Street no longer needed to worry whether or not his business would be outlawed, and he could continue to focus on the day-to-day operation of his brewery. He could also turn his attention to expanding the physical plant of his brewery.

D. G. Yuengling was proud of his small business. The brewer, like most successful businesspeople, sought to record the fruits of his hard work, on canvas and, later, in pictures. Businessmen often commissioned drawings or paintings of their properties to hang in company offices, reception halls, or homes. The brewery founder

Business owners in the nineteenth century frequently ordered portraits of their company to immortalize their accomplishment. This depiction of the Yuengling Brewery was produced around 1844. The fenced-in field ascending Sharp Mountain (right) would eventually be the site of D. G. Yuengling's home and, later, the company's current business office. (D. G. Yuengling and Son, Inc.)

arranged to have at least two artists capture the brewery in operation during its first two decades. One of the earliest lithographs represents the brewery as it appeared around 1840. It shows several rustic, wooden frame buildings with horse-drawn beer wagons entering and exiting the brewery. The hillside next to the brewery is an open field where horses from the brewery grazed. Photographs taken at the same location about thirty years later set a different tone. D. G. Yuengling was not camera shy and posed in several of the early pictures taken of his brewery. The old-world image in the lithograph transformed to an increasing industrial scene as profits allowed the brewery to complete several additions, renovations, and modernizations.[84]

Early photographs of the brewery bear a very close resemblance to the brick structure on Mahantongo Street today. By the 1870s, the wooden brewery had transformed into, by Civil War-era standards, a modern complex geared for increasing beer production. Significant changes include the removal of a tall grain elevator that had once dominated the brewery's physical plant. Several stories were added to the brewery itself, or what company documents refer to as the "Old Brewhouse." Early photographs show that the upper stories were comprised of louvered panels that allowed the beer to breathe and cool after it was boiled in a large kettle. Like most nineteenth century brewers, D. G. Yuengling felt it was important to be as close to his business as possible, so he built his residence right next to the brewery. The Yuengling family home, known as the "Old Homestead," was constructed in the 1840s. The upper floors of the home would eventually serve as the office for the company.

Yuengling made every effort to prevent the brewery from becoming an eye-

One of the earliest photographs of the brewery, probably from the Civil War era. The building at the right is the home of D. G. Yuengling and his family. In the nineteenth century, brewery workers sometimes boarded on the brewery premises or at nearby homes. (D. G. Yuengling and Son, Inc.)

sore. A typical nineteenth century brewery has been described as "a particularly conspicuous establishment. Various obstructions, such as old beer wagons, empty kegs, or retired brewing vats often littered the premises. Spent grains, soaked with half-fermented beer were routinely discarded indiscriminately, left to rot in the sun. And, perhaps worst of all, the unmistakable odor of a thriving brewery tended to hang relentlessly over its neighborhood."[85] Yuengling worked to avoid friction with Pottsville residents and borough officials, as a commentary on his life in the *Miners' Journal* indicates: "[N]obody was more careful to respect borough ordinances in the spirit as well as in the letter, and if all the other citizens of Pottsville were as particular as he in keeping their pavements in repair and in curbing and guttering along alleys and vacant lots, they would have much less grumbling to do about the miserable condition of the borough streets and sidewalks."[86]

While it would seem that he had more than enough work to do with the growing brewery, he somehow found time to become involved in other business ventures. Pottsville's community leaders "almost always engaged in a number of entrepreneurial activities that encompassed the primary sectors of the local and regional economies."[87] Yuengling provides an example, as he assumed the presidencies of the Pottsville Gas Company and the Pottsville Water Company. From the beginning of the coal boom until the 1860s, Pottsville developed an "upper stratum" of community leaders. The "anthracite aristocracy" that emerged in larger communities was comprised of men who had achieved financial success in not only the coal industry, but also in coal-related industries like small-scale iron and steel manufacturing, transportation, lumber production, and machine shops. Wealth was also made in banking, insurance, utilities, and manufacturing. And in brewing, too. D. G. Yuengling's business and community activities in Pottsville over the years certainly placed the Yuengling family among the most prominent in the community. And a large family it was.

According to marriage records in the German newspaper *Stimme des Volks*, a Rev. Kroll married Yuengling and Elizabeth (Betz) of nearby Schuylkill Haven on Valentine's Day, February 14, 1841.[88] The couple eventually had three sons (David Jr., Frederick, and William) and seven daughters (Elizabeth, Mary, Sophie, Theresa, Carrie, Emma, and Laura). The household next to the brewery was busy. However, Yuengling also found the time to become involved in charitable activities in Pottsville. As the *Miners' Journal* noted, "[H]e gave away many a dollar in unostentatious charity, of which no one knew except the beneficiary and the all-wise Creator."[89] As a result of his community involvement and the growing fame of his products, D. G. Yuengling's name probably surfaced in political circles as a possible candidate for federal, state, or local office. He was, after all, an influential Democrat. But Yuengling's personality was more suited for running a brewery than making speeches on the campaign trail.

Elizabeth (Betz) Yuengling (1823–1894), wife of D. G. Yuengling and the mother of ten children. (D. G. Yuengling and Son, Inc.)

In times of crisis, Yuengling responded. During the Civil War, the Pottsville brewer was among the beer makers in the Union states who were required to pay a federal tax of $1 a barrel. The tax, instituted to help finance the war, was something entirely new to the brewing industry and went into effect on September 1, 1862. Yuengling also aided the war effort on a local level. When the struggle erupted and Schuylkill County was called upon for the requisition of troops, "subscriptions and funds for the aid of the families of the volunteers" had to be raised. On the evening of April 16, 1861, a meeting was held at the Schuylkill County courthouse to organize the fundraising. D. G. Yuengling was among a long list of community leaders who each contributed $100. Significantly, as the nation was split by the slavery issue, a brick house on Mahantongo Street, about two blocks from the Yuengling Brewery, was a station for the Underground Railroad. Quaker James Gillingham offered aid to escaped slaves in the basement of his home at the northeast corner of Seventh and Mahantongo streets. He provided provisions for them as they made their way to the next station and to freedom in Canada.

Following the Civil War, Yuengling was approaching the age of sixty, but he would continue working for at least another decade. If he took the time to reflect on his past, he could look back on an eventful, active life. He had not only overcome the challenges faced by an immigrant in a new land, but he had gone on to play a vital role in the Pottsville community at a time of rapid growth, becoming, in the words of one newspaper commentary on his life, "one of the solid foundations of society." As a brewer, he did not give in to discouragement when faced with growing competition and serious setbacks like fires. He continued working to develop a solid reputation as an honest, industrious businessman:

> By the death of Mr. Yuengling Pottsville loses one of her most useful citizens. He added materially to both the material wealth and the business prosperity of the town.... Quiet and unostentatious, he was a worker rather than a talker; but what many others contented themselves with merely talking about he went ahead and did.... The business established by Mr. Yuengling on a modest scale grew by attention and good management until it reached colossal proportions and brought into town a revenue whose loss would be sensibly felt. He attended strictly to his business and sought profit not by making the cheapest article he could, but by making the best, thereby winning and holding an extensive market. His career is another example to young men about engaging in business, showing that the key to success is simply industry, intelligence and honesty.[90]

In perhaps an indication of the brewer's stature, the words of praise, published on the day of his funeral, appeared in the *Miners' Journal*, the very paper that had posed a threat to the brewer years earlier with its campaign for total prohibition.

A year before D. G. Yuengling's passing, the nation had marked a turning point in its history with a centennial celebration. Down the Schuylkill River where the canal once flowed, the Centennial Exposition was held in Philadelphia, attracting millions who came by train to see it. The Centennial Exposition in 1876 saluted successful individuals— self-made men like Yuengling— and their contribution to America. It also sent a message about America's future. New machinery was on display— dynamos and large engines— symbolizing a new mechanical age. The light bulb, the telephone, and the typewriter were among the new wonders on display. Significantly, visitors to the exposition would have found Brewers Hall, a two-story building that cost $20,000 to construct. Members of the Yuengling family were among the major beer makers who planned the exhibit, and the Pottsville brewery showcased its products there. Despite the protests of prohibitionists, Brewers Hall, with its statue of King Gambrinus (the patron saint of brewers) over the entrance, showcased the scientific and technological improvements in methods of malting and brewing and even featured an operating "Centennial Brewery" to provide samples to visitors. "Mechanical refrigerating devices," as well as Adolphus Busch's new refrigerated railroad cars, were proudly displayed and provided a hint of the technological and scientific changes would lead to radical shifts in the brewing industry. The strong foundation that D. G. Yuengling had built would be tested in the near future as the brewery entered a new phase in its history.

Two

The Sons and the Saloons

"There is no easier way possible to make the unfortunate or oppressed worker content with his misfortune than a couple of glasses of beer."
— Thomas L. Lewis, president of the United Mine Workers of America (1908–1911) and native of Locust Gap, Pennsylvania

German-Americans in the nineteenth century viewed the family as the cornerstone of their lives and believed close family ties led to financial and social well-being. The German family could not be considered egalitarian, however. The head of the household was the father, and his domineering role extended into business decisions as well. So D. G. Yuengling faced few questions at the dinner table as he enthusiastically described his ambition for each of his boys to attend brewers' schools in Germany and become beer makers. Arranging for a male successor to continue the day-to-day operation of a company was a common practice among successful commercial enterprises in the Gilded Age. Private assets eliminated the need for external capital and infiltration from those outside the family. Internal succession along familial lines was particularly prevalent among beer makers so breweries throughout the country passed to sons, sons-in-laws, and grandsons.

In Pottsville, the three Yuengling sons began to develop brewing skills under the watchful eye of their father. When they were old enough and weren't occupied with their schoolbooks, David Jr., Frederick, and William could be found at the brewery adjacent to their home working with the other employees among the vats, kettles, and barrels. Eventually, as their teenage years came to a close, the young men expanded their training and assumed responsibility for the brewery's national reputation as a leader and innovator in the industry. This challenge — highlighted by ambitious business ventures outside Pennsylvania — resulted in continued success as well as deep disappointments.

The second generation of the Yuengling brewing dynasty was fortunate. They would be part of the "golden age" of the industry between the Civil War and World War I, when the nation's beer consumption tripled and fortunes were made.[1] Still, brewers who adopted a complacent business approach were at risk, according to industry figures. The high point in the number of breweries in the nation — 4,131 — came in 1873. But a devastating economic depression began that same year and

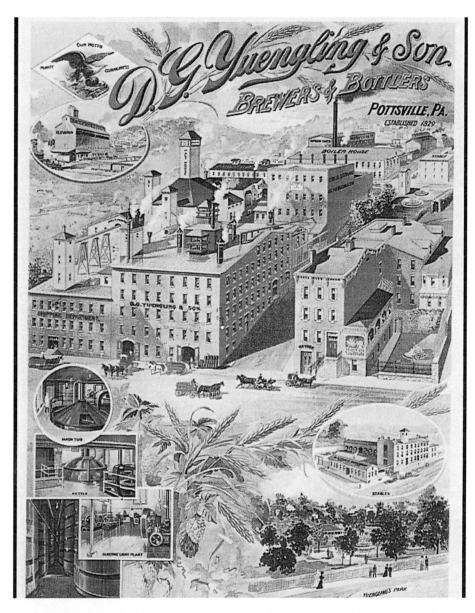

A lithograph of the Yuengling Brewery produced in the late nineteenth century by the Louis J. Porr Company of New York. The lithograph provides important clues about the modernization of the brewery under Frederick Yuengling's direction. (D. G. Yuengling and Son, Inc.)

caused a drastic drop to 3,000 by 1875. Internal Revenue Department records show 2,830 breweries in 1880. By 1910, the figure would drop to about 1,500. Why were breweries going out of business if consumption was on the rise? Developments in the science, technology, and marketing of beer presented brewers with vastly improved methods of production and distribution. They could not only make more

The sons of D. G. Yuengling. From left, David Jr., William, and Frederick. The sons expanded Yuengling's national reputation for producing quality beer. (D. G. Yuengling and Son, Inc.)

beer but could also expand their customer base. The age of the national brewer had arrived.

Larger breweries became possible largely because of improved methods of keeping beer cold. Indeed, if there was one factor that moved a brewery into the modern age, it was the day artificial refrigeration came to the plant.[2] The cost and availability of natural ice had always been a major concern for America's pioneer brewers. Records indicate that D. G. Yuengling had to schedule deliveries of ice from the Knickerbocker Ice Company at the other end of the Schuylkill River in Philadelphia. He also had to worry about how long the ice would last if it needed

The brewery around 1876. D. G. Yuengling and his son, Frederick, posed by the lamppost for the photographer. (D. G. Yuengling and Son, Inc.)

to be stored in ice houses. Mechanical refrigeration made these inconveniences a thing of the past. Brewers could get out of the cramped, moldy caves which limited production. Now the sky was the limit, as capacity could be expanded above ground. In the United States, the first patenting of an ice machine for brewery refrigeration was granted in 1860. Over the next few decades, dramatic improvements continued to be made in brewery refrigeration, including the development of air-cooling machines. Artificial refrigeration made virtually every stage of the brewing process easier, from the cooling of wort to storage.

Advances in the fight against the spoilage of beer also boosted the industry. In the postbellum period, efforts by scientists to preserve beer for longer periods ended in failure. At least that was the case until Louis Pasteur — who actually preferred wine to beer — turned his attention to the matter. The famous scientist published a study in 1866 that showed how wines became diseased by bacteria. He then developed a process to eliminate bacteria — pasteurization. What about beer? Pasteur wanted to make French beer better than German beer — supposedly as an act of revenge for the French defeat at the hands of the Germans in the Franco-Prussian War. His experiments revealed that heating checks bacteria growth in the beverage, and in 1876 Pasteur published a paper — *Etude sur la Bière* — demonstrating that pasteurization could also keep beer from spoiling. The scientist's breakthrough would have a major impact on the brewing industry, and what seemed like a footnote to the story turned out to be extremely significant. One beer producer, Adolphus Busch of Saint Louis's Anheuser-Busch brewing dynasty, somehow was a few years ahead of the release of Pasteur's important findings.

Busch stands as the classic example of the late nineteenth century beer baron. He rose to become a powerful force in the industry due to a combination of Germanic thrift, aggressiveness, good business sense, and a willingness to invest in his breweries. Did the brewer gain insight into Pasteur's studies during his travels to Europe after 1868? Or did he learn about them through his older brother, Anton, who was active in the wine business? Researchers are uncertain. Still, as early as 1872, Busch was extending the shelf life of his beer through the use of primitive tub pasteurizers. The end of the bacteria problem opened the door for bottled beer and widened the path to nationalization. By 1876, bottled beer from Anheuser-Busch in Saint Louis was being enjoyed by thirsty German immigrants on ranches in Texas or in Colorado mining camps. Busch's bold attempt to increase sales was a first. Prior to this time "no American brewer had ever dared venture outside his local markets."[3] Brewing was a regional business, and the product still needed to be enjoyed within less than a dozen miles of where it was produced. But that would no longer be the case. In Pottsville, D. G. Yuengling lived to see the warning signs of nationalization, but guiding the Schuylkill County brewery through this period of dramatic change fell to his second son.

Born on January 26, 1848, Frederick Yuengling's education and training made him very well prepared to join his father in a leadership position at the brewery.[4] A graduate of the public schools in Pottsville, he attended Pennsylvania State College (in State College, Pennsylvania) for three years and also attended a private school on Staten Island. The young man then continued his education at the Eastman Business School in Poughkeepsie, New York. In 1871, he learned more about brewing quality beer when he was sent to Europe to study the craft in world-famous breweries in Munich, Stuttgart, and Vienna. He gained additional brewing experience when he returned to the United States and worked for the Bergner and Engle Brewing Company of Philadelphia — a leader and innovator in the rise of lager in the United States.[5] At the age of 25, with his training complete, he returned to Pottsville in 1873 and worked once again beside his father. He did not return alone.

Frederick Yuengling most likely met his wife, Minna Dohrman, of Brooklyn, while attending private school in New York. The couple exchanged vows on April 3, 1873. The new Mrs. Yuengling then faced the prospect of life in the anthracite coal region — a bit different from the social scene to which she had grown accustomed. The Gilded Age is romanticized as a period of opulence and elegant life. Members of America's wealthiest families— the Astors, the Vanderbilts, and the Goulds—characterized high society in their top hats and tiaras. The anthracite region as a whole did have some millionaires in the late nineteenth century, but the "uppermost social class" that had made fortunes in the northeastern Pennsylvania coal region did not live there. Those who grew the wealthiest from the industrial growth in the region were "the capitalists, chiefly New York and Philadelphia

men, who controlled the dominant railroad and mining corporations of the region"[6]
Still, while it couldn't rival the splendor of the upper classes of New York, Pottsville,
as well as other large cities in the region, had a reigning aristocracy with upper-
crust customs. At places like Mahantongo Street in Pottsville, the River Common
in Wilkes-Barre, and "Quality Hill" in Scranton, there was a mannered social scene,
dominated by a few dozen well-to-do families. Annual balls, masquerades, con-
certs, art lectures and exhibits provided opportunities for displays of "wit, beauty,
and grace."[7] When sons and daughters came home from finishing school or college, the occasion was marked by "brilliant private parties," or "at homes."[8] A fashionable party to mark the return of Frederick Yuengling and his young bride would
undoubtedly have been in order in 1873.

Frederick Yuengling (1848–1899), son of D. G. Yuengling. After extensive training in the craft of brewing,
Frederick used his skills to bring important technological changes to the Pottsville brewery. (D. G.
Yuengling and Son, Inc.)

The couple purchased a townhouse at 606 Mahantongo St., within easy walking distance of the brewery. The house had six bedrooms, formal living and dining rooms, a music room, a tiled entryway, a Spanish crystal chandelier and German stained-glass windows.[9] Over the decades, Mahantongo Street would grow to sixteen blocks as Pottsville's older monied families abandoned their manor houses in other parts of the city and moved to high-toned homes in the blocks above the brewery. Most American cities in the late nineteenth century had a street which suggested opulence. In Pottsville, it was Mahantongo Street, richly described by author Finis Farr:

> Along here the town houses gave a metropolitan air to the street, built as they were
> to form a continuous façade with party walls, just as in London, Philadelphia, or
> Baltimore. A short distance further up, the town houses gave way to large free-
> standing structures, some with mansard roofs, conservatories, and driveways, on
> ample lawns amid magnificent trees. In good weather one could see gardeners,
> coachmen, and grooms at work around these houses, and ladies driving out in car-
> riages to shop or pay calls. For these were carriage folk, families of established
> wealth and unassailable position. On its upper reaches, Mahantongo Street gave its
> message plain and clear: in this part of Pennsylvania, life followed an established
> course, and was quiet, dignified, and gilt-edged.[10]

In this setting on Mahantongo Street, the young couple raised two children. Frank

D. was born on September 27, 1876. A daughter, Edith Louise, followed on March 18, 1878. Sadly, the couple's daughter passed away on October 6, 1883. Frederick and Minna socialized with other prominent Pottsville families like the Archbalds, the Shaefers, the Ulmers, the Luthers, the Carpenters, and the Russells. They shared good times and participated in church groups, the school system, clubs, community organizations and a variety of charitable endeavors. D. G. Yuengling instilled his sons and daughters with a sense of community involvement. Frederick, for example, devoted a considerable amount of time to the Children's Home in Pottsville. The Children's Home provided shelter for neglected and orphaned children not only from Pottsville but also from

Minna (Dohrman) Yuengling, wife of Frederick Yuengling. A native of Brooklyn, New York, Minna played a significant role in the management of the brewery following Frederick Yuengling's death. (D. G. Yuengling and Son, Inc.)

communities throughout the county. Frederick was also actively involved in Pulaski Lodge, No. 216, F and A. M., and provided important support for the Trinity Episcopal Church, a cause that was also dear to his wife.

The years following Frederick Yuengling's return to Pottsville were very challenging for the nation's economy. Like most areas of the country, the anthracite coal region was left seriously weakened in the aftermath of the Panic of 1873. Schuylkill County, in particular, struggled with a negative national reputation for lawlessness fostered by the notorious Molly Maguire episodes and the coinciding labor struggles like the Long Strike of 1875. The Yuengling Brewery somehow continued to post respectable production numbers for a regional brewery, despite the hard, troubled times. Throughout the decade, about 15,000 barrels rolled out the doors annually.[11] The firm also continued to be one of Pottsville's main employers, providing jobs for about 100 workers. Frederick was officially appointed his father's partner in October, 1873. No longer D. G. Yuengling's Eagle Brewery, the company's new name, "D. G. Yuengling and Son," was displayed in large letters on the front of the brick structure on Mahantongo Street. The new official name could also be spotted on the horse-drawn beer wagons trotting throughout the area. Not long after being named a partner in the company, Frederick Yuengling lost an important advisor when his father passed away. But he could also turn to his mother, whose opinions on business dealings probably carried a considerable amount of weight.[12] D. G. Yuengling's will stipulated that his wife "succeeded to his interest in the firm." According to the Pottsville *Republican*, Frederick was willed "one-third" ownership in the company. The other "two-thirds" of brewery

Frederick Yuengling at work on the family farm at Bull Head's area of Pottsville. (D. G. Yuengling and Son, Inc.)

ownership went to the "estate" of D. G. Yuengling—the other members of the family.[13]

Like his father before him, Frederick maintained an interest in a variety of business ventures. He was president of the Pottsville Gas Company, vice president of the Schuylkill Real Estate, Title, Insurance and Trust Company, and a director of the Safe Deposit Bank and of the Pottsville Water Company. As vice-president of the Schuylkill Electric Railway Company, he was among several dignitaries who tried their hand at operating the city's first electric trolley car when it was formally opened on December 23, 1890. About a month later, the second-generation brewer was active in the planning of the Pottsville Armory to provide a headquarters for the military units active in the city. The Yuengling Brewery was among a host of businesses providing financial support for the project, which was not completed until 1914. To escape the stress of these responsibilities, Frederick tended to the chores at the Yuengling Family Farm located in the Bull's Head area of the community.

Under Frederick Yuengling's tenure, the physical plant of the brewery continued to grow. The most helpful illustration of the architectural changes in the late nineteenth century is found in a lush, multicolor lithograph. Portraits of industrial scenes were common in the Gilded Age. Industrialists sought to immortalize their success. This was particularly true of brewers, who considered lithographs and art prints key media for creating the image of an ultramodern, successful operation. The illustrations were usually distributed to saloons, but also became significant in labeling and packaging.[14] Of course, factory portraits should be judged carefully. Artists (no doubt prompted by business owners) embellished or exag-

Top: The Yuengling blacksmith shop at 5th and Norwegian streets. (D. G. Yuengling and Son, Inc.) *Bottom:* Yuengling employees post in front of the brewery. (D. G. Yuengling and Son, Inc.)

gerated certain features of the actual site. The lithograph of the Yuengling Brewery was produced at the dawn of the twentieth century by the Louis J. Porr Company of New York City. The unknown artist sought to create the impression of architecture of vast size that was also aesthetically pleasing. While some artistic license was taken, the colorful print, for the most part, accurately captures the brewery.

The lithograph presents D. G. Yuengling and Son as a sprawling, bustling industrial complex, smoke billowing from about a dozen smokestacks. Workers in the shipping department also had easy access to Mahantongo Street, where fully loaded, horse-drawn delivery wagons make their way. More structures rested up the steep northern slope of Sharp Mountain, emphasizing modernization: an ice department, the cold storage building, the malt house, a boiler house, an electric light shop, and a paint shop. Reaching higher into the hillside, stables and wagon sheds were maintained that included a blacksmith shop and wheelwright shop. Along Mahantongo Street, the former Yuengling home has transformed into an attractive, two-story red-brick office building.

While images of industrial progress dominate the Yuengling lithograph, important clues indicate that the brewery is in harmony with nature. Businesses owners often included "cornucopia or other symbols of prosperity" in company paintings because they wanted to "minimize the impression that industry disturbed nature."[15] The bottom of the factory portrait captures the natural ingredients used to make beer—hops and barley. It also attests to the brewery's important link to the people of the community through the depiction of "Yuengling Park"—in reality the brewery's spring reservoir several blocks away on Mahantongo Street. At the "park," attractively dressed young couples and families enjoy a leisurely afternoon courtesy of the Yuengling family as they stroll past the grounds and its rich green grass and trees. Despite the addition of natural imagery, the lithograph contains hints that industrial technology cannot be ignored. Upon very careful examination, a train, barely visible in the hills beyond Sharp Mountain, can be seen making its way toward Pottsville. In a separate smaller drawing of the brewery's grain storage building, brewing ingredients are delivered by the iron horse. While the trains are minuscule in the lithograph, the mode of transportation loomed very large in the brewing industry.

For at least the first 75 years of the Yuengling Brewery's history, virtually everything depended on the horse and wagon. Not only did the teams make their way through Pottsville and labor on the hills around Mahantongo Street, but local deliveries of beer to retailers in developing communities in Schuylkill County were also made with horse-drawn wagons piled high with wooden kegs. At one point, Yuengling had at least thirty teams of horses and wagons.[16] An important part of the brewery's operation was a blacksmith shop at Fifth and East Norwegian streets, where horses were shoed, fed and groomed. The brewery also had the opportunity to lease animals from various livery stables in Pottsville or have the horses treated by the veterinary dentist in town.[17] Caretakers also tended to the animals on the family-owned farm.

In the initial years of the brewery's operation, the horse and wagon was used to bring ingredients to Pottsville. John Gaul, one of the pioneer maltsters in Philadelphia, delivered his product to Mahantongo Street by guiding his horse and wagon on a 96-mile trip through the winding, hilly roads of eastern Pennsylvania. The Schuylkill Canal was also an important transportation link in the brewery's early history. For example, a major Philadelphia malt producer, the Francis Perot's Sons Malting Company, delivered malt by using the canal, making the approximately 100-mile journey in about six weeks.[18] Before long, the use of the canal to deliver brewery products became antiquated, as coal mining activities spurred the development of a substantial rail system in the lower anthracite region.

The tremendous expansion of railroads in the post-Civil War era presented brewers with a superb opportunity. They would not have been able to expand the market for beer without advances in distribution and transportation, particularly the shipping of draft beer. Initially, however, transporting beer by rail was an expensive, wet, sloppy proposition. Unpasteurized barrels of beer would be rolled onto rail cars, and workers would then cram the cars with as much natural ice as possible to prevent the brew from spoiling — a challenging task when freight cars were headed south in the summer months. Railroad operators often complained that brewers added too much weight to the cars by overloading them with ice. Several brewers, who were also frustrated by variable freight rates, responded by forming their own rail lines to gain greater control over shipping conditions.[19] As the 1890s approached, technological advancements in refrigerated boxcars eased cooling problems during shipping. As a result, competition in the national market continued to intensify.

Brewers who worked to extend their range had to deal with expenses that much smaller regional brewers didn't face. First, they had to pay for the round-trip transportation of beer barrels. They then needed to develop a distribution system in the nation's major cities. The primary feature of the distribution system was a small icehouse, usually near railroad depots, where beer could be stored. The more successful brewers could afford to include offices and warehouses and hire personnel not only to sell the beer from the icehouse but also to take orders and then make local deliveries. Despite the added expenses, some efforts to capture a national market were successful. One of the strongest examples of the trend is Captain Frederick Pabst of the Pabst Brewing Company in Milwaukee, Wisconsin. Through national distribution and the absorption of another brewery, the company reached the coveted one-million barrel annual sales figure in 1893. Anheuser-Busch provides another convincing example of nationalization. In 1872, it produced about 23,000 barrels. Two decades later, thanks to advances in technology and transportation, the Saint Louis brewery produced over 700,000. Other brewers pursuing a national market included August Uihlein, president the Joseph Schlitz Brewing Company, Christian Moerlein of Cincinnati, and W. J. Lemp of Saint Louis.

The emergence of national breweries did not present an immediate threat to the Yuengling Brewery. True, in the last quarter of the nineteenth century, sales agents for the new national brewers like Anheuser-Busch entered Pennsylvania and came uncomfortably close to the heart of Yuengling's local market. In Philadelphia, for example, three businessmen attempted to franchise and sell Adolphus Busch's beer in the 1890s.[20] The time had not yet come, however, when beer from Saint Louis and Milwaukee would infiltrate the anthracite region. The changes in the industry in the postbellum period presented the greatest danger to breweries in major American cities with very large populations and easier rail access. Successful regional beer makers could still grow, but not at the pace of the national brewers. Northeastern Pennsylvania brewers like Yuengling were in a particularly good position, because the anthracite coal industry, despite periods of labor unrest and market instability, continued to grow until shortly after World War I, reaching a peak in production in 1920. The demand for black diamonds, particularly its impact on transportation, benefited regional brewers.

As early as the 1840s, Schuylkill County had 65 miles of incorporated railroad, and as the decades passed more rail lines and stations honeycombed the area. Regional brewers took advantage of the development of several large railroads, such as the Philadelphia and Reading and the Lehigh Valley, and rail became the preferred method of bringing supplies to breweries. For example, railroads delivered malt to the Yuengling Brewery as early as 1842. Eventually, the brewery opted to install larger malt storage, because railroad cars could deliver more of the vital ingredient. The storage tanks had the capacity to hold nearly eight railroad cars of malt. Ice was also delivered via rail. Perhaps the most significant development in rail transportation in Schuylkill County and one which had an important impact on regional businesses like the Yuengling Brewery, came in 1855 with the development of railroad "planes," an engineering feat which allowed railroads to cross mountains.

Plane engineering provided rail access to northern Schuylkill County, most notably into the Mahanoy Valley over Broad Mountain. Within a decade of the new innovation in railroad transportation, nearly half of the coal shipped from Schuylkill County came from the northern rim. So just as Pottsville was a coal boomtown a few decades earlier, the advance in transportation led to new boomtowns in Ashland, Shenandoah and Mahanoy City, as well as the Northumberland County communities of Mount Carmel and Shamokin. Mine operators and miners migrated north, and the population of northern Schuylkill County grew substantially over the next three decades in comparison with the southern part of the region. Shenandoah, for example, briefly topped Pottsville's population in the 1890s, and Ashland and Mahanoy City grew more rapidly as well. The economic expansion of northern Schuylkill County presented the Yuengling Brewery with a strong opportunity, as rail technology allowed beer to be transported safely over long distances.

If Frederick Yuengling wanted to learn how his brand was selling in the developing Ashland–Mahanoy City–Shenandoah region — or in any other part of the country for that matter — he would have few problems. Advances in communication brought the nation closer together. Frederick Yuengling had evidence of this everyday at work. A telephone was installed at the brewery in 1877 to connect the brewery office with the plant. The new device established the company as the first continuous telephone user and subscriber in Pottsville. The use of the phone at this early date is particularly remarkable since telephones were first offered for commercial use in May of 1877. Advances in communications are also evidenced in the fact that Yuengling called upon dozens of firms in New York, Chicago and Philadelphia to provide advertising supplies and technical equipment.

At some point during his presidency at the brewery, Frederick Yuengling had come to the realization that the times his father knew—the times when brewers respected the territory of fellow brewers—were fading. For decades, the brewery on Mahantongo Street's main competition came from the other breweries in the city, the Rettig Brewery and Lorenz Schmidt's Orchard Brewery. These breweries, however, understood their boundaries and generally avoided cutthroat sales tactics. One sign of cooperation among regional brewers was the formation of the Anthracite Brewers Association around the turn of the century. The association helped prevent bitter price wars by reaching agreements on the cost of a barrel of beer. An association document from about 1900 set the price of a barrel at $6.50 for licensed dealers. The association also shared information regarding labor problems and created blacklists of tavern owners who failed to pay for their beer or fell behind on their payments.[21] Still, competition intensified. The advances in both communication and transportation before the close of the nineteenth century brought about a different approach to business, and regional brewers were forced to expand their markets.

Frederick Yuengling was among many beer makers who imitated the distribution pattern established by the national brewers. Yuengling cold storage depots sprung up along rail lines in key communities not only in Schuylkill County but in neighboring counties as well. By 1896, Yuengling beer was shipped via rail to depots in Shamokin, Hazleton, Girardville, Mount Carmel, Ashland, Tamaqua, Mahanoy City, and Shenandoah. The old-time distributor's depots were simply ice houses where Yuengling's wooden barrels could be kept cold as they awaited further delivery. The structures presented the opportunity for the company to spread its brand name among travelers as "D. G. Yuengling and Son" was painted in large letters on the depots. Sales agents also promoted the Yuengling brand in these communities.[22] Yuengling was available to wholesalers in Northumberland, Dauphin, Lebanon, Luzerne, and Lycoming counties and could be enjoyed in taverns in major cities on the Eastern Seaboard like Philadelphia, New York, and Boston.

Rail lines, of course, move boxcars in two directions, and Frederick Yuengling may have been concerned as changes in transportation gave aggressive brewers the opportunity to capture customers in Pottsville. To the south, in the city of Reading, breweries operated by Frederick Lauer and his sons expanded their market, thanks to rail transportation, and posted high production numbers. To the north, the thirst of potential customers in the developing communities was satisfied through new breweries—several of which, to Frederick Yuengling's dismay, were quite successful.[23] The most significant and enduring example of a northern

A Yuengling beer wagon on the streets of Philadelphia. (D. G. Yuengling and Son, Inc.)

Schuylkill County brewery is the Charles D. Kaier's Brewery in Mahanoy City. The company was established as a retail liquor business during the Civil War by Charles D. Kaier, a native of Biningan, Germany. Kaier, in his early years, was also a sales agent in Mahanoy City for the noted Bergner and Engel Brewing Company in Philadelphia, importing beer from the city into Schuylkill County. By 1880, he would open his own brewery at 67–69 North Main Street. Kaier's business became a limited stock company in 1894. Like Yuengling, Kaier branched out into a variety of business ventures, including the operation of an ice company, a grand opera house, a hotel and a restaurant. The Mahanoy City businessman was also a bank president and controlled the operation of the Anthracite Light, Heat and Power Company. He passed away on May 31, 1899, but, aided by a legendary number of taverns in Mahanoy City, the brewery he founded continued to successfully market ale, porter, lager and weiss beer. After a few decades of operation, it became one of the largest breweries in the state and employed about 150 workers. By 1899 it had reached the very respectable 100,000-barrels-per-year capacity, a figure that the Yuengling Brewery would not reach until 1918. As early as 1896, advertisements for Kaier's "Kaiser Export Beer" were appearing in the Pottsville *Miners' Journal*. The ads were tagged with a note that "[m]ail orders will receive prompt attention."

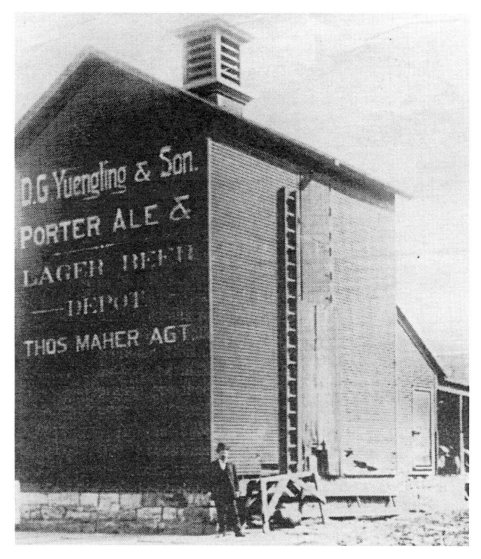

Frederick Yuengling stands before a company storage depot in Shamokin, Pennsylvania. The Yuengling Brewery took advantage of advances in rail transportation. The company successfully expanded its market by using the depots to keep its beer cold and fresh for thirsty customers in key communities throughout the region. (D. G. Yuengling and Son, Inc.)

Another notable brewery in the southern anthracite coal field—the Fuhrman and Schmidt Brewery in Shamokin—had a significant tie to the Kaier's Brewery. Founded in 1854 as the Eagle Run Brewery (because of its location near the Eagle Run stream), the beer-making operation would approach the 40,000-barrel production figure in the 1890s through the popularity of a variety of beers, including ale, bock, porter, and half and half. The growth was due in large measure to the brewing expertise of Max Schmidt and Philip Henry Fuhrman. The latter was plant superintendent at the Kaier's Brewery and a friend and mentor of Charles D. Kaier. That was before 1895, when the two men had a serious disagreement about the management of the company. Kaier bought Fuhrman's stock in the brewery, reported to be worth $25,000, and the former plant manager at Kaier's went to Shamokin, where the Fuhrman and Schmidt Brewery, also known as F & S, was formed.

Further north, in neighboring Luzerne County, Yuengling was getting pressure from brewer Charles Stegmaier. Like D. G. Yuengling, Stegmaier was a native of Württemberg and had developed his brewing skills there. The brewer was undoubtedly familiar with the Yuengling brand, because he had left Wilkes-Barre for a few years in the 1850s to work at the Orchard Brewery in Pottsville. He returned to the Luzerne County city in 1857. The Stegmaier Brewery briefly ceased operation under the depressed economic conditions of the 1870s. But it made a very strong rebound as the economy slowly improved. By the 1890s it was producing about 100,000 barrels annually, and, in the early twentieth century, was reaching some of the same counties that Yuengling had targeted. By the time Charles Stegmaier died in 1906, the company employed a few hundred workers. To deliver its products, Stegmaier had a stable with over two hundred heavy draft horses, several delivery trucks, and numerous refrigerated railroad cars. A partial listing of its cold-storage plants and depots indicate Stegmaier's growing influence in the brewing market. Trains were delivering the Stegmaier brand to places throughout northeastern Pennsylvania like Sayre, Towanda, Dunmore, Pittston, Bloomsburg, Nanticoke, Plymouth and Lehighton. The Wilkes-Barre plant produced twice as much as any brewery in Luzerne County, closing in on the 170,000-barrel mark. The brand also gained a reputation for quality, winning eight gold metals at major beer expositions in Paris, Brussels and Rome between 1910 and 1913. In an indication of the competitiveness of the industry, Yuengling's ads invited customers to compare its brew with other brands on the market. "By Testing Yuengling's Wiener Beer, Porter, Ale and Brown Stout, You will pronounce them Superior to any in the market," stated an ad in the April 21, 1896, Pottsville *Republican.*

The stability at the Yuengling Brewery in these increasingly competitive times was due in part to its ability to keep pace with several advancements in the science and technology of brewing. A description of the brewery written around 1893 praised a host of modernizations inside the plant. The business continued to utilize its cavernous storage cellars, but modern ice machines and cooling equipment were in place:

> The buildings of the brewery are of the superior kind, and are fully equipped with the latest improved apparatus, appliances and machinery, including a kettle of 300 barrels, ten pumps, three steam boilers, of 400 horse-power respectively, and six steam engines. There are also two Mayer ice machines, with an aggregate capacity of about eighty-five tons, in active operation. The vats, mash-tubs, coolers, boilers, etc., in fact all the superior interior equipments commend the admiration of brewing experts, as well as those who have a less intimate knowledge of apparatus of this kind. The storage accommodations of the brewery are very extensive, so that ale and lager are not hurried from the vats to the consumer but are kept in good cellars until they reach the proper maturity. The brewery is noted for its cleanliness, and

Early refrigeration equipment at the Yuengling Brewery. (D. G. Yuengling and Son, Inc.)

> the general care which is characteristic of the minutest part of the process. The ale brewed here is equal to the best imported. The entire product of this firm is unrivaled for purity and quality, and possesses a delicacy and flavor rarely found in other brands.... In everything related to the process of brewing, Mr. F.G. Yuengling is regarded as a high authority.[24]

The brewery added its own electric light plant, and the power source also ran pumps and motors. The installation of a stained-glass ceiling in the brewhouse in 1881 also indicated that the brewery was profitable under the initial years of Frederick's management.

The Yuengling Brewery also kept pace with the advances in the chemistry of brewing and efforts to curb spoilage problems. Important discoveries regarding yeasts and bacteria reduced the chances of failures in the brewing process. Brewmasters could address most chemical problems, but many of the larger breweries began hiring research chemists as an important part of their staff. They maintained up-to-date laboratories to bring greater uniformity to their product. Smaller brewers could not afford to take these measures; however, Frederick Yuengling recognized the improvements scientists were bringing to the brewing process and took measures to have his beer inspected to maintain quality. He enrolled the brewery into "The First Scientific Station for the Arts of Brewing" in New York and could

The bottle shop at the Yuengling Brewery in its infancy — around 1895. (D. G. Yuengling and Son, Inc.)

then send samples of his beer to the facility for chemical analysis. The services were provided for a fee of $260 per year.[25]

Of all efforts to modernize, perhaps the most important addressed changes in the packaging of beer. It can be argued that Frederick Yuengling's key contribution to the brewery's longevity was his focus on bottling beer. The dramatic growth in the popularity of bottled beer was the most important development in the brewing industry during the last decade of the nineteenth century. Originally, brewers only produced beer to be sold on draft. Pasteurization did put bottled beer on the path to popularity; however, its acceptance would be gradual. Problems in the bottling process lingered even after Pasteur's contribution. One difficulty was the expense. Bottles were handmade in the nineteenth century, and they were not cheap. The special embossing of the brewery's name added to the cost. The bottles were "returnables," often embossed with statements like "This Bottle Must Be Returned" or "This Bottle Not to be Sold." Of course, for a variety of reasons, bottles disappeared, and the brewer was then forced to pay for more. Thus, bottling was done sparingly, and, prior to the 1890s, sudsmakers often preferred to leave the bottling to someone else under a separate operation. Barrels of beer would be sold to independent bottling companies, who would then resell it to thirsty consumers. For this reason, most nineteenth-century beer bottles carry two names—

Rare Yuengling beer bottles, including several from New York. (D. G. Yuengling and Son, Inc.)

the brewer and the bottler. One of Yuengling's independent bottlers, for example, was the Bender family in nearby Minersville.[26]

Independent bottling worked well for a time, but more and more beer drinkers came to expect uniform packaging and consistent quality — something that could not be guaranteed under independent bottlers. In addition, a competitor's brew could mistakenly be placed on the market under the Yuengling name, a great risk for a brewer who took great pride in his beer and had worked hard to develop a solid reputation. Brewers could no longer leave the important packaging process in the hands of others. They had to overcome two challenges, however, in order to successfully meet the public demand for the new packaging.

Early bottling caps, even those produced in the 1880s and early 1890s, were far from reliable. The bottling operation was almost entirely a manual job as well. Beer bottles were filled by hand by workers who drew the beverage from a rubber hose attached to a keg. The cork stopper was inserted with a pressing apparatus as foam flowed around the neck of the bottle. There was no shortage of attempts to

The racking shop where barrels of beer are filled. This photograph was taken around 1900. (D. G. Yuengling and Son, Inc.)

find alternatives. American brewers experimented with at least 1,500 bottle-stopping methods, and none were very successful. They either allowed dirt in or carbonation out.[27] Brewers dreamed of a stopper that could be applied by machine. A key development toward realizing this dream occurred in 1892 when William Painter patented the "crown" bottle cap. The crown top extended the shelf life of beer even further, and advances in bottle manufacturing led to uniformity. Breweries became even noisier as machine-made bottles clanked their way through automatic bottling and capping equipment.

Tax laws further complicated the bottling process. The government dictated that brewing and bottling beer could not take place on the same premises. The separation of the bottling department and the brewery forced brewers to go through the wasteful, time-consuming process of filling up kegs so tax stamps could be affixed. Then the kegs were transported across the street to a bottling house, where they were emptied into bottles. In a significant development, however, Captain Frederick Pabst led a successful effort to change this regulation of the Internal Revenue Act. The June 1890 change allowed brewers to construct pipelines from the storage cellars to bottling houses. With the capping problem solved and tax laws relaxed, the production of bottled beer began to increase to meet high demand. In the name of quality control, D. G. Yuengling and Son fell in line with a trend in the brewing industry and established its own bottling works in 1895.

A nineteenth century Yuenglng business card featuring a variation of the company's eagle logo. (D. G. Yuengling and Son, Inc.)

Packaging beer in labeled bottles meant that names, trademarks, and logos became more visible and more important. Brewers were prompted to take action to protect their brand names and trademarks. In fact, about a decade after Yuengling opened its bottling works, it found itself defending its rights to the eagle-and-barrel logo before the United States Patent Office. The office was concerned because several brewers used the same emblem. A Yuengling document states that at least three breweries, including the Jacob Ruppert Brewing Company, used an eagle and barrel logo and had attempted to register the image as their trademark. Yuengling's attorney, Titian W. Johnson, argued that Yuengling was the earliest to register the eagle and barrel logo as its trademark. He submitted as an exhibit a Yuengling beer label used in 1895 and provided a summary of the use of the image throughout the company's history. Johnson's brief states that Yuengling was "the first of all of the parties ... to adopt as a trade-mark for beer the representation of an Eagle and Barrel and actually apply the same to goods, and if the question of priority is to be considered by the Patent Office, then registration should be given to D. G. Yuengling and Son." Johnson also stated that the company had no objection to the use of the same figure by the other brewers involved in the case, because their eagle-and-barrel logos were "so different in appearance as to preclude the possibility of deception or confusion in the trade."[28]

Customer confusion concerning the eagle-and-barrel image was probably not a major concern to Yuengling. Beer drinkers in the anthracite region, for the most part, were more than content with the brew being turned out by their hometown brewery and remained fiercely loyal. Still, brand identification would become increasingly important, a point illustrated by a rare case of local residents rebelling

A group photograph of Yuengling employees. (D. G. Yuengling and Son, Inc.)

against the hometown brand. One of the most serious acts of violence in American labor history, the Lattimer Massacre of 1897, occurred on September 10 in a small coal patch near Hazleton, Pennsylvania. The fatal shooting of nineteen striking coal miners by sheriff's deputies signaled the emergence of Slavic immigrants as a force in the American labor movement. When a murder trial ended with a verdict of not guilty, the deputies who were charged left the courthouse in Wilkes-Barre and went directly to the Old Hazle Brewery on Hazleton's south side to get beer to celebrate. The immigrant population of the area, which was devastated with the verdict, then labeled Hazle Beer as "Deputies Beer." The boycott caused the brewery to go bankrupt in six months.[29] The protest by Hazleton's immigrant beer drinkers might not have been successful if they did not have beer from other breweries to drink. As brewers took advantage of advances in transportation, occasionally quaffing a brand different than the hometown brew was no longer out of the question. The founder of the Yuengling Brewery could probably have been satisfied with word-of-mouth promotion or allowing the brewery name to be boldly painted on the side of the beer wagons as they made their delivery. His sons would be forced to turn to more aggressive advertising tactics.

As early as the seventeenth century and for most of the nineteenth century, beer marketing was limited to small, dull ads in the hometown newspapers or local city directories. The ads did little more than list the name and owner of the business. As the market for beer expanded, however, so did newspaper advertising. D.

"The Proof of the Pudding is in the Eating,"
::::AND::::
"The Test of the BEER is in the Drinking."

By Testing ✦✦✦✦

YUENGLING'S
Wiener Beer, Porter, Ale and Brown Stout,

You will pronounce them Superior to any in the market.

Our *Porter* and *Brown Stout* are *Celebrated* for being the Best Brewed in this country and as Tonics are much better than any other Malt Extracts.

When drinking any of these goods you can depend upon their being

PURE, CLEAN & WHOLESOME
For we use only Clean Malt, Clean Hops, Clean Water and have a Clean Brewery.

A Yuengling ad from the Pottsville *Republican* in the 1890s. Early beer advertisements emphasized the health benefits of beer drinking as well as the cleanliness of the brewery. (D. G. Yuengling and Son, Inc.)

G. Yuengling and Son also used newspaper advertising extensively in order to protect and expand its markets. Most towns had a local newspaper in the nineteenth century, and, in addition to Pottsville papers, Yuengling promoted its products in papers in Shenandoah, Ashland, Girardville, and Shamokin. Advertisement for the foaming treat could also be found in larger urban papers, as well as in ethnic papers like the *Amerikanski-Slovenski Union* in Pittsburgh and one of the leading German newspapers in the anthracite region, the *Jefferson Democrat*.[30]

Early beer ads often emphasized the idea that beer was a key to good health because it provided both carbohydrates and protein to the body. Beer was also recognized as a "tonic" for "easing tension and providing nutrition."[31] Brewers also tried to enhance the image of beer by emphasizing "family, health, friendship, and the nation" in their ads.[32] One study of advertising in the Gilded Age notes that beer advertisements were similar to patent medicine ads that had been effective and popular a few decades earlier. For example, a Schlitz ad in *Harper's Weekly* from 1903 pictured a doctor recommending Schlitz to one of his patients. The copy in the ad detailed why:

> It is good for anybody. The hops form a tonic; the barley a food. The trifle of alcohol is an aid to digestion. And the custom of drinking beer supplies the body with fluid to wash out waste. People who don't drink beer seldom drink enough fluid of any kind. A great deal of ill health is caused by a lack of it.[33]

Evidence suggests that doctors in several states were also recommending Yuengling to their patients. The Yuengling ad in the Pottsville *Republican* on April 21, 1896, notes that the porter and brown stout could be used for medicinal purposes because these brews are known "for being the Best Brewed in this country and as Tonics are much better than any other Malt Extracts."[34]

Another theme in early newspaper ads reflected public pressure for pure food and drug laws during the Progressive Era. Yuengling's simple motto during this period was "Purity ... Cleanliness." Advertisements proclaimed the brewery's products were "pure, clean, and wholesome.... For we use only Clean Malt, Clean Hops, Clean Water and have a Clean Brewery." For some brewers, exaggerated claims of superiority or propaganda phrases were not enough, and they were compelled to move beyond newspaper advertising to promote their products. National magazines allowed some beer barons to spread the word about their product across the land. Fred Pabst, in an example of the impact of rail transportation on brewing, placed a full-page advertisement in *Harper's Weekly* in 1895 which announced that "2 trains, 15 carloads of Pabst Milwaukee Beer are shipped daily." Even magazine ads did not reach a wide enough audience for some brewers, and more aggressive promotional measures were needed. Enter the brewery salesman: When he entered a saloon, he had more than a few weapons in his arsenal.

Sales agents for breweries were popular figures at the neighborhood bar and not only because they could offer discounts and rebates to the tavern owner, or free samples for the crowd. They gave other things away, too. They provided advertising literature and even promotional material, including items found hanging outside over the door or on the barroom wall: signs, bar posters, and calendars. Early signs were simple and made of wood, but as point-of-sale items became more important, glass and electrified signs became more common.

When artwork supplemented the printed word in the late nineteenth century, brewery advertising material became more ornate and colorful. This is particularly true of posters and calendars that brewers supplied free of charge to taverns, hotels, and restaurants. Yuengling calendars and posters date at least as far back as the 1870s and feature a variety of colorful scenes in which the pride of Pottsville is being enjoyed. Like other brewery calendars of the period, Yuengling's calendars were hard on the eyes of beer drinkers who couldn't remember the date. The months occupy small squares on the calendar while the artwork and the brewery name dominate. One of the most notable examples of a Yuengling calendar is one created by Wolf and Company of Philadelphia in 1907—the "puppies" painting titled "A Good Story." The calendar is reminiscent of and probably inspired by Cassius Marcellus Coolidge's famous "Dogs Playing Poker" series of portraits. Coolidge's dog paintings were very popular at about the time the Yuengling painting was done by an anonymous artist. The four puppies in the Yuengling poster share the latest gossip as they enjoy cigars, cigarettes, and, most importantly, Yuengling Weiner beer, ale, and porter. The social nature of beer drinking is also emphasized in other Yuengling calendars and posters. Popular promotional scenes included romanticized elderly gentlemen hoisting a frothy glass of Yuengling beer, serving as a reminder of the German tendency toward beer drinking. Portraits featuring attractive, elegantly attired women, another industry trend, are featured as well. Early Yuengling beer posters and calendars also proclaimed Yuengling beer as a "tonic of tonics." They often noted the variety of beers marketed by the company as well.

As competition continued to intensify, salesmen sweetened the sales pitch by offering more lavish "gratuities." Old promotional items that carry a brewery's name—also known as "breweriana"—are now treasured by hobbyists and collectors. Adolphus Busch pioneered the use of gratuities to promote his beer, providing tavern owners and customers with items like playing cards, inkblotters, hooked metal bottle openers, corkscrews, match boxes, pocket knives, and postcards, theatre and ballpark programs, and storybooks. The Yuengling Brewery followed Busch's lead and offered many of the same gratuities. This includes what is probably the most prized item among breweriana collectors.

Beer trays were first produced by a few brewers around 1900. Within a decade, any brewery interesting in attracting and retaining customers was providing trays as part of its lineup of point-of-purchase offerings.[35] Some of Yuengling's most impressive beer trays can be dated from 1939 to 1948; however, some Yuengling trays are dated as early as the first decade of the twentieth century. Perhaps the earliest Yuengling beer tray features a traditional scene depicting two colonial women being assisted as they prepare to step off a carriage at the end of a journey. The tray notes "Yuengling's Celebrated Porter" in its lettering. Other Yuengling trays emphasize the company's classic eagle logo.

Brewers also knew that word of mouth could help boost sales. One of the major methods of getting potential customers throughout the nation talking was by presenting beers at the various national and international fairs, as well as industrial and trade fairs, that took place in the late nineteenth and early twentieth centuries. Awards for brewing excellence provided the opportunity for brewers to document their claims of superiority to other products. A good showing at these competitions could also find a place in subsequent advertising. The Yuengling Brewery staff planned and participated in events like the Centennial Exposition of 1876 in Philadelphia; however, the 1893 Columbian Exposition in Chicago went a long way to giving the Pottsville brewery more name recognition.

Pottsville resident Charlie Guetling made a trip to the 1893 World's Fair. Of

The cover of a promotional storybook, *Sylvan Scenes*, that was distributed by Yuengling. The Pottsville brewer, like other beer makers, produced and distributed more and more gratuities like playing cards, calendars, and post cards. (D. G. Yuengling and Son, Inc.)

course, many people went to the spectacle. But Guetling and his dog, Prince, walked the entire distance from Pottsville to the Windy City — almost 900 miles — pushing a wheelbarrow and a barrel of Yuengling beer. An advertising campaign? Probably. The keg, painted patriotically in red, white and blue with gilded hoops, weighed 30 pounds when filled with beer and was clearly inscribed on the side, "Yuengling and Son, Pottsville, Pa." Guetling also took a .38 pistol along. Enthusiasm was high in Pottsville when he set off on the journey on July 19. His wife

Charles Guetling and his dog Prince. The pair delivered a barrel of Yuengling beer to Chicago from Pottsville — via wheelbarrow. (D. G. Yuengling and Son, Inc.)

waved goodbye to him, probably saddened by the fact that it was their 12th wedding anniversary. And two of his six children tagged along with their father and the dog for a short way. On the first day, he did not stop until he reached Ashland, where crowds lined the streets to cheer him. He rested at Billy Campbell's saloon in Ashland, and the next day he left Schuylkill County and made his way into the mountains. His shoes and clothes were in tatters, but he made it a few days early:

> It was Wednesday, August 16, 1893, and a tattered, tired man wheeling a sextel of beer showed up at the 57th street entrance of the World's Fair.... He had been afoot

over Pennsylvania, Ohio, Indiana, and Illinois for 28 days, three days earlier than his schedule called for. The keg of beer was intact; that had been one of the requirements.[36]

Frederick Yuengling did reward Guetling with $25; more significantly, however, Guetling and his dog won the admiration of his fellow beer lovers in Pottsville upon his return (via train) from Chicago. The effort by Guetling and Prince no doubt helped spread the word about Yuengling beer and made the pair local celebrities. One example of a national celebrity endorsement has also been documented. "The March King," John Philip Sousa (1854–1932), and his highly popular concert band made Pottsville a regular stop on their national tours because they "looked forward to the opportunity of enjoying the wonderful Pottsville Porter."[37]

No matter what the advertising method used, nothing could ensure sales like the "tied house system." First, brewers purchased properties—preferably corner locations near heavy pedestrian traffic. Then, they found a prospective saloon-keeper who would rent or manage the property with the agreement that the owner-brewer's beer would be the only brand available.[38] The practice of producer-controlled retail outlets began in England where, beginning in the 1790s, brewers like Guinness monopolized pub licenses.[39] In antebellum America, a very limited number of breweries owned taverns, but more and more brewers became involved in the retail end of the trade under the intense competition in the industry from the 1870s to the 1920s. The "saloon period" in American bar history had arrived.[40] In the earliest stage of the system, saloonkeepers rented from the brewer-owner the saloon's fixtures, plate-glass mirrors, sideboards, bars, stools, storage cabinets and other items. Gradually, brewers owned an entire establishment or built new saloons. It has been estimated that in the early twentieth century brewers owned or controlled between 70 and 85 percent of all the retail drinking establishments in the United States. An example of the large scope of the tied-house system is found in Milwaukee, where, as early as 1887, Schlitz owned approximately 50 drinking establishments.[41] Controlling what was sold in saloons through direct ownership of the property proved to be extremely profitable and resulted in great brewing fortunes. In addition, if a brewer couldn't find a way to own the local taproom or hotel, he would limit competition at the bar by offering an exclusive distributorship contract. The beer maker offered special financial deals to the business owner with the understanding that the brewer's brand would be sold there exclusively.

In the anthracite region, the use of the "tied-house system" met or exceeded the national trend. The Yuengling Brewery owned several local taprooms, saloons, and hotels, not only in Pottsville, but also in neighboring communities. The Black Cat Saloon in Pottsville, the Buckhorn Cafe in Saint Clair and the National Hotel in Tremont were among the properties controlled by the brewery, and, considering Frederick Yuengling's position as vice president of the Schuylkill Real Estate, Title, Insurance and Trust Company, it is reasonable to assume that the company had many more real estate holdings. Other Pottsville breweries, as well as other Schuylkill County beer makers, utilized the tied-house system. Yuengling's competitor in northern Schuylkill County, Charles Kaier, owned an estimated 40 taverns in Mahanoy City. In its coverage of the Prohibition movement and its impact on local businesses, the Pottsville *Republican* made a distinction between "brewery-owned" bars and other drinking establishments in the city. The description implied that the practice was commonplace and widely recognized by the general public.

While competition among brewers in the anthracite region was heating up, Yuengling's reputation for producing quality beers spread to other parts of the country, thanks to D. G. Yuengling's skills as both a brewmaster and mentor. Today, brewers typically learn to make beer at brewing schools, studying subjects such as organic chemistry and chemical engineering in laboratory setting. The concept of a brewing school would have been foreign to the founder of the brewery on Mahantongo Street.[42]

John Frederick Betz (1831–1902), a wealthy Philadelphia brewer and brother-in-law of D. G. Yuengling. Betz developed his skills as a brewmaster at the Yuengling Brewery and maintained personal and business ties with the Yuengling family throughout his life. (The Library Company of Philadelphia.)

He was an old-time brewer who believed that the art was best learned in working breweries at the side of a master craftsman. Not surprisingly, he allowed the brewery to become a place where the fine art of brewing could be studied by those hoping for a career in the business. Among those who learned at the brewery were John Frederick Betz, Henry Clausen (as well as his sons George C. and Henry Clausen, Jr.), William Woerz of Beadleston & Woerz of New York City, and George W. Robinson of the Albany (New York) Brewing Company. Two men who learned beer making at the Yuengling Brewery — Betz and Clausen — went on to become leading figures in nineteenth-century American brewing history.

Betz not only had the benefit of learning about brewing under a highly skilled craftsman, but he also became related to that craftsman.[43] Betz was born in Mohringer, near Stuttgart, Germany, on April 8, 1831, the son of John George Betz and Rosine Elizabeth Ulmer. When John Frederick was only a year old, the family immigrated to America, settling in Schuylkill County. There is some evidence that Betz and his wife became hotel operators.[44] Fortunately for Betz, his sister, Elizabeth, married David Gottlieb Yuengling. As a member of the family, albeit an in-law, the young German immigrant probably had an easier time obtaining an apprenticeship at the Yuengling Brewery. As apprentices at the brewery, young men virtually became part of the Yuengling household. Brewery workers often boarded at houses near the Brewery selected by the brewery owner. There is also a possi-

John Frederick Betz's Eagle Brewery at 347–355 West 44th St. in New York around 1890. Betz, the brother-in-law of D. G. Yuengling, learned the brewing craft in Pottsville. D. G. Yuengling's son, David Jr., worked here early in his brewing career. (D. G. Yuengling and Son, Inc.)

bility that they found lodging inside the brewery itself — a common practice in the nineteenth century. In the 1850 census, Betz is among 20 people listed as part of the Yuengling household. This includes, in addition to the immediate Yuengling family, other brewers, teamsters, and laborers. Betz's occupation is listed as "brewer" by the census enumerator. He completed his apprenticeship at the age of 21 and then further developed his brewing skills in Europe, where he practiced his craft under some of the most noted brewmasters: Paul Kolb in Stuttgart, Germany; Count Archor, near Sultzberg, Austria; and Anton Dreher in Vienna, Austria. When he returned to America, the young businessman opened a brewery at 347–355 W. 44th St. in New York in 1853. In what is perhaps a tribute to his experience in Pottsville under David Yuengling, Betz named his brewery the Eagle Brewery. He was also affiliated with the Bauer and Betz Brewery at 140–150 East 58th St. between Lexington and 3rd from 1876 to 1882. The Schuylkill County native then successfully operated it independently from 1882 to 1884.

Betz achieved even more success in Philadelphia, where he first leased William Gaul's Brewery at 401/421 Newmarket and Callowhill in 1867. He added lager to the brewery's existing portfolio of ales and porters. In 1869, he purchased the brewery and operated it under his name until 1880. Figures show that the operation was successful. It placed third among Philadelphia's 85 breweries in 1878, selling a very respectable 52,891 barrels. In an expansion move, a brewery at 415 Callowhill and 5th and Lawrence streets was completed in 1880. This brewery was operated in partnership with his son, John F. Betz Jr., and the firm became known as John F. Betz and Son. The father and son team's heavy investments made it one of the largest in the country.[45] The Betz brewing operation in Philadelphia also included the manufacture of its own malt in a building on Saint John Street. Betz personally supervised the malthouse, which was seven stories high and had a capacity of 250,000 bushels of barley. The Betz family's other Philadelphia brewing venture included the takeover of the Germania Brewing Company at Broad and Columbia avenues in 1886. Also, in Jersey City, New Jersey, Betz went into partnership with Henry Lembeck to establish a brewery at 164–182 9th Street in 1869. Again, perhaps as a tribute to his roots, the name Lembeck and Betz Eagle Brewery was adopted in 1890. The Jersey City brewery had a large capacity and had an estimated value of $900,000.[46]

Brewers built great fortunes during this time, and Betz provides a chief example. He supplemented his brewing profits with astute real estate investments and rose to great prominence in Philadelphia, becoming one of its wealthiest citizens. He owned property in nearly every ward and constructed large office buildings, magnificent hotels and theatres. His contributions to the German-American community were particularly noteworthy. At the corner of Broad Street and South Penn Square, he erected the Betz Building at an estimated cost of $1.5 million. The office building included an old world-style Raths-Keller where customers could enjoy a wide variety of foreign and domestic beers, dine on fine German cusine, and browse the directories and newspapers of major European cities.

Betz established another landmark around 1880 when he built a new home. During the Gilded Age, mansions rose like palaces, thanks in part to monopolies and government corruption. Major beer makers also built impressive homes, but few could rival the estate that Betz built just above Norristown on the Schuylkill River. Known as Betzwood, the 364-acre country estate was probably without equal in the Philadelphia area. It included a one-hundred-room Gothic mansion, fishing ponds, a giant conservatory, an arboretum, a deer park, a bear pit with live bears, and a Victorian boathouse on the river.[47] Betz traveled extensively with his wife, the former Countess von Beroldingen. He became well known among European royalty and was granted two private audiences with Pope Leo XIII. Throughout his life, he maintained close personal and business ties to the Yuengling family, and he never forgot his mentor in Pottsville who had taught him the craft of brewing. The report of the funeral of D. G. Yuengling in the Pottsville *Miners' Journal* notes a floral contribution sent by the Betz family: "The floral contributions were rare and in great profusion, among them a large cross and crown of tuberoses, lillies ... sent by Mr. and Mrs. [John F.] Betz of Philadelphia were generally admired."

The prominent Philadelphia business leader died from Bright's disease in New Jersey on New Year's Eve, 1902, leaving his considerable fortune to his son, John F. Betz II.

Another former Yuengling apprentice, Henry C. Clausen Sr., became a significant force in the New York brewing market.[48] Sources indicate that Clausen was a Schuylkill County native. There is also strong possibility that he knew Betz while in Pottsville because the pair had maintained business ties in New York City early in their careers. A brewery, Clausen and Betz, opened in about 1857 at 235 West 44th St. and 250 West 45th St. Clausen's independent operations included Henry Clausen's Phoenix Steam Brewery at 309–313 East 47th St. which opened in 1855. Soon afterwards, Clausen brought his son, Henry Clausen Jr. (1838–1893), into the family business while the boy was still in his late teens. The H. Clausen and Son Brewery produced about 90,000 barrels in 1877, making it the sixth largest brewery in the country. In 1888, it merged with Flanagan, Nay & Company and became known as the New York Breweries Company. A few years later it was purchased by an English syndicate, an industry trend in the late nineteenth century. The younger Clausen founded the U.S. Brewers' Association and served as its president from 1866 to 1875. He remained a prominent figure in the association throughout his life. Like the Betz family, the Clausen family purchased some notable real estate. In 1890, not long before his death, Henry Clausen Jr. purchased what would become known as Clausen Farms in Sharon Springs, New York. The area was known for its hop production and featured a view over the Mohawk Valley into the Adirondacks and the Green Mountains of Vermont. The prominent family turned it into a country estate, complete with a Victorian gentlemen's guesthouse, a pool and a single lane bowling alley.

The success of Betz and Clausen in the urban markets may have convinced D. G. Yuengling that his sons could have better success as brewers outside of Pottsville. He also may have recognized as early as the 1860s that Pottsville's economy was changing and that the city would not become the industrial center he had once imagined. The coal trade was shifting to northern Schuylkill County. Pottsville was further weakened by the monopolization of the coal industry in the southern region by the Philadelphia and Reading Railroad. Many coal entrepreneurs, several of whom were Pottsville's key leaders, got out of mining. The Panic of 1873 also dealt a blow to Pottsville's standing as a business center. When Yuengling's sons were completing their training as brewers in the 1860s, the city was already beginning to experience outmigration. Many of its most promising young citizens felt their prospects for a prosperous future did not rest in Pottsville's slowly declining business climate. They looked to other communities outside the region for better opportunities.[49] Similarly, D. G. Yuengling had reasons to think about the growing market for beer in urban areas beyond Pottsville.

The challenging task of taking the Yuengling brewing tradition to other parts of the country fell to the eldest son. David G. Jr. was born in 1842. He was educated in Pottsville schools and then successfully completed his apprenticeship as a brewer under the direction of his father. In his youth, he was active in the Good

D. G. YUENGLING, Jr.   CHAS DUNCKEE,   LEON H. MICHEL.

JAMES RIVER STEAM BREWERY,

YUENGLING & CO.

BREWERS.

AND DEALERS IN MALT AND HOPS,

ROCKETTS, RICHOND, VA.

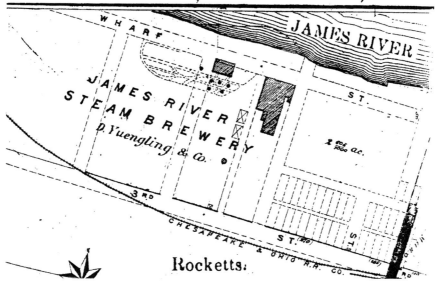

A newspaper ad for the James River Brewery. (D. G. Yuengling and Son, Inc.)

Intent Fire Company No. 1 of Pottsville. In fact, he is listed among the applicants for the charter for the organization.[50] He would move from the city at an early age in an effort to widen his experiences in the craft of brewing. At the age of 19, he accepted the position as foreman at John Frederick Betz's brewing operation in New York City. D. G. Yuengling obviously encouraged his sons and other apprentices to learn more about brewing in Europe. Like his brother, Frederick, and like Betz, David traveled to Europe. He enhanced his skills by taking courses at famous breweries in Munich and Stuttgart as well as at the Dreher brewery in Klein-Schwechat near Vienna. He returned to Pottsville when his additional training overseas was completed and once again worked with his father. He would move again before long, and this time he would take the Yuengling brewing tradition south.

When David Jr. stepped out of his father's shadow, he undertook some ambitious projects. In 1866, he helped manage the construction of a five-story brick

David Yuengling Jr.'s James River Steam Brewery. (D. G. Yuengling and Son, Inc.)

brewery at 912 East Main Street in Richmond, Virginia. The beer-making facility was located along the James River near what was then Wharf Street in the former capital of the Confederacy, and the setting offered a new mode of transportation for Yuengling beer. Barrels of brew could be rolled out from the five-story brick building to riverboats tied up and waiting at the brewery's dock. The original name of the brewery — Betz, Yuengling, & Beyer — indicates that the venture was possibly a partnership between David G. Jr., John Frederick Betz, and another brewer of the mid-nineteenth century, Louis Beyer. However, the records of the brewery's initial years of operation are sketchy. In 1869, the name of the brewery changed to James River Steam Brewery, D. G. Yuengling Jr. and Company. Like the anthracite region of Pennsylvania, the Richmond–James River region had plenty of beer-loving coal miners. Mines in a basin just west of the city produced a significant amount of bituminous coal in the nineteenth century. The brewery remained under the direction of David Jr. until 1878 when the Yuengling family sold the Richmond operation to the Richmond Cedar Works, an ice-cream freezer manufacturer.[51] This did not mean, however, that David Jr. was ready to return to Schuylkill County and make it his home.

David Jr. had not forgotten his experience working in New York City a decade earlier. Perhaps drawn by the highly competitive but lucrative beer market, the young brewer moved to New York with his wife, Catherine. The couple had three

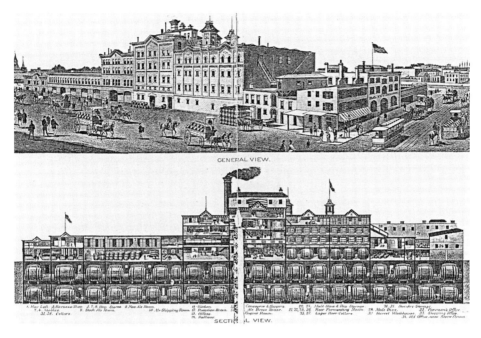

A portrait of David Yuengling Jr.'s brewery in New York. It was located at 128th St. and 10th Avenue. (D. G. Yuengling and Son, Inc.)

children, Kate, Lena, and Frederick. It was around 1870, and the city had already moved ahead of Philadelphia to become the nation's top beer producer. Brooklyn, in particular, was one of the leading brewing centers, with nearly 50 breweries, many in a section of the borough that would become known as "Brewers' Row." David Jr. operated an ale brewery at 5th Avenue and 128th Street, in partnership with W.T. Ryerson, beginning in 1871. In the same area of the city, at 10th Avenue and 128th Street, he purchased a second brewery in 1875 for making lager. Originally known as Yuengling and Company-Manhattan Brewery, the facility produced a brand name known as New York Lager Beer. On the 17th of October, 1882, at Albany, Mr. Yuengling was elected as the first President of the New York State Brewers' and Malsters' Association.

Production figures indicate that David Yuengling Jr.'s business endeavors were initially successful. The New York City brewing operations posted some strong production numbers. For example, numbers from 1879 provide an indication of the continuing growth of the popularity of lager over ale. The lager brewery on 10th Avenue sold 58,316 barrels and the 4th Avenue ale business sold 29,390 barrels.[52] Probably in reaction to the continuing popularity of lager, the ale brewery at 5th Avenue was closed around 1884. At this point, David Jr. turned his full attention to the 10th Avenue lager brewery as he expanded and upgraded the plant. The brewery was worth about $1,000,000 in 1884. A portion of the financing for the development of the sprawling brewery came when Yuengling formed a partnership with William Belden—a man whom at one time was an associate of one of the richest men in the country, robber baron Jay Gould. Belden had a very questionable reputation among investors on Wall Street. According to one source, Belden and his brother were under suspicion of stealing securities from Gould to the tune of $3 million in the late 1870s, helping to bring Gould to the brink of financial disaster.[53] Belden was also known as a man with extravagant taste who maintained a fast-living lifestyle in New York social circles.

David Jr. and Belden wielded enough influence to make the brewery the focus of an article in the *New York Times*—an article that seemed to have the sole purpose of promoting the brewery. The article carried the headline, "A Model Brewery. The Establishment of David G. Yuengling, Jr.—Acres of Cool Cellars." In flowery language loaded with superlatives, the anonymous author, who was given an extensive tour of the brewery, expresses amazement at both the spaciousness and cleanliness of the "well appointed" brewery. The brewery's modern equipment draws most of the praise:

> A storage place for ale, which does not require as cool a temperature as lager in which to mature, is to be found on the ground floor measuring 200 by 60 feet, filled to its utmost capacity. Passing through this, one next enters the refrigerating room in which there are three of the largest ice machines ever made. They were constructed by the Empire Refrigerating Company of Saint Louis, Mo. and have each a cooling capacity equal to that produced by one hundred and fifty tons of ice per day. They are based upon the ammonia absorption principle, and so intense is the cold produced as to form a thin coating of ice on the floors of the five cellars in which the lager is stored until it is fit for use. Of these cellars more will be said later on. Still on the ground floor is the cooperage where somewhere about a score of workmen were busily employed. In one of the wide spacious yards was an unimposing little Knowles pump, which forces water from a well 130 feet deep. This well was sunk by Mr. Yuengling and the water which it yields is absolutely pure.[54]

At the time the article appeared, David Jr. was counted among the top businessmen on the New York City social scene.[55] In the 1880s, newspaper reports place him among the city's elite at important dinners and social affairs. The article about the brewery in the *Times* closed with words of praise for the "gentleman brewer":

> The counting room is filled up in a rich and most elegant manner, and everywhere is seen evidence of an able, energetic, competent head. And that head is Mr. David G. Yuengling Jr. to whose alone and unaided the phenomenal growth of the business is to be traced. And not only is Mr. Yuengling a man of business, but he is also a gentleman of culture and refined artistic taste. This is most strikingly illustrated in the elegant suite of private apartments which are situated over the office. Here Mr. Yuengling has gathered together many valuable works of art in the way of paintings and costly bric-a-brac, together with a complete library of standard authors. Connected with the main apartment are one or two sleeping rooms and Russian and plunge baths. The furnishings are all in perfect harmony of color and material, and well suited as surroundings of a gentleman brewer.[56]

The same newspaper was less kind a decade later. Following the Panic (or crash) of 1893, David Yuengling Jr. fell victim to a variety of financial troubles and business problems, eventually leading to bankruptcy in October, 1905. In one

A beer wagon from David Yuengling Jr.'s New York operation. (D. G. Yuengling and Son, Inc.)

instance, David Jr. faced a case in which he failed to pay a judgment of $685.50. According to the *Times* account of the testimony at the hearing, Yuengling provided an overview of his financial problems, stating that most of his woes began when he took a trip to Europe:

> When he left this country the firm's indebtedness was about $400,000, but when he returned it had been increased to $1,800,000. This, he said, he had never been able to explain. Notes were in the hands of thirty-four banks. The crash came, and the firm was put in the hands of a receiver, subsequently being made a corporation, with a capital of $1,000,000 in stocks and $100,000 in bonds.... Yuengling claimed that at this time he had no property, and from 1885 to 1893 his expenses had not been over $10,000 a year. He said his home was owned by his wife, and had on it a mortgage of $35,000.[57]

Of course, David Jr. preferred not to have his business trouble spelled out in the press, and he probably wished that his son, Frederick D. Yuengling, received less press coverage, too. A reading of the young man's press clippings provides at least one source of his father's financial woes.

Popularly known by the Americanized version of his name, "Fred" Yuengling was born in 1870. He was a good brewmaster, perhaps one of the best in the country, as well as one of the best paid. But not long after he started his career, while he was in his early twenties, he found himself involved in a variety of scandals. His reputation as a skilled brewer faded, and he became "known from one end of the city to the other for his lavish expenditures and luxurious life" and reportedly occupied the "handsomest bachelor apartment in the city."[58] The *New York Times* covered Fred Yuengling's exploits in detail and published the following example of his lifestyle in 1908:

> Yuengling on one occasion took a party of friends to Europe at his own expense, and then brought them all back to New York, and during all the time they were away Yuengling never allowed them to spend a cent. On the top floor of the Yuengling brewery there was a famous room where Yuengling was wont to entertain his friends on a lavish scale.[59]

Reports indicate that he became romantically involved with a woman, "Baroness Blanc," in the early 1890s. A divorce suit, with Frederick Yuengling named as a co-respondent, was filed by Baron Blanc. The controversy was heightened when the "Baroness" produced and starred in a play called *Deception* on Broadway at the Fifth Avenue Theatre in the winter of 1892–93. "The venture was not a success," wrote an anonymous *New York Times* reporter, "and in the course of the attending tribulations Mr. Yuengling discharged the manager of the company, thrashed a coachman who was impudent, threw out a lawyer's clerk who had come to serve papers on the star, and was finally arrested for passing bogus checks upon the actors in the company."[60]

In the wake of the scandals, Fred Yuengling traveled extensively and eventually took up residence outside of the country in South America and British Columbia. He utilized his brewing skills for a time at a brewery in Trail, British Columbia. He then returned to New York in the late 1890s, and problems with the law continued, including an appearance before a judge on charges of non-support. He died in 1908 while being transported to the prison ward of Bellevue Hospital, following his arrest on charges of passing a bad check to an automobile agency. "F.D. Yuengling Dies, Bellevue Prisoner," roared the headline on the front page of the *New York Times*: "Son of Retired Brewer Victim of Alcoholism After a Wild Career."[61]

Even his death was marked by controversy. Yuengling was very sick prior to his arrest, and at the West Side Prison he was in a partial coma and running a temperature approaching 106 degrees. Doctors at the prison insisted that the brewer be taken to Bellevue Hospital immediately; however, the prison warden refused, claiming he did not have a prison guard available to send with the ambulance. Delays continued despite the doctors' insistence that Yuengling was in no condition to attempt an escape. Finally, a guard was assigned to accompany the ambulance, but Yuengling died on the way to the hospital despite a valiant attempt by doctors to save his life.

The impact of Frederick Yuengling's difficulties on the family business is difficult to assess. A report on Yuengling's arrest on embezzlement charges in October, 1900, notes that he "is alleged to have been largely responsible for the financial troubles which befell his father."[62] The beginning of David Jr.'s business woes did coincide with the beginning of his son's scandals in the early 1890s. The economy of the entire nation, however, was reeling from the Panic of 1893 at the same time. Late in that year, the D. G. Yuengling Jr. Brewing Company at 10th Avenue was purchased by Samuel Untermeyer at a foreclosure sale. A reorganization plan was implemented, and David Jr. stayed on board as a member of the new board of directors. The brewery also retained his name, but only for a few more years. Business problems continued, however, and the brewery was sold in 1897. The brewery maintained indirect ties to the Yuengling family, since the purchaser was John Frederick Betz, D. G. Yuengling's brother-in-law. Betz and his son, John, operated the brewery under the name Betz's Manhattan Brewery until 1903. Following the sale of his brewing operations in the city, David Yuengling Jr. moved upstate and opened a smaller brewery in the community of Hudson at Second and State streets. The facility was named Yuengling's Hudson–New York Breweries and was operated by the Yuengling family in partnership a bottler, Edward F. McCormick, for only a year—1903 to 1904. Newspaper reports indicate that David Jr. was still alive at the time of his son Frederick's death in 1908. He maintained an apartment in New York but also spent time in Philadelphia, where he assisted the Betz brewing operations.

The promotional material for David Yuengling's New York brewing operations provides information about the Yuengling family that needs to be considered carefully. While company commemorative programs cannot be accepted uncritically, an undated souvenir publication from David Jr.'s brewery, probably written in the 1880s, describes the Yuengling brewing tradition as a large "dynasty" that extends back to Germany. "The Yuengling family of good old German stock, forms a real dynasty of brewers," states the booklet, "at one time there were about 28 breweries in the family, and it is not to be wondered at that Mr. Yuengling followed in the footsteps of his forefathers."[63] While the Yuengling family did expand brewing operations to other states, there is little evidence to support the claim of 28 breweries in the family at one time.

A document from another brewer describes David Yuengling Jr. and raises another significant question. Did D. G. Yuengling have relatives in the United States before he emigrated from Germany? Horton Pilsener Brewing in New York, which eventually took over D. G. Yuengling Jr.'s brewery at 128th Street and Amsterdam Avenue, produced a pamphlet that provides a short history of its company. A few intriguing sentences are devoted to the origins of the Yuengling brewing tradition:

> The history and traditions of this great brewery dates [sic] back to the earliest days of ale and lager beer in America. The original founder was Jans Yuengling, who came to the United States about 1770 and founded his brew tavern in Richmond, Virginia. The original Yuengling ale and lager were famous in the pioneer days of our country. They were the favorite beverages at important social functions thruout Virginia and Maryland.[64]

Who was Jans Yuengling? Did D. G. Yuengling have a relative — an uncle or grandfather — who was brewing beer in America decades before him? It's certainly a pos-

sibility; however, the document makes no reference to D. G. Yuengling Sr. as a pioneer brewer, and additional references or records about Jans Yuengling have yet to
be found. Did he even exist? Of course, the Richmond, Virginia, reference is
significant because David Jr. operated his James River Brewery there. Perhaps David
G. Yuengling Jr. embellished his family's brewing tradition while promoting his
beer and a myth crept into the family brewing tradition. The mystery has yet to
be solved.

David Jr. was assisted in his New York brewing operations by his brother, the
youngest of D. G. Yuengling's children, William G., who was born in 1862. William Yuengling was educated in Pottsville schools. In addition to developing brewing skills at the Pottsville brewery, he "spent several years in New York, where he
studied the business in all its branches in the brewery of his brother, David G.
Yuengling Jr."[65] In addition to providing valuable assistance with the New York
operations, William would go on to manage a branch depot/brew pub called the
D. G. Yuengling Summer Garden Brewery and Hotel Todd on Broadway in Saratoga
Springs. He returned to Pottsville in 1895, to use his impressive brewing experience to assist his brother, Frederick, who was in the process of opening the bottling shop at the brewery. The future appeared to be bright on Mahantongo Street
for the two brewers and their families. Life, however, brings times when families
are personally gripped by sadness — and this includes members of the social aristocracy. In the 1890s, the Yuengling family faced more than its share of difficult
moments. The matriarch of the family, Elizabeth Yuengling, passed away at the family home at 501 Mahantongo St. on January 9, 1894, at the age of 71. Her four-line
obituary in the *Miners' Journal* simply noted that she was the "widow of the late
David G. Yuengling." The equally concise notice in the *New York Times* only added
that her death came "after a lingering illness."

By nineteenth-century standards, Elizabeth Yuengling had lived a very long
life. The same could not be said for William, who passed away on August 7, 1898,
at the age of 36. In contrast to the brief accounts of his mother's death, several
columns of newspaper copy detail William Yuengling's passing, further evidence
that the Yuengling family was one of the most prominent in the community. The
young brewer's death was described in the *Miners' Journal* as "one of the saddest
that ever occurred in the community."[66] Like other members of the family, he had
been very active in the community, assisting with a variety of charitable endeavors:

> The social side of Mr. Yuengling's life was a happy picture. He was a favorite every-
> where and being possessed of a fine baritone voice and rare musical talents he shone
> as an entertainer. For many years he was a member of Trinity Episcopal Church
> choir. He was always ready to help any charitable movement and his musical talents
> and his purse were at the disposal of any worthy cause.[67]

William Yuengling was ultimately "the victim of diseases involving the stomach,
liver, kidneys and lungs."[68] He had been ill for approximately two months and suc-
cumbed despite the efforts of doctors from Philadelphia. The tragedy was partic-

ularly moving, since he had married Clara R. Bannan only two months earlier. Following a month-long honeymoon, the couple had settled into life on Mahantongo Street, residing in the 800 block of the thoroughfare. "He leaves a widow, his fair bride of only two months, who has been left prostrated by his death," noted the moving account of William's passing. "The people will mourn his loss, but their hearts turn in sympathy toward this young wife, whose grief is inconsolable."[69]

Just as the family was beginning to recover from the untimely death of William, another passing jolted the household. Frederick Yuengling passed away on January 2, 1899, after struggling for several weeks with complications from typhoid pneumonia and peritonitis. According to his obituary notice in the *New York Times*, he was "at the time of his death one of the best known citizens in the city of his birth." Significantly, the notice also points out that he "was nearly as well known in this city [New York] having for many years spent much of his time here."[70] Frederick Yuengling's public service was noted in the account of his death in the *Miners' Journal*:

> He was public spirited in the broadest sense of the term and was always ready to lend aid to any movement that had for its object the advancement of Pottsville and he never turned a deaf ear to any charitable movement. Through his integrity, uniform courtesy and eminent fairness in the management of a large business concern he won for himself the respect and confidence of all with whom he came in contact. As citizen or business man he had attained an enviable position in the community, and Death could not have chosen one who would be more missed and more sincerely mourned in Pottsville than Frederick G. Yuengling.[71]

Like the funeral of his father and brother before him, memorial services for Frederick Yuengling attracted friends and relatives from throughout the anthracite coal region as well as Philadelphia and New York. Brewery employees played an important role in the funeral as well. The active pallbearers were all Yuengling workers, and the entire work force "followed the body of their manager to the grave in Baber cemetery."[72]

With Frederick's passing, the brewery then entered a transitional period in which his wife, Minna, and son, Frank, managed the brewery and worked in close consultation. Together they made a formidable team. Indications are that Minna, described as "a strong person and very capable business woman," took the lead.[73] Frank Yuengling, however, was certainly qualified to provide important input. A letter that he wrote to Santa Claus in 1885, when he was only nine years old, shows not only that he was excited about the forthcoming arrival of Saint Nicholas, but also that he was familiar with activities at the family business just down the street. "Dear Santa," he wrote, "I want a nice large horse and I want a nice brewery wagon with barrels on top...."[74] Clearly a boy with a polished upbringing, he signed the correspondence to the North Pole "Master" Frank Yuengling.

The education of the third-generation head of the brewery might have indicated that he would take a different career path. After beginning his education in Pottsville schools, he went on to attend the highly prestigious boarding school, Phillips Academy, in Andover, Massachusetts. Finally, he entered Princeton University, where he took courses in pursuit of a Bachelor of Science degree. Upon his father's untimely death, however, he made the ponderous decision to return to Pottsville and pick up the reins of the family business. The Pottsville *Republican*, in its report of Frederick Yuengling's death, expressed confidence that his son would be a capable successor. "Frank D. Yuengling, the only son and living child of F.G. Yuengling is a young man of 22 years of age and is possessed of much of his father's manly ways and business energy," noted the newspaper report. "Although young in years and only for a few months regularly connected with the brewery management he has thus early demonstrated his ability to carry out the plans and practices of his father."[75] There are indications that the young man went through a period of apprenticeship, shifting titles through his first decade at the brewery. He was manager in 1905, then general manager in 1906. The most significant challenge faced by Frank Yuengling came almost immediately after he assumed the presidency of the company.

Three generations of the Yuengling brewing family as pictured in the major book on brewing, *One Hundred Years of Brewing*, which was published in 1903. (D. G. Yuengling and Son, Inc.)

D. G. Yuengling's will had stipulated that the brewery would be passed to all ten of his children when his wife passed away. When Elizabeth Yuengling died in early 1894, Frederick Yuengling was placed in the difficult position of keeping all the family members satisfied. On March 23, 1894, he arranged to buy out his siblings' interest in the business. The first payment was made on July 1, 1895. But before a second payment was made, Frederick Yuengling passed away. Officially, it was left to Frank Yuengling to follow through on the agreement reached by his father and complete payments to the original heirs. Most likely, he discussed the matter with his mother and then decided to follow through on his father's agreement by borrowing half a million dollars. Over the next few years, a conscious effort was made to pay off the loan quickly. According to Edith

Yuengling's account of the brewery during this period, "[Frank Yuengling] once recalled that he and his mother allowed themselves the amount of $50.00 a week for all living expenses, no matter what profit the brewery made; that money went to repay the loan. He also made the decision not to assume the responsibilities and expense of marriage and family until this was accomplished."[76]

At the same time that Yuengling's out-of-state brewing operations were experiencing devastating financial troubles, Frank Yuengling's business ventures in Pottsville were running smoothly. The beer business in Schuylkill County was booming in the first decade of the twentieth century.[77] Production levels at the Pottsville brewery were quite high at this time. Thanks in large part to the efforts of Frederick and William Yuengling, the brewery's output in 1900 reached approximately 65,000 barrels—a sharp increase from the 15,000-barrel average production in the 1870s. A highly skilled brewmaster, Nicholas Dennebaum, assumed duties in 1906. The firm was officially incorporated as D. G. Yuengling and Son, Inc., and Frank Yuengling was elected president of the company in 1914, the same year that America's beer consumption had reached an all-time high, with sales reaching 66 million barrels. Also in 1914, Frank Yuengling was elected head of the Pennsylvania National Bank and Trust Company, replacing the late D. H. Seibert.

Frank Yuengling also had a very busy personal life. He married Augusta C. Roseberry on April 24, 1907. The couple was "well known and popular among the young people of Pottsville."[78] Within a few years of their wedding, Frank and Augusta had a growing family and needed more space. The Yuengling townhouse at 606 Mahantongo St. was no longer large enough, and they decided to construct a home a few blocks up, at 1440 Mahantongo St. To move beyond the townhouses and further away from the brewery on Mahantongo Street was a step up. Construction of the new Yuengling home started in 1911. The structure was designed by an architect from Reading, Harry Maurer, and is regarded as a fine example of early twentieth century Tudor-Jacobean Revival architecture. The home was completed in 1913, and the family moved in.

One of Frank Yuengling's sons, David G. Yuengling, recalled the "mansion with spreading lawns and a lovely sunken formal garden that was my mother's pride and joy."[79] By 1915, twins, Richard and David, would join their brothers and sister, Frederick, Dorhman, and Augusta, and add more liveliness to the household. "I am sure my mother and father lavished their affection upon me as much as upon my other brothers and sisters who preceded me into this world," recalled David. "We were a rough-and-tumble group, my brothers and sister and I, whose main preoccupation during these primary years seemed to be tussling or fighting on the hall or living room floor."[80] If there was a scuffle between siblings, there was usually somebody on hand to referee. The family had a full-time cook, four servants, a chauffer and gardener. When the home was constructed, craftsmen did not put a doorbell on the front of the house, since it was assumed that members of the hired staff at the home would intercept visitors. Deliverymen were usually directed to the kitchen door at the rear of the home. As they made they made their way through the spacious front yard, deliverymen hurried to avoid the boxers that served as watchdogs on the property. In the carriage house behind the home, the chauffer was fortunate enough to be able to wash the car with a "built-in car washing system." Times were good. Frank Yuengling, however, would have some reasons to be concerned not long after he moved the family into the new home. In response to the growth of the brewing industry and the proliferation of saloons, reformers in favor of temperance and prohibition emerged once again. And "dry forces" could point to the anthracite region of northeastern Pennsylvania as evidence of the need for reform. This time, however, it was a different ethnic group bearing the brunt of the criticism.

Despite legislation and campaigns by organized labor to limit the importation of foreign workers to the United States, immigrants continued to be attracted to Pennsylvania and jobs in the hard and soft coal mines, as well as the iron and steel industries. Significantly, the ethnic composition of those coming to region took a noticeable shift, but it didn't necessarily spell bad news for the region's brewers and saloon operators. In 1880, immigrants from Ireland, England, and Germany still comprised the majority of the foreign-born population in the anthracite coal region of northeastern Pennsylvania. Subsequent census data, however, points the immigration pattern in the direction of the mountains and plains of Eastern Europe and the Balkans. By the turn of the century over 50 percent of the immigrants to the anthracite region were Italians, Czechs, Austrians, Poles, Ukrainians, Slovaks, Serbians, Croatians, Russians, Russian and Polish Jews, and dozens of other nationalities.[81] The specific nationality didn't seem to matter. English-speaking and American-born citizens generally referred to them as "Slavs." The steady flow of "new immigrants" had a notable impact on ethnic composition of the larger cities and towns in the region like Pottsville; however, the change was even more dramatic in the smaller mining villages. Within a few short years, coal patches, at one time dominated by either the Irish, English, and Welsh, were populated exclusively by new immigrants.

The new wave of immigration to the anthracite region was spurred by economic rather than political conditions. The Slavs and non-Slavic immigrants hoped for better living and working conditions in America. These new "foreigners," mostly Roman Catholic or Greek Orthodox, were very poor and often illiterate. They brought a babel of new languages to the region. They were also unskilled laborers, a feature attractive to coal operators looking for a cheap source of labor. In fact, mine owners encouraged the new nationalities to come to the region and work at the collieries. As workers, the Slavs did not complain about long hours like the English-speaking miners. As miners, they were more willing to endure the difficult working conditions and the danger. What the coal operators may not have immediately realized, however, was that the most recent arrivals to the region in many cases shared the same fondness for the bottle demonstrated by the ethnic groups that comprised the "old immigration." Indeed, the Slavs had a significant impact on the region's liquor businesses and breweries, a fact well-documented by the work of a noted sociologist who provided an eyewitness account of life in anthracite coal communities.

Peter Roberts (1859–1932) was born in England but lived most of his life in the anthracite coal region. He had received a doctorate in divinity from Yale University in 1886. For the next two decades, he held pastorates as a Congregational minister in Scranton, Olyphant, and Mahanoy City, and he joined hands with agencies working to assist coal miners and their families.[82] He proved to be particularly helpful to immigrant workers during labor struggles and brought aid to strikers as a member of the Anthracite Committee of the Young Men's Christian Association (YMCA). Because a series of coal strikes at the dawn of the twentieth century disrupted the national economy, interest in conditions in the region grew across the country. Roberts believed in the power of the pen and responded to events surrounding him by writing two books and several articles to enlighten the general public about the coal industry and its employees.

Roberts' books and articles have been praised as the most detailed and accurate accounts of life in the region.[83] His first book, *The Anthracite Coal Industry* (1901), focused on economic history, and, in part, attempted to provide an explanation of the labor problems in the area. It wasn't long before the minister had a subject for a second treatise. He was deeply troubled by the suffering of strikers during the Anthracite Coal Strike of 1902. The strike, which lasted from May to October, had a devastating effect on the economy of the region. As the battle between the mine operators and the United Mine Workers dragged on, determined men, women, and children with no income were brought to the brink of starvation. If there was food, women and children had to scavenge the culm banks surrounding the coal communities to get fuel to cook. In desperation, thousands of young men and women in their teens had to leave the family so their younger siblings could survive. They usually found themselves in New York or Philadelphia, desperately trying to find work or begging for food.

Roberts hoped a book addressing "the social and moral life of the anthracite mine employees" would lead to sense of cooperation and understanding that would help avoid future labor unrest.[84] The result was *Anthracite Coal Communities* (1904), which was subtitled, "A Study of the Demography, the Social, Educational and Moral Life of the Anthracite Regions." The manuscript was written inside his parsonage during the time Roberts was leading an evangelical Protestant congregation in Mahanoy City. To support his assertions about the social culture of the region, Roberts consulted a wide variety of books and articles, as well as government statistics, federal and state reports, and records from county courthouses in the region. His background as an academic and sociologist is also apparent, as he includes ideas from works by such authors as Thomas Carlyle, Karl Marx, Adam Smith, and Herbert Spencer. Perhaps most importantly, Roberts, while careful to avoid use of the first-person in the body of his scholarly book (except in the preface), clearly attempts to support some of his ideas by drawing on personal observations and conversations with area residents.

While Roberts' scholarship has proved to a vital secondary source for historians of the anthracite region, the tone of his books and articles have drawn criticism. In fact, Roberts has faced the same charges levied against *Miners' Journal* editor, Benjamin Bannan, who had focused his attention on the Irish several decades earlier. Bannan, according to his critics, was a nativist who despised Catholics and slanted his articles accordingly. Similarly, Roberts' detractors find that his professional writing is seriously biased and intolerant of the ethnic group that is the main focus of his studies—the Slavs. For example, Michael Barendse in his dissertation on Slavic immigrants in the region, argues that Roberts tried to be objective but failed. "[T]he biases of his culture colored his account," states Barendse. "While he was not openly anti-Slav his commentary on the data presented shows that he thought they were somehow inferior. He presented a picture of the Slavic immigrants that was full of negative stereotypes."[85] True, Roberts' commentary about working-class Slavic immigrants does exhibit a degree of Anglo-American, middle-class elitism. In the opening paragraph of "The Sclavs in Anthracite Coal Communities," Roberts notes that "[e]ach race has it particular genius.... The genius of the Sclav differs widely from the Anglo-Saxon." He adds, however, that certain "influences" have "clogged the Sclav's advancement so that he is the creation of a less progressive civilization than our own."[86]

Despite the accusations of ethnocentrism, Roberts' actions indicate that he genuinely cared about all immigrants. In addition to seeking to improve living conditions for the nation's newcomers, he developed a host of education programs for immigrants, including lessons in civics, English, and history. Described as a person with considerable energy, Roberts also authored his own textbooks that detailed what became known nationwide as "The Roberts Method" for teaching foreigners. He also wrote a songbook for immigrants. In his frequent tours around the country, Roberts demonstrated his innovative teaching methods at schools, churches, businesses and prisons. After leaving the anthracite region, he wrote two more books dealing with the immigrant experience, *Immigrant Races in North America* (1910) and *The New Immigrants: A Study of the Industrial and Social Life of Southeastern Europeans in America* (1912). In *Anthracite Coal Communities*, he sympathetically depicts "Sclavs" as hard workers who are victims of living conditions thrust upon them by mine operators and businessmen. He is more critical of the recent arrivals, however, when he turns his attention to social problems in the region.

Reverend Peter Roberts, author of *The Anthracite Coal Industry* (1901) and *Anthracite Coal Communities* (1904). An authority on immigrant life in the coal region, Roberts was highly critical of alcoholic beverage consumption in the mining communities and called for reform. (Courtesy of the YMCA of the USA and Kautz Family Archive, University of Minnesota Libraries.)

Roberts devotes considerable space to alcohol consumption in his writing.

An entire chapter of *Anthracite Coal Communities*, entitled "The Men at the Bar," attempts to provide insight into the saloon business in the coal region. Alcohol use is also addressed in other sections of the book dealing with temperance efforts and crime. While Roberts embraced puritan values and clearly encouraged temperance reform, there is some evidence that he attempts to be balanced in his approach to the subject. He points out, for example, that the "vast majority of mine employees are industrious, and although they frequent the saloon either for social purposes or to quench their thirst, they neither neglect their homes nor their families."[87] Still, the author felt that drinking in the mining towns and villages was excessive, noting that coal region towns and villages had "many confirmed drunkards ... men dead to all paternal and marital obligations, and slaves of a depraved appetite."[88] In the spirit of a temperance crusader, the minister emphasized that drinking leads to misery for the workers for two principal reasons: They spend too much of their wages on drink, and their income is further reduced because alcohol abuse leads to absenteeism. While these points are debatable, the details in the sociologist's books and articles leave little doubt that business was very good for many of the region's brewers at this time.

Temperance advocates in northeastern Pennsylvania who read *Anthracite Coal Communities* would have been pleased with at least one point in the book regarding alcohol consumption. The work-site drinking which could be observed in the mines decades earlier was no longer being condoned, largely due to the considerable financial investment in the collieries. Mining equipment was increasingly expensive, complex, and potentially dangerous. If there had been any tolerance for the workplace boozer in the past, it was replaced by strict discipline, as mine owners embraced the cause of temperance reform:

> Every plant in the anthracite coal fields to-day represents an investment of hundreds of thousands of dollars, and operators cannot afford to put drinking men in charge of these costly concerns. Many efficient mine officials have been discharged because of drink, and the tendency is to exercise greater discipline in this regard among the miners. Fifty years ago, it was nothing unusual for a miner to take a quart of whiskey with him into the mines; to-day no one would think of such a thing.... Men half drunk are not allowed around the mines and a debauch may cost an official his position.[89]

While the threat of unemployment kept miners away from the temptation of drink during work, many apparently quenched their thirst immediately after the shift ended. Beer wagons still came to the collieries in the late nineteenth and early twentieth centuries, only now instead of beer tapped from kegs, bottled beer was for sale. Of course, business was particularly brisk on paydays.

Miners were usually paid at the colliery with the visit of the "pay car." When the pay car arrived, a beer wagon wasn't far behind. "As soon as the company pay car backs into a colliery a line of wagons take stands along the roads of the pay car," noted one temperance publication. "As miners leave the pay car they are confronted by the speakeasies on wheels and bottled beer and pints of whiskey are handed out, just like the peanut vender disposes of his goods on circus grounds."[90]

While it is possible brewers sponsored the beer wagons, local bottlers and whole-sale liquor dealers had closer ties to these business ventures. Roberts described the beer wagon as "nothing less than a portable saloon which follows the pays, and works an injury which frustrates the laudable attempt of those who aim at shutting out all saloons from certain sections of the coal fields."[91] He complained that the wagons did a "flourishing business" on pay-days and even provided alcohol to "boys." Such complaints about drinking near the collieries were not the major focus of reformers, however. Miners could always get a drink elsewhere.

At the time *Anthracite Coal Communities* was being written, about 3,000 retail liquor licenses were granted in the coal mining towns of northeastern Pennsylvania each year.[92] On average, mining towns in the anthracite region had one license for every 175 inhabitants, the equivalent of a drinking establishment for every 58 adult males.[93] Statistics from specific towns were astonishing. In some anthracite communities, one saloon was open for business for every eight men who were qualified to vote.[94] Clearly, the region's brewers realized they could boost sales tremendously under the tied-house system. They also knew the importance of local politics. For example, brewers demonstrated enormous clout, as they helped potential saloonkeepers secure liquor licenses. In one town the court refused a license to five saloons. But the "boss" of the town — who happened to be a brewer — applied political pressure to members of the council, and a vote went in favor of granting the licenses. The councilmen then "waited on the judge and the licenses were granted."[95] One of Roberts' contemporaries, Frank Julian Warne, also wrote a book on conditions in the coal region, *The Slav Invasion and the Mine Worker: A Study in Immigration*. Warne, who covered the Anthracite Strike of 1902 as a staff reporter for the Philadelphia *Public Ledger*, described a similar incident. Five or six saloon-

A beer wagon making its rounds in a mining village. The photograph is among several illustrations in Peter Roberts' study of the immigrant laborers, *Anthracite Coal Communities* (1904). Roberts was an outspoken critic of the drinking patterns among immigrant groups in the region and sought to curb the popularity of the beer wagon and the local saloons. The beer wagon regularly made trips to local mines in search of customers. The practice gradually diminished as concern over work-site drinking grew. (From the book *Anthracite Coal Communities* by Peter Roberts published in 1904.)

keepers in Mahanoy City were deprived of their license because the establishments they operated had a very poor reputation. "The brewer [possibly Charles Kaier] who was 'backing' these saloonists put political and other "influences" to work at Pottsville, the county seat," wrote Warne, "and within a very short time these saloon-keepers were back at their old business."[96] Warne charged regional brewers "of the English-speaking races" with exploiting bar owners, pointing out that nearly every immigrant tavern owner in the anthracite region secured a liquor license through the efforts of a local brewer, who then required the saloonkeeper to pay for the service. Warne noted that the brewers influence "extends into the ordinance-making bodies of the mining towns; they not infrequently dictate municipal and even county control of the liquor system."[97]

One of the striking features of *Anthracite Coal Communities* is the extensive use of statistics and charts to illustrate points. Data, including figures from specific towns, was apparently gathered through legwork, because information from "license court" was only available at county courthouses. In addition, information was possibly drawn from the Report of the Anthracite Coal Strike Commission (1903), which also devoted some attention to the use of alcohol among miners in the region. Roberts' study includes the region's two other principal counties, Lackawanna and Luzerne, but comes to the conclusion that the "saloon evil is greatest in Schuylkill County."[98] Mahanoy City earned the dubious title of the county's drinking capital. With a population of 13,725, the town could boast 143 barrooms, or one for every 98 residents. The rival northern Schuylkill County community of Shenandoah was not too far behind. Its 20,700 residents had 174 drinking establishments from which to choose, or one for every 119 residents. In 1902, the smaller northern Schuylkill County community of Ashland, with a population of 6,348, had 42 licensed saloons, or one for every 151 residents.

The city of Pottsville provides a significant contrast to the towns to the north over Broad Mountain. The city's population in 1902 stood at 15,869 and it had 72 saloons, or one for every 220 residents. Why were there fewer saloons in Pottsville? Roberts accounts for the fact by pointing out the city's role as a business center stating that a "large number of professional men reside there" and that "[m]any retired and wealthy families make it their home."[99] In contrast, New Philadelphia, a mining town near Pottsville, gained notoriety for an intersection where a saloon could be found on every corner. Significantly, statistics stored at the county courthouses only include *licensed* drinking establishments. Because a license cost $265, it is reasonable to conclude that the county also had a considerable number of unlicensed establishments, or speakeasies. While there are no estimates on the number of unlicensed establishments in Schuylkill County, Roberts terms the prosecution of speakeasies an important measure in curbing the "drink habit" among workers in the county.[100]

The anthracite region's immigrant saloons could be found in any part of town, but they were generally clustered along the main street in the business district of the community. It was not unusual to spot about a half-dozen drinking establish-

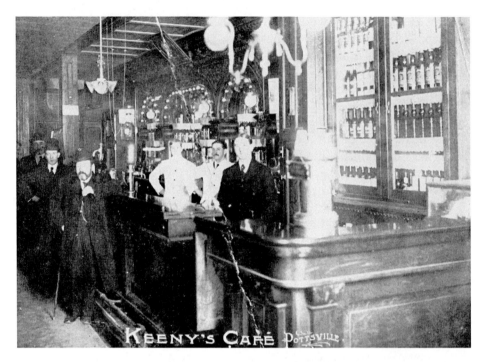

Keeny's Café in Pottsville around 1895. This drinking establishment was one of many in Pottsville and Schuylkill County. (From the collection of the Historical Society of Schuylkill County.)

ments in a single block. The sizes of the businesses and their "character" varied, depending on the proprietor. Some saloons were crude shacks where a bar was nothing more than a wooden plank atop a few empty beer barrels. Others could be described as "kitchen barrooms," which were part of the proprietor's home. One "saloon" in the region was operated by a man who "carried on the business on a small scale in one of the rooms of the house which he owned, and secured the services of his wife and children when he could not attend the bar."[101] Some saloons were well kept, but others had not seen a broom or a mop in some time. Peeling paint, chipping wood, and rundown tables and chairs provided more evidence of a lack of upkeep. Behind the bar, sullied beer mugs and shot glasses waited for another customer in front of a streaked, cloudy mirror.

Other saloons were spacious, with plenty of rooms for tables and chairs. Photographs of bars during this period indicate that many taprooms were very well-appointed, thanks in large measure to brewery financing and the emergence of bar-equipment manufacturers. The centerpiece of the saloon, of course, was an intricately carved mahogany bar with brass footrails, and even handrails, which people used while standing. Behind the bar were large plate-glass mirrors and plenty of shelves and cabinets, where bottles and glasses stood for the bartender. If a customer needed to use the facilities, they were usually located in the rear of the building. In the summer, a large fan helped cool the saloon. In the colder months, the chill in the air was replaced by the warmth of burning anthracite coal as it blazed in a stove in the corner.

Larger drinking spots, with their back rooms and tables and chairs, were a convenient meeting place for organized groups, such as unions, fraternal organizations, political parties, and religious and charitable organizations. At the saloon, members of these organized groups would plan events or meet with the members of the community they were aiming to assist. Developing labor unions, for example, needed space to conduct organizing and recruiting campaigns, and they turned to the local saloon. Of course, saloonkeepers welcomed union members, because they knew that glasses of beer were enjoyed before, during and after the meetings. Such gatherings also helped spread the word about the business. When anthracite coal miners wanted to meet to "debate the questions of the day…. The saloon in these coal fields afford better opportunity for this than any other institution."[102] Eventually, the relationship between organized labor and the saloon became estranged. As unions were viewed as increasingly radical, harassment from the police, a headache that barkeepers wanted to avoid, sometimes resulted. Successful unions, when they became large enough, often accumulated enough money to build their own halls, and these halls often had liquor licenses.

Employers also found the saloon to be beneficial. In the time before state-run employment agencies, it was a common practice for unemployed workers to try to find a job through contacts at the local saloon. When there was plenty of work in the anthracite coalfields, the local bar took on the important function of a hiring hall. During the saloon's convenient business hours, coal operators and mine foremen could find plenty of cheap, unskilled labor. And the workers and their prospective employer could negotiate a wage scale over a few brews. Immigrants often arrived with a job already provided for them by a sponsor, but if they had no prospects they could often find employment by going to the local public house.

In addition to serving as a meeting place, the saloon provided a basic necessity for the working-class immigrant: free or cheap food. As breweries took command of more and more saloons, they ushered in the period of the famous "free lunch" to maintain a steady stream of customers. Out of concern for the intoxicating effects of alcohol, temperance advocates pushed for food in barrooms. Saloonkeepers were more than willing to oblige. Many offered free lunch counters that included vast quantities of bread, meats, vegetables, cheeses, frankfurters, egg sandwiches, and clams. The bait to increase traffic at the saloon proved to be extremely popular and became a major source of daytime sustenance in America. A contemporary observer of this phenomenon in Chicago noted that the free or inexpensive meals offered at saloons fed more working-class poor than all charitable institutions in the city combined. While not all saloons offered free lunches, many in the anthracite region did. A description of the saloons in Schuylkill County written in 1933 reminisced about saloons decades earlier and the food available:

> Few people, especially those of the present generation, remember a great deal about the old time saloon where several kinds of sandwiches, many varieties of cold lunches and some types of soups and hot provender, were obtained free of charge,

with a big schooner of beer for only a nickel. The saloons of Pottsville and Schuylkill County were notorious throughout the state. Our county had the reputation of having more drinking places to the square foot than any other section of the Commonwealth.[103]

Some saloons in Pottsville were noted for their particular foods or beverages. For example, one had a reputation throughout the community for its swiss- and limburger-cheese sandwiches. Another proprietor operated a saloon noted for its "use of syrup beverages putting out a lemonola of his own manufacture, which added much to his reputation."[104]

Each saloon seemed to have its own peculiarity that attracted customers. The strongest example is undoubtedly a caged bird that once lived in "Billy" Soell's saloon on Pottsville's North Centre Street:

> The big green parrot, swinging in its cage, in the barroom for years shrieked anathemas and profanity, day and night. Its vocabulary was most remarkable for a bird, and vied with the most notorious of human trouble-makers in the town. The parrot was brought here and given to Soell by Captain Crawford F. Glover, Scotch commander of a sailing vessel…. The precocious bird lived to a good old age.[105]

Occasionally, it wasn't pets, but proprietors that were the key to an establishment's appeal. Mrs. Fred Hoehn, who operated a beer saloon on Laurel Street, was known among Pennsylvania Germans for her "sonorous bass voice, having a richness and depth seldom to be found anywhere in the state."[106] John "Jumbo" Trout, who stood six feet, six inches, and weighed nearly 400 pounds, was known for "possessing prodigious strength." Before opening a saloon in Pottsville, Trout was a prominent volunteer fireman and a beer wagon driver.[107] The colorful Frederick Portz operated one of the city's most popular bars, the "Lafayette House." An active Democrat in the city, Portz was "a genial and witty Pennsylvania German, who could take a joke and did take many which were played on him."[108]

In addition to drink, food, and a good time, the saloon offered other important services that were particularly helpful to immigrant families. Some were reminiscent of the assistance offered at the stage taverns of the early American period. The saloon provided temporary lodging. An interpreter or translator was usually available. If an illiterate person needed a letter sent home, there was someone on either side of the bar that could help. Papers could be notarized, and arrangements for transportation could be made. Most important, however, were the financial services available at the saloon. Saloonkeepers would forward money orders home or offer generous credit to newcomers from their homeland. They also cashed workers' checks on paydays, providing another reason the local bar was commonly referred to as the "immigrant bank."

Working-class immigrants generally felt out of place next to the cool marble and onyx counters of the local bank, and they were often confused and intimidated by banking forms and receipts. So where could they cash their checks? The saloon offered an alternative. The check-cashing practice began in urban areas, where many companies became increasingly uneasy about paying their workers in cash. Using cash made bookkeeping more complicated and created security risks, particularly in neighborhoods of questionable character. Laborers on their way between factory and home usually stopped at the local saloon anyway, so it seemed to be the ideal place to cash their checks.

The saloon's reputation as the "poor man's bank" helped the tavern owners and brewers, too, because patrons customarily sprung for a few drinks to repay the favor of cashing the check. The proprietors of some saloons did not have sufficient funds to bankroll such a service, but brewers often did. On paydays, many beer makers made sure there were large sums of money at their tied-outlets. After closing time on payday, the operator of the tied-house saloon simply signed the cashed check over to the beer maker.[109] It comes as no surprise that brewers in the late nineteenth and early twentieth centuries were closely affiliated with local banks.

Check cashing at local saloons did not appear to be as prevalent in the anthracite region. Most coal companies continued to pay their workers in cash, and payday generally came once a month. Still, miners had several reasons to gather at the local saloon on pay day. First, the saloonkeeper did provide a service by accepting larger currency from the miners and "accommodating these men with change."[110] In addition, a contract miner was responsible for paying his immigrant helper, about one third of the miner's earnings. It made sense as well for this transaction to take place at the local saloon. Often on paydays, saloon owners attracted customers by supplying attractions like music and dances. For many miners, payday marked a bout of binge drinking. Now a term commonly used to describe excessive drinking behavior on college campuses, binge drinking is a periodic ritual in which a person drinks to intoxication. Coal miners generally participated in "communal" binge drinking with their fellow workers.[111] Not surprisingly, residents of many anthracite communities did not need to ask if paychecks had been issued. They only had to count the beer barrels. "After payday the empty kegs in mining patches are many," wrote Roberts, probably after looking out on the street of a coal community from the window of his parsonage.[112]

Miners short on cash did not necessarily have to wait until payday to have a beer or buy a round for their friends. Anthracite region drinking establishments were notorious for using a system that was also customary at saloons in other parts of the country—allowing patrons to pay on "tick." Because employment in the coal industry was irregular in the late nineteenth and early twentieth centuries, these credit accounts for neighborhood regulars were important for a successful business. In fact, saloons strictly conducting business with cash were the exception rather than the rule. One proprietor of a successful coal-region saloon, when asked about the keys to attracting steady patronage, responded, "I keep good stuff, give good measure, keep a clean place and sell on tick."[113] Those who drank at the bar on "tick," a truncation of "ticket," were obliged to pay down their account on a regular basis. Significantly, this custom at the local saloon was also referred to as "getting trusted" and, inevitably, there were some bar patrons who failed to earn this privilege.[114] Most bar owners started to get nervous when a customer's tab hit the $50 mark. At this point, some imbibers decided to take advantage of the considerable number of drinking establishments in town. They moved on to a different neighborhood tavern without paying their tab at their old barroom. The swindler became known as a "sticker." "[T]he man behind the bar must watch his P's and Q's if he expects to stay in business," warned Roberts. "The 'sticker' is skillful. He drinks heavily and each month pays a part of what he owes. When the arrears reach the $50 mark he makes a change and opens an account in another saloon."[115]

While the criminal offenses of the "sticker" could be considered petty, there were other activities at the local saloon that diminished its reputation. Several pages in *Anthracite Coal Communities* are devoted to the darker side of the saloon, describing it as the greatest "evil" in Schuylkill County. Many saloons permitted or encouraged gambling in various forms. For laborers who worked long, hard hours and lived paycheck to paycheck, the lure of financial gain through gambling was great. Card-playing in the back rooms of saloons proved to be very popular, particularly among the immigrant population after the 1890s. Playing cards were inexpensive, portable, and provided a leisure activity that carried over from the Old World. Card games at times became large, and no doubt added to the foul language which occasionally echoed into the streets near the saloon. Dice games were also quite popular in the local saloon. Pocket billiards came into vogue during this period, but many of the smaller bars in the region could not afford the space. Another form of gambling, cockfighting, was less popular in the region and, if it did take place, it was usually beyond the limits of the boroughs. Some saloon-keepers, however, did devise "cock-pits in their cellars where matches are frequently carried out."[116]

The form of gambling of greatest concern to reformers in the anthracite region was the slot machine. The machines were first brought into area saloons by a corporation, and profits were divided equally between the owner of the machine and the proprietor of the saloon. Soon, bar owners bought their own machines so they could keep all the profits. Youngsters in the area were particularly addicted to the machines, which could also be found in stores and barber shops. "Boys from ten to twenty years of age, when they have money, cluster around these and, infatuated with the whirl and click of the machine, they stand there until the last penny is spent, and then curse the machine," wrote a concerned Roberts. "They will steal from home, take money from their pay, borrow from their friends, and devise cunning schemes whereby they may get the means to carry on the game."[117] Young men devised creative ways to "beat" the slot machines, using wires to stop the wheel at a winning combination, or using washers from the local hardware store instead of currency. Slot machines in bars became such a problem in some counties in the region that the courts ordered their removal. In Schuylkill County, applicants for liquor licenses had to swear that their proposed saloon did not harbor a slot machine.

Reformers voiced concern about the impact of the saloon on women. In the Victorian era, most women would not have thought of passing through the swinging doors of the saloon. But some young ladies, often of questionable virtue and hygiene, did find a place at the end of the bar or in the saloon's back room. Roberts expressed concern about "bastardy" and the "licentiousness" of young girls in northeastern Pennsylvania and implicated the neighborhood bars:

> On summer evenings it is nothing unusual to find young girls parading the lonely walks near mining towns until past midnight. In some instances their shamelessness reminds one of conditions which must have prevailed at Sodom and Gomorrah, or the practices which prevailed in the groves surrounding the temple of Aphrodite. In all our towns there are "chippies" and some saloons open their doors to traffickers in lewdness. When one of these young girls was asked if she was not afraid, her reply was: "Not as long as the drug store is handy."[118]

What was particularly problematic about this immoral behavior was that young children were sometimes exposed to it. Saloons still had their "take-out" customers, and they were often boys or girls who came to have the "growlers" from home filled with beer.

Saloon ownership in the coalfields increasingly passed into the hands of members of the Slavic immigrant community. Like the Irish before them, Slavs viewed saloonkeeping as "a stepping-stone whereby the enterprising can get out of the mines."[119] Regional brewers, recognizing the popularity of beer among the new arrivals, took advantage by bringing Slavs into the saloon-keeping business under the tied-house system. The business strategy certainly yielded positive results, as beer sales continued to grow. Germans and Slavs provided the main market for lager, with the English leaning toward ale and the Welsh ordering ale and porter. The Irish had no real preference and would order whatever the saloonkeeper was promoting that week.

Of all the ethnic groups, the Slavs, in Roberts' view, were the "the heaviest drinkers in the coal fields" and frequented the saloon more than any other.[120] He claimed the new immigrants were "addicted to drink in their native country" and "keep up the practice here."[121] The minister's writing, loaded with generalizations, certainly contributed to a growing stereotype held by non-immigrants that the Slavs were a hard-drinking people:

> All Sclavs drink. Temperance organizations are pooh-poohed by the people. A few Sclavs occasionally pledge themselves to total abstinence for three or six months, but these generally count the days when the fast will come to an end. The Sclav never has a good time unless there is plenty of beer and whiskey flowing.... The Sclav does not know how to enjoy himself save by getting drunk; he does not know how to show kindness to his friends save by making them drink.[122]

He expressed shock at seeing "both women and men of the Sclav races" entering the local saloon and maintained that many Slav saloonkeepers operated "nothing more than a beer den, where riot, ribaldry and rowdyism prevail."[123] Another description of a Slavic saloon is less than flattering. "These grimy saloons," wrote a reporter for the *New York Herald*, "present little pictures of a life that is not of this age.... They carry you back into the Burgundian taverns of the fourteenth century, into the bandits' dens of Upper Hungary."[124]

Certain cultural practices contributed to the reputation of the Slavs as heavy drinkers. Celebrations of wedding, christenings, and holidays involved a notable amount of drinking — raising the eyebrows of conservative Protestants. At a Polish marriage in Mahanoy City, "[t]he neighbors watched the wagons bringing provisions and drink into the home, and the general remark was, 'See the amount of drink carried in.'"[125] One reporter described a Slavic baptism celebration following the church ceremony. The family hosted a celebration at home and started by making what is called "polinki," a mixture of two jugs of whiskey and a handful of hot peppers in a huge vat of beer. The celebration became so raucous that it became necessary to place the newly baptized baby in the outhouse.[126] Another drink of notoriety with a Slavic connection is "boilo." The drink remains especially popular as a Christmas treat and has a potent reputation. Recipes vary from family to family, but the usual ingredients in the concoction are whiskey, honey, lemon and orange slices and cinnamon. It is usually served warm in a shot glass. A few shots can bring even the most experienced guzzler to his knees.

Significantly, some ethnic drinking took place on the Lord's Day, much to the dismay of evangelicals who believed in a sober Sunday. This Protestant concept was contrary to the practices of many Slavs, and, as a result, Sundays were the banner day for drinking in the region. Temperance reformers successfully pushed for a law prohibiting the sale of alcohol on Sunday, but the law was widely ignored and little enforced. Only the saloon doors changed when the seventh day of the week rolled around. On the first six days, customers used the front door of the bar. On the seventh day, they went in the back door. "There are more drunkards seen on the streets on Sunday than on any other day, " complained Roberts.[127] Even at outdoor activities, beer was consumed on Sundays. From the turn of the century until the 1940s, anthracite coal companies sponsored baseball teams for their workers, believing that the sport encouraged teamwork and diverted employees from labor agitation. After Mass on Sunday, crowds drifted to ballfields to watch the games and relax with a few beers. Players also enjoyed their share of the keg after the games were over.

In the minds of some of the region's industrialists, there was nothing wrong with drinking on Sunday — until Monday came. Absenteeism was reportedly high at the coal mines on the first day of the workweek. Miners who were nursing hangovers could argue that they were just perpetuating a tradition. In colonial times, when workers were more independent and had more control over the pace and progress of their jobs, it was often permissible to skip work on what was referred to as "Saint Monday" or "Blue Monday."[128] Groggy working-class immigrants in the late nineteenth century apparently may have felt the same way when the weekend came to a close; however, the pre-industrial custom did not fit well with the demands of mining coal. Mine operators, aware of the behavior of some employees away from the colliery, monitored absenteeism, particularly on Mondays. Miners who regularly missed work in the aftermath of paydays were considered suspect and often fired. If a miner lost his job due to alcohol, his wife often pleaded for his job with the mine foreman or superintendent. The appeal often failed, however.

A depleted workforce was not the only problem related to Sunday drinking. Workers who showed up for work with their minds clouded from weekend festivities presented a danger. Roberts pointed out that more accidents occurred in the mines on Monday than any other day of the week.[129] Like Benjamin Bannan before him, Roberts expressed concern about the impact of the alcohol trade on the efficiency and quality of work performed by the region's coal miners. "If left to the unrestrained influence of the saloon, which today plays so prominent a part in their social and economic life," Roberts wrote, "what type of worker will be evolved, upon whom will rest the obligation of faithful and efficient workmanship in the risky business of digging coal? Indeed, we need not limit this question to the Sclav; it applies to the mine workers in general."[130]

Coal mine operators and foremen were not alone in seeking reform. Businessmen from more and more industries were coming to anti-liquor sentiments. Perhaps more than the mining industry, railroad magnates faced public pressure to keep their workers sober in the wake of wrecks and passenger injuries. Rules on employee sobriety tightened, and workers were directly ordered to stay out of saloons. Employers also argued that drinking resulted in poor craftsmanship and poor health among employees. Under the precept that alcohol led to less efficiency among workers and lower profits, workplace rules grew tighter and tighter.

More storm clouds darkened the horizon for the nation's brewers. Perhaps the surest sign of serious trouble could be found in the positions being adopted by labor unions. Not only were lawmakers and employers taking steps to keep workers sober, but unions were also taking action against the saloon. Some early labor organizations, most notably the Knights of Labor, denied union membership and worked against the employment of individuals who used or sold alcohol or other intoxicants:

> It was John B. Chisholm, a Pennsylvania miner, who authored the restrictive clause on strong drink in the Knights of Labor constitution. He gave as his reason, "I want to save this Order from the evil which has been the curse of every organization of miners in the history of the Labor movement.... The saloon has no real sympathy for labor, and only robs the worker of the hard-earned money which ought to go for the comfort of wife and little ones at home."[131]

In earlier times, the neighborhood bar was a friend to union members, but labor soon found the saloon to be problematic. If a meeting was held at a saloon, drinking men occasionally disrupted meetings. The saloon weakened the public image of labor. Major labor figures like William "Big Bill" Haywood and Eugene V. Debs were encouraged to curb their fondness for the bottle and stop visiting bars.[132] In northeastern Pennsylvania, the United Mine Workers apparently realized the popularity of beer and whiskey among its rank and file. When pressed on the alcohol question, the UMW adopted a position in favor of temperance reform; however, union leadership did not actively work to bring about reform. The UMW's half-hearted approach to alcohol use among its members was notice by Roberts, who encouraged the union to take "a pronounced stand" on temperance and suggested union leaders should "totally abstain."[133]

Roberts, in his suggestions for social change at the conclusion of *Anthracite Coal Communities*, encouraged others to take up the fight against alcohol abuse in the region: "Against this great evil both the economic and moral interests of our communities should protest and wage war."[134] He also argued that the failure of temperance efforts was predictable because it did not get to the "root of the evil," adding that "the nature of the industry and conditions of domestic life have much to do with the curse."[135] The sociologist pointed out that improving the living and working conditions of miners would be an important step in ending problems with alcohol:

> In it are involved the question of better homes, greater dissemination of knowledge, education of public opinion and the instruction of youths, and the evolution of a better type of manhood. Until these counts are taken into consideration and work begun along these lines, the evil of intemperance in our towns and cities will go annually increasing.[136]

While Roberts believed attention to bread and butter social issues was the key to curbing alcohol abuse in coal communities, other individuals and organizations were working toward legislative action to bring about reform. And, slowly, they were gaining significant support from the business barons of America like Henry Ford, Andrew Carnegie, Gustavus Swift, and Cyrus McCormick. These men were major employers who were coming to understand that a dry workforce was not a bad idea. They were forgetting about workers in another industry, however.

On Mahantongo Street in Pottsville, about 100 employees were still making real beer as the echoes of war drew the curtain on the Progressive Era. The Yuengling Brewery stood among the regional breweries that had passed a test that many other beer makers failed. It had kept pace with a host of technological, scientific, and marketing changes that had transformed the beer industry. But just as it posted some its highest production numbers thanks to the crowded saloons, one of its greatest challenges loomed. "The Great Killer of breweries in America" would try to stop the flow of beer across the land.[137]

Three

Prohibition ... and Perseverance

Mother's in the kitchen, washing out the jugs;
Sister's in the pantry, bottling the suds;
Father's in the cellar, mixing up the hops;
Johnny's on the porch, watching for the cops.
     —*Collier's Weekly*, September 1, 1928 (Poem
     by a New York state Rotary Club member)

When national Prohibition went into effect on January 17, 1920, the brewing industry suffered. Many brewers—some whom had devoted their entire lives to their businesses—found investments wiped out.[1] About a year earlier, Frank Yuengling approached the dark times for American brewers with a sense of calm as he read the newspaper headlines proclaiming the ratification of the Eighteenth Amendment. "He saw the news, shook his head back and forth and let out a deep sigh," as the story goes among members of the Yuengling family. "Slowly, he took the newspaper, folded it, and set it on the desk. He then predicted that, 'this will last ten years, at the most, and we'll be making beer again.' With that he went right back to work."[2] The third-generation brewery owner's prediction about the duration of what became known as "the noble experiment" wasn't quite right, but he clearly understood the changing times. Unlike many other beer makers, Frank Yuengling persevered. He gave no consideration to the idea of bringing the family brewing tradition to an end. Instead, he made a less potent version of the Yuengling product: near beer. He also recognized the importance of diversification in a changing economy and courageously initiated new enterprises. As the nation turned "dry," his perceptive business decisions were the key to the brewery's survival.

Looking back, the first quarter of the twentieth century could be considered Pottsville's glory days. The city approached the high point in its population — about 25,000. Its residents kept up on the latest happenings through two daily papers, the *Republican* and the *Journal*. Many readers, no doubt, wanted to read about the details of the action during games played by the Pottsville Maroons, their NFL team that claimed the championship in 1925.[3] Business boomed, and the city "burgeoned with four furriers, five department stores, seven jewelry shops, nine shoe

103

stores, eleven furniture stores, thirty-seven clothing shops."[4] The county seat was also the region's entertainment center, featuring six movie theatres, three-a-day vaudeville acts, and lyceum programs. Large audiences enjoyed attractions like circuses, orchestras from New York and Philadelphia, light opera performances, and college glee clubs, which regularly scheduled Pottsville on their tours.[5]

Other aspects of the social and cultural scene in Pottsville benefited the city's brewers. The community continued to retain a substantial immigrant population that enjoyed beer. As late as the 1920s, 30 percent of its population was comprised of either first- or second-generation immigrants (those with at least one foreign-born parent). Pottsville's German community also stood by its traditions and held a variety of social gatherings and clubs. One of the most noteworthy was the Pottsville Liederkranz (songfest), which showcased the musical talents of its members until at least the 1920s. The club formed in the Civil War era, and the earliest accounts of the organization's meetings were written in German. The singing group successfully competed against other male glee clubs throughout the anthracite region and in Reading, Williamsport, Allentown and Philadelphia. Of course, the large, annual Liederkranz, marked by song, instrumental performances, and oration, had a German flavor, as the "waltz, polka, schottische and quadrilles were danced in true German manner, with noted elderly people being prevailed upon to participate in them…. Feasts, comprising German dishes and relishes, were always enjoyed." Among the members of the Pottsville Liederkranz were Frank Yuengling and Nicholas Dennebaum, the Yuengling brewmeister.[6]

Pottsville had a large number of taprooms, and beer was sold in many of the city's nine hotels and over twenty lunchrooms and restaurants.[7] The town had also developed "a reputation among the prep-school and Ivy League as a great party town during the Christmas holidays."[8] Probably contributing to this reputation was "a red-light district that drew high rollers from New York and Philadelphia."[9] But even as plenty of beer was being brewed on Mahantongo Street, in the early part of the twentieth century, storm clouds hung over the Yuengling Brewery. If Frank Yuengling was reading his local paper carefully and paying attention to the attacks on the brewing industry on the state and national level, he had to be worried about the future of his business. Slowly, the temperance movement was gaining steam.

A significant force in the fight against the nation's liquor traffic was the Women's Christian Temperance Union (WCTU).[10] The organization was founded in late 1873 in Cleveland, Ohio. Under the leadership of dynamic figures like Frances E. Willard (1839–1898), the WCTU brought moral, family-related, and religious arguments into the alcohol debate and worked to persuade states to prohibit the sale of alcoholic beverages. One of the group's main techniques was to go directly to saloons and ask the saloonkeeper to join its cause. The saloon visitations were marked by the singing of hymns and prayer. From Ohio, the WCTU spread into Pennsylvania within two months of its founding. In Pittsburgh, the Allegheny County WCTU drew support from prominent citizens like steel manufacturer and philanthropist Felix Brunot. The sidewalk services and street campaigns and the encounters with saloonkeepers drew extensive press coverage. Saloonkeepers often took extreme measures to dissuade the women's campaign. They would set their dogs on the crusaders, roll beer barrels at them, or brush their beer wagons against them. In some cases, the reformers "found themselves kneeling in cayenne paper which had been scattered all over the sidewalk or inhaling fumes and smoke of burning refuse set afire in vaults under the pavement."[11] Despite very limited success in shutting down saloons, the visitations continued to annoy saloonkeepers in the Pittsburgh area for several years.

Frank D. Yuengling (1876–1963). (D. G. Yuengling and Son, Inc.)

At the other end of the state, in Philadelphia, WCTU activists were more successful. According to one statistical report, the WCTU of Philadelphia was successful in shutting down 143 saloons and encouraged 121 bartenders to give up their jobs in its first five weeks of operation in 1874. Later, the organization founded the Home for the Reformation of Inebriate Women on North 13th Street in the city. The WCTU of Philadelphia also opened a coffee house, called the Holly Tree Inn, near the Centennial Grounds. The coffee house provided meals at low prices for workers on the street railway system. The services at the Holly Tree Inn offered an alternative to the free lunch offered at the local saloon. The crusade against alcohol spread from Pittsburgh and Philadelphia to other areas of the state, particularly the western and central portions of the commonwealth. On March 3, 1875, local branches of the WCTU in the state came together to form the Pennsylvania WCTU. The organization worked for a state constitutional prohibitory amendment. While it has been argued that the Pennsylvania WCTU "did little to harm the liquor industry," it was successful as a "temperance propaganda mill" and at keeping the issue of temperance reform before the public.[12]

Significantly, another one of its major objectives of the WCTU was carry the temperance campaign to the immigrant population. Surveys regarding the nationalities of liquor dealers led the WCTU leadership in Pennsylvania to create a separate department to promote temperance education among immigrants. In the 1880s, temperance tracts were prepared and distributed to the French, Germans, Italians, Chinese, Welsh and Scotch. Organization members seemed to be particularly concerned about German immigrants and devoted time to meeting with German ministers and organizations. One WCTU member stated, "We sometimes sigh over the difficulty of reaching them [Germans and other foreign-born]; but just here, woman with her personal influence can do what others cannot."[13]

The Pennsylvania WCTU also worked to increase temperance education in the state's public schools. Compulsory education began in Pennsylvania in 1873 and temperance education became part of the curriculum in 1875 under the "Scientific Instruction Bill." At approximately the same time, some Pennsylvania college students, in a trend that would astonish contemporary college educators, began falling under the temperance banner. Students at Westminster College in New Wilmington, Pennsylvania, pushed for courses that addressed the liquor problem and education programs that prepared them for careers in temperance organizations. By 1920, similar programs were in place at 28 Pennsylvania colleges and universities. The State Grange also conducted a vigorous campaign against the use of alcohol in the Commonwealth.

Temperance advocates were successful at bringing about renewed attempts to pass legislation that would curb alcohol abuse. In the 1870s, "local option" legislation passed, allowing certain areas of the state to vote independently to eliminate the alcohol trade. Once again, areas with heavy immigrant populations remained in the "wet" column. Temperance forces also sought to limit the number of bars and saloons by raising license fees. The "high license movement" started in 1881 in Nebraska and spread to Missouri and Illinois in 1883. The Pennsylvania legislature responded to public pressure by passing the Brooks High License Law on May 13, 1887. Other main provisions of the legislation, in addition to creating higher fees for liquor licenses, included stiffer penalties for illegal selling and other alcoholic beverage violations, and more uniform regulation of the liquor business in the commonwealth. In addition, the new law gave exclusive power to grant liquor licenses to court judges rather than political boards.

The Brooks High License Law went into effect on June 1, 1888, and remained virtually unchanged as the commonwealth's major piece of alcohol control legislation until national Prohibition. The Committee of Fifty, a group of scholars and businessmen who were interested in promoting temperance and the study of the liquor problem, investigated the impact of the law in the mid-nineties. A subcommittee of the organization, led by John Koren of Boston, gathered information from throughout Pennsylvania from October 1894 to January 1895, focusing largely on Philadelphia, Pittsburgh, Wilkes-Barre, and Reading. The final report, published as *The Liquor Problem in Its Legislative Aspects*, noted that the law succeeded in reducing the number of licensed drinking establishments in Pennsylvania, particularly in urban areas. But it did little to curb alcohol consumption. Beer sales in the state, for example, rose by 600,000 barrels from 1888 to 1896. The law also increased illegal liquor traffic. The speakeasy became a Philadelphia institution after the Brooks High License Law went into effect. One police officer in Philadelphia estimated that 6,000 speakeasies existed in the city in 1894. The illegal operations were largely located in the city's poorer districts and slums, but illegal sales also increased at many fashionable social clubs.

The impact of the Brooks Law was mirrored in Pittsburgh. In the Steel City, there were an estimated seven speakeasies for every licensed saloon. Illegal sales took place regularly at soft-drink places, cigar stores, and newsstands. Similar stories could be found elsewhere in the state. The study noted that in the "Pennsylvania Dutch" region of the state — Berks, Bucks, and Lancaster counties — liquor licenses were liberally distributed, thanks in large measure to the brewers, who wielded considerable political and social power. In contrast to Philadelphia and Pittsburgh, the "German" counties in the south and central areas of the state had little or no decrease in liquor licenses under the Brooks Law. In addition, other liquor regulations, such as the ban on Sunday sales, were essentially ignored.

A similar situation was found in northeastern Pennsylvania. The coal region's disregard for the Brooks Law was renowned. According to Koren's report, the liquor interests maintained tight control over the immigrant vote. Hence, they wielded tremendous influence over the regional politicians as well as the police. As a result, local legal authorities were generally lax when called upon by the state to enforce the Brooks Law. The Koren study called attention to an increase in the number of unlicensed saloons in Luzerne County, particularly Wilkes-Barre. The city had a population of 37,718 in 1890, and about 600 speakeasies operated with little or no interference from police. The situation was worse in other large coal mining towns like Pittston, Nanticoke, Plymouth, and Hazleton. The liquor traffic was equally powerful in Lackawanna, Carbon, and Schuylkill counties.

The findings in *The Liquor Problem in Its Legislative Aspects* regarding the anthracite coal region were substantiated a few years later in *Anthracite Coal Communities*. Peter Roberts observed that high license did "not succeeded in reducing the number of saloons in our towns" and "laws prohibiting the sale of intoxicants to minors and on Sunday are openly violated in every town, while the number of 'holes in the wall' is great."[14] Prohibitionists and temperance organizers apparently faced a great challenge in the mining towns. True, statewide organizations, which were largely evangelical Protestant in nature, focused most of their energy on urban communities. This does not mean, however, that heavily Catholic northeastern Pennsylvania was not touched by the growing crusade. Churches, mine operators, and specific temperance reform groups provided speakers who attempted to awaken the region to the evils of alcohol; however, their message did not have a lasting impact. "[A]s soon as the speaker leaves, the enthusiasm dies away and the reformed seek the old paths," complained Roberts. "Labor organizations and operators are also advocates of temperance because of economic considerations, and their power and influence can be exerted to a greater degree than they are in behalf of temperance reform."[15] Slavs were particularly resistant to temperance efforts:

> An effort by one of their pastors to organize a temperance club failed, for the people did not see the use of it. Public sentiment among them regards temperance agitation pretty much as Anglo-Saxons did fifty years ago. They look upon it as a craze of fanatics, and regard it as uncalled for, unwise and contrary to good social habits. Their saloon keepers are leaders in social and religious life and their business is held in honor. Sclav women as well as men drink a social glass, and no gathering is complete which has not a plentiful supply of whisky and lager on hand.[16]

The Roman Catholic Church, and specifically the Father Mathew Society, won some praise for enlightening "strictly sober young men, who hold positions of trust and responsibility in the anthracite industry as well as in other spheres of usefulness in these coal fields."[17] Another Catholic group that was active in the region was the "American League of the Cross." This organization had three divisions. Members of the first division were pledged to total abstinence. The second division members could drink socially, but could never buy rounds of drinks or accept a glass from another saloon patron. Members of third division pledged not to frequent saloons.[18] Protestant organizations were also formed: Bands of Hope, Blue Ribbon Leagues, Rolls of Honor, Sons of Temperance Societies. Roberts, however, concluded that temperance efforts by Protestant churches were "weak" and ultimately "must fail."[19]

Citizens eventually became more active and organized in attempts to enforce the state's liquor laws. Across the nation and the commonwealth, temperance advocates monitored the enforcement of existing alcohol regulations by forming "Law and Order Committees." In Schuylkill County, a committee, comprised of community leaders from eight of the principal mining towns, became very active. Roberts described the members of the committee as "law-abiding citizens" and "patriotic sons" of the county. The operations of the group included hiring detectives to gather evidence of liquor law violations. Members also attended the trials of violators to expose "the incidental evils of the liquor business."[20] The Law and Order Committee also attended hearings of applicants for liquor licenses and provided maps of communities for the court, to ensure that the proposed saloon would not be located near a church or a school.

The campaign by the Law and Order Committee was initially successful. Even Slav saloonkeepers, who had a reputation for operating particularly loathsome bars, were beginning to respect Pennsylvania's laws, thanks to the efforts of that citizen organization. "The fruit is already seen," wrote Roberts. "Some twenty Slav saloonkeepers came this month to the Law and Order Society to express their wish to obey the law and their anxiety that violators be brought to justice.... The same is true of English-speaking men in the business. The more responsible men in the business feel they must obey the law. Men who have from ten to twenty thousand dollars tied up in their saloons cannot afford to risk their license."[21] While there were some successful efforts to enforce license laws, most temperance advocates recognized that high license legislation was a failure and only succeeded in increasing the number of speakeasies in the state. They felt that the time had come for the more drastic measure that other states had adopted — statewide prohibition.

Another strong push for a statewide constitutional prohibition amendment occurred during the 1880s, culminating with the issue being put before the voters in 1889. The state's brewers — with Frederick Yuengling probably among them — banded together to defeat the referendum. Led by Brewer Harry Crowell, beer makers from across the state stockpiled a war chest of $200,000. The funds were raised by assessing ten cents for each barrel of beer sold. Large hotels controlled by brewers under the tied-house system were assessed $1,000. In addition, each brewer "was required to solicit money from all kindred interests ... every man ... with whom they had dealings."[22] The money was distributed to politicians, newspapers, and public speakers. By Crowell's own admission, weekly newspapers sought $50 to $500 to publish material favorable to the liquor interests. Larger urban newspapers demanded and received between $1,000 and $4,000 each. Soon, Pennsylvanians were reading bogus articles about the evils created by prohibitory liquor laws in other states. The brewers also paid Kate Field, a noted propagandist, $250 a day for taking the stump and telling listeners why Prohibition would be bad for the Commonwealth.

Those favoring the amendment worked for almost a year organizing committees, promoting their position in the press, and garnering support from churches and clergymen. Prohibitionists also gained an ally among organized labor — most notably the Knights of Labor. The Knight's official publication encouraged members to vote in favor of constitutional Prohibition, stating that the amendment was in the "best interest of the toilers of the Keystone State."[23] Even the Knights of Labor's noted leader, Terence V. Powderly (1849–1924), said he intended to vote for prohibition. "We are now forced to choose between the poverty and distress upon one side, brought about by the Drunkard and unprincipled rumseller, and Prohibition on the other," declared Powderly. "Of the two, I prefer Prohibition."[24] Powderly, a native of the northeastern Pennsylvania community of Carbondale, near Scranton, was a teetotaler and supporter of temperance causes. During his tenure of leader of the Knights, from 1878 to 1893, he helped form an alliance between the union and the WCTU. As the date for the vote — June 18, 1889 — drew closer, temperance forces grew confident. When the polls opened, many WCTU members were serving buttermilk and wearing white badges inscribed, "For the Prohibition Amendment." In some towns and cities, WCTU members arranged for church bells to ring periodically through the day to remind people to vote. The efforts would not be enough.

The lobbying by the brewers carried the day. The statewide vote was overwhelmingly against Prohibition — 484,644 to 296,617. Three-fourths of the vote against the amendment came from three areas of the state: the brewing centers of Philadelphia and Pittsburgh, and Berks County, with its heavy German population.[25] Other significant wet counties included Lehigh, Lancaster, and Northampton. Voters in Schuylkill County and the rest of the coal region helped bring victory to brewing and liquor industries. "The attempt made in 1888 to bring the State of Pennsylvania in line with other states of the union, where the sale of intoxicants is prohibited, was overwhelmingly defeated," stated a disappointed Peter Roberts about the fate of the prohibitory liquor law, "and in no part of the commonwealth was the vote for the dram-shop more pronounced than in these coal fields."[26]

A few years later temperance forces took another swing at the state's brewers by backing a bill to tax beer. The Bliss Bill of 1896 passed the state house and was expected to easily pass the Senate. The weekend before the vote, however, the brewing lobby went to work. Pennsylvania's brewers rented a floor in a Philadelphia hotel and invited selected members of the Senate to occupy the rooms. The expense-

An illustration from Henry Malcolm Chalfant's 1920 book, *Father Penn and John Barleycorn*. The book celebrates the victory of prohibition forces in Pennsylvania. Prohibitionists considered northeastern Pennsylvania the most difficult area to reform. (From Henry Malcom Chalfant's 1920 book *Father Penn and John Barleycorn*.)

paid weekend festivities somehow convinced Senate members to rewrite the bill — now titled the Merchants Tax Bill. In an intriguing reversal, the new legislation taxed everything *except* beer. Republican Governor Daniel Hartman Hastings (1849–1903) ultimately vetoed the bill, but there was no more talk of a tax on beer. A few years later, a grand jury investigation of political activities by brewers and distillers in Pennsylvania was conducted. The probe resulted in hundreds of indictments on charges of bribing legislators to vote against dry laws.[27]

If setbacks on the legislative front taught prohibitionists anything, it was that they needed to more politically active and skillful. This was particularly true among members of what would ultimately become the most powerful temperance organization — the Anti-Saloon League of America. The roots of the organization are found in Ohio in 1893. Under the cry of its slogan, "The Saloon Must Go," the Anti-Saloon League took direct aim at the nation's brewers and liquor producers. The organization worked to spread anti-alcohol sentiment, enforce current liquor laws, and most significantly, press for further enactment of anti-alcohol legislation. It was largely interdenominational, and it used churches to get its message before the public. Members worked to coordinate and centralize various temperance organizations.

By working through the political party in power, the Anti-Saloon League scored a host of victories on the legislative front across the country. The association entered Pennsylvania in the summer of 1896 and opened district offices in Pittsburgh, Wilkes-Barre, Erie, Philadelphia, Altoona, and Harrisburg. Ultimately, the organization's efforts in Pennsylvania would become unnecessary, because its campaigns in other parts of the nation were already bearing fruit. As the years passed, its ultimate goal, national Prohibition came closer. By the dawn of the twentieth century, a change to the United States Constitution to bring about reform came into sight, and it came even closer to becoming a reality when World War I broke out in 1914.

The United States was officially neutral at the beginning of World War I, but the mood of the nation was not. After 128 American citizens were killed in 1915 when a German submarine sank the British passenger ship *Lusitania*, anti–German sentiment was very high. Groups in favor of Prohibition saw an opportunity, and beer and brewers came under attack as pro–German. "Dry propaganda said all patriots must be prohibitionists," observed Herman Ronnenberg in his description of America's anti–German mood. "German-Americans were guilty of spying and beer-drinking, and German armies committed atrocities while drunk. World peace demanded the outlawing of the *Deutsch* brewers. German-style beer would keep American soldiers from shooting straight and thus hurt the country."[28] It seemed that anything with a German name created suspicion. Pretzels were removed from saloons. Sauerkraut was referred to as liberty cabbage. Americans were no longer eating frankfurters but hot dogs. At the market, it was no longer a pound of hamburger but liberty steak. Similarly, German measles was liberty measles. The pet dog was no longer a German shepherd but an Alsatian. In some cases, families with German names attempted to hide their ethnic identity by changing their names.[29] For German Americans operating breweries, the rampant anti-German sentiment created fear and uncertainty. If brewers had any hopes that the prohibition movement in the country would be stopped, those hopes were crushed when America entered the war in 1917. The industry was dying.

Even before America entered World War I, alcoholic beverages were outlawed in thirteen states, and twenty-six had passed prohibitory laws of some nature. For brewers in Pennsylvania and other remaining "wet" states, this troubling legislative trend, which began around 1913, grew into cause for alarm. Action by lawmakers in Washington, D.C., and additional measures against alcohol on the state level signaled that national Prohibition was imminent. There were some red-letter days for avid prohibitionists, but for brewers and their employees, including the Frank Yuengling and his workers, the legislative trend was troubling:

- **March 1, 1913:** Congress passes the Webb-Kenyon Interstate Shipments Act. Prior to this action, thirsty people in search of beer, wine, and whiskey in dry states could simply order it by mail from wet states. The Webb-Kenyon Act (which is quickly passed by Congress overriding the veto of President William Howard Taft) outlaws interstate transportation of liquor into states where intoxicants are banned.
- **December 10, 1913:** The Anti-Saloon League marches on Washington and presents Congress with petitions calling for Prohibition by 1920.
- **December 11, 1917:** Following America's entry into World War I in April 1917, President Woodrow Wilson obtains power under the Food Control Act to save grain for the war effort. He has the option of limiting or prohibiting the manufacture of beer and wine as he sees fit. On December 11, he reduces the grain supply allowed for brewing by 30 percent. Perhaps more significantly for brewers, the president also reduces the legal alcoholic content of beer to 2.75 percent. Brewers usually made beer with at least 4 percent alcohol, but some beers went as high as 8 percent.
- **December 18, 1917:** Congress passes the Eighteenth Amendment and submits it to the states for ratification.
- **January 8, 1918:** Mississippi becomes the first state to ratify the Eighteenth Amendment.
- **January 16, 1919:** Nebraska becomes the 36th state to vote in favor of Prohibition, providing the three-quarters necessary for ratification.
- **October 10, 1919:** The apparatus to enforce the Eighteenth Amendment is set into place with passage of the Volstead Act. President Wilson vetoes the bill. He argues that it is unconstitutional, because it contains provisions drafted for "wartime" prohibition. The war had ended on Armistice Day, November 11, 1918. Congress quickly overrides Wilson's veto.
- **January 5, 1920:** The U.S. Supreme Court decides the Ruppert Case and upholds the establishment of the legal content for beer at one-half of 1 percent by volume. New York beer baron Jacob Ruppert, who was also owner of the New York Yankees, had led brewers in challenging the legislation. Attorneys for the brew-

ers argued that the 2.75 percent alcoholic beverages manufactured during World War I did not come under the heading of "intoxicating beverages," because "in order to get drunk one would have to drink more liquid with that amount of alcohol in it than the human system could take."[30] The Supreme Court does not see it this way and, for all practical purposes, brewing real beer comes to an end.

- **January 17, 1920:** National Prohibition goes into effect at 12:01 a.m.
- **November 23, 1921:** Congress passes the Willis-Campbell Bill. A few breweries had been licensed to manufacture beer with an alcohol content higher than 0.5 percent for medicinal purposes. However, this practice is outlawed under the new law.

Pennsylvania and other leading industrial states with significant immigrant populations reluctantly fell in line with the move to change the constitution. The Keystone State, New York, Illinois and New Jersey were among the last to act on the Eighteenth Amendment. In fact, the Pennsylvania legislature took up Prohibition *after* enough states had voted in favor of ratification. House ratification bill No. 1 was read into place on January 27, 1919, and came up for debate the following week. Deliberations were heated, with organized labor among the few groups voicing opposition to the measure. A spokesman for the United Mine Workers of America argued that over 90 percent of the coal miners opposed Prohibition, and the American Federation of Labor and the Pennsylvania Federation also stood in opposition.[31] Countering this position was Robert Wallace, an attorney from Lawrence County, who noted that 1,500 members of the Brotherhood of Railroad Trainmen in Harrisburg had passed a resolution in favor. When the time came for legislators to vote, the result was close, 110 to 93 — just six votes over the constitutional majority needed for passage.

Once the bill was in the hands of the state Senate, the Law and Order Committee scheduled a public hearing. The major organizations that had been working for Prohibition in Pennsylvania — the Anti-Saloon League, the Dry Federation of Pennsylvania, and the Woman's Christian Temperance Union — turned up the heat. The Anti-Saloon League brought in its big guns for the hearing — Wayne B. Wheeler, general counsel for the organization, and William Jennings Bryan, former presidential candidate, noted speaker, and avid prohibitionist. Speaking against prohibition were James H. Maurer, a former House member from Reading, and J. N. Ritchie, a Philadelphia labor leader. Ritchie argued that the matter should be decided by referendum vote when all of Pennsylvania's soldiers had returned from France. The Anti-Saloon League immediately put anti-German sentiment to use, as Wheeler countered, "I can't believe that the boys who were willing to sacrifice their lives on the battlefield are going to support the liquor traffic which was one of the most ardent supporters of the German alliance."[32] The bill passed the Senate on February 25 without debate, making Pennsylvania the 45th state in favor of ratification.

As constitutional Prohibition drew closer, Yuengling and other Schuylkill County breweries continued to produce the 2.75 percent beer that was legal under the Food Control Bill. Regional beer makers sold enough of this lower alcohol beer to continue normal operations and make regular deliveries to the county's approximately 1,200 saloons. Customers complained about the mellower brew, however. One beer lover, in a letter to the Pottsville *Journal*, humorously vowed that he was giving up drinking because "the two and three-quarters beer is too hard on the elbow."[33] In 1919, more changes were on tap to irritate customers. On July 1, the official beginning of "wartime prohibition," fewer bottles could be found behind the bar. The manufacture and sale of hard liquor — whiskey, gin, vodka, and other spirits — was officially forbidden. Some bar owners saw no reason to stay open without the "hard stuff." Significantly, the Pottsville *Republican* noted that most of the "privately owned" saloons "closed tight" while the "brewery controlled" saloons, which had plenty of 2.75 percent beer to sell, remained open. Still, the ban on hard liquor in taprooms drove away more potential customers and quieted the cash registers in the saloons.

A few months after the start of wartime prohibition the power to enforce national Prohibition was set in place with the passage of the Volstead Act. Yuengling and other brewers now had to reduce the alcohol content of beer from 2.75 percent to the requirement set forth in the new law — one-half of 1 percent. The legal, low-alcohol alternative became popularly known as "near beer." Actually, this change had been brewing for some time. In 1917, Carl A. Nowak, secretary of the Master Brewers' Association of the United States, published a book, called *New Fields for Brewers*. The book offered advice for adapting breweries to low-alcohol beverages and suggested other commercial ventures. Even before the publication of Nowak's book, national brewers had prepared to market near beer. In 1916, Anheuser-Busch moved forward with a considerable investment to construct one of the largest bottling plants in the world expressly for the production of "Bevo," its new, non-alcoholic beverage. The following year, other beer makers were lining up to register their near-beer trade names, and about 200 variations of the product found their way onto store shelves.

Yuengling Special. A version of "near beer" that posted respectable sales in the 1920s. (D. G. Yuengling and Son, Inc.)

Promising markets prompted the national brewers' early near-beer ventures. With the emergence of bottled beer, household consumption rose, and a significant market for beer emerged among women. Most women would not put a foot inside a saloon, but packaged beer allowed them to enjoy the beverage at home. In many cases, women favored a beverage with less alcohol content than regular beer. In addition, low-alcohol products gave brewers new retail outlets, such as soda fountains, drug stores, grocery stores, and movie theatres. Another benefit for brewers was near beer's classification as a soft drink by the federal government. It was not subject to high taxation like traditional beer. The tax on beer, which was first set at $1 a barrel during the Civil War, had risen rapidly in the Progressive Era. By late 1919, smaller regional brewers like those in northeastern Pennsylvania recognized the factors that were changing the market. Many decided it would be necessary for them to produce near beer as well if they were to stay in business and save local jobs.

The direct result of Prohibition was tens of thousands of very worried workers—those who labored honestly to make, deliver, and sell alcoholic beverages. Before the ban on alcohol went into effect, the Yuengling Brewery was estimated to be worth about a million dollars, and it employed about 100 people. There was cause for concern, but Frank Yuengling was confident that the public would eventually clamor to overturn the Eighteenth Amendment. In the meantime, his primary goal was to keep the plant operating so it would be ready when real beer returned. Near beer was the sensible alternative, because it required few changes to the plant on Mahantongo Street. Employees performed essentially the same duties as before with existing equipment and supplies. The only change necessary was the installation of a de-alcoholizing machine to boil off excess alcohol. As soon as the demise of "John Barleycorn" became a certainty, Frank Yuengling and his brewmaster committed themselves to the challenging task of finding a near beer recipe that would satisfy the public and post respectable sales. Predictably, early reactions by Pottsville-area beer drinkers were not promising.

A "general test" of near beers by Schuylkill County brewers began at the end of October, 1919. Newspaper reports acknowledged that the future of the breweries hinged on the results:

> The general condition is viewed as being a race between the different manufacturers to get the most acceptable substitute and it is a question whether the public will take kindly to the non-alcoholic stuff or not. The dealers are hopeful that a drink that will meet the demands of both the government and the people will be produced. The fact that this country has always stood up to the test of necessity being the mother of invention is looked upon as the possible salvation of the trade.[34]

The response to near beer by many is best summed up in a popular quotation from the period, "Whoever named it near beer was a damned poor judge of distance!" The problem was the "boiling method" used to de-alcoholize the beer. As the beer boiled, its alcohol level was gradually lowered until it met legal standards. Unfortunately, the brew's flavor also evaporated into the air along with the alcohol. Newspaper reports indicated that Schuylkill County beer drinkers were not at all impressed with what the area breweries were turning out. Within less than a week the "general test" of near beer in the Pottsville area was looked upon as a failure:

> The new stuff, according to reliable information, is not meeting with a hearty reception, the executor of John Barleycorn being any thing but agreeable to the palate of those used to stronger and better things. According to reports the brewery teams hauling the stuff out are bringing it back, the sale falling way below the usual beer sales.[35]

The region's beer lovers could only be pessimistic about the dry years ahead.

So much anticipation had built surrounding the official beginning of Prohibition that when the moment finally arrived it was anticlimactic. Schuylkill County quietly entered the new era. The Pottsville *Republican* reported some breweries had beer "with a hefty punch in it" and were distributing it to their "favorite customers" in anticipation of Prohibition; however, the breweries denied the rumor and insisted that they only had near beer. Illegal sales of "whiskey or so-called whiskey" at the saloons in Pottsville's neighboring communities of New Philadelphia and Cumbola were also described. The paper predicted that saloons could "experience very hard sledding" if near beer sales failed. At the Yuengling Brewery, pressure mounted to develop a near-beer formula which would satisfy the taste buds of the public.

The elderly Nicholas Dennebaum — who had been brewmaster at Yuengling since 1906 — felt utilizing the latest technology could solve the problem. The company decided to invest in new equipment that could make near beer under an "expensive vacuum distillation process."[36] Under the "distilling method," the flavor of the beer did not vanish into thin air; rather, it stayed within the vacuum system and retained most of the original, pre–Prohibition taste that Yuengling drinkers enjoyed. Indeed, the brewery worked to imitate the formula for success that had worked for generations and introduced two near beers in the hopes of striking a note of familiarity with its faithful customers.

"Yuengling Special" was the best selling of the low-alcohol near beers. "Brewed and Aged the Old-Fashioned Way," the new brand closely imitated the taste of traditional beers and had a flavor similar to today's light beers. "Yuengling Special" won praise from those who had drunk Yuengling brands before Prohibition. It continued to develop a loyal following as a "snack beverage" in the Prohibition era. Stanley Shevokis, a former Yuengling employee, recalled enjoying "Yuengling Special" in 1928:

> It was really a good tasting beer. Me and my buddies used to run downtown at lunchtime at the brewery and eat a candybar and drink a Yuengling Special. I remember that we were not allowed to shoot pool because of our age, but that we all used to drink beer and it was good.[37]

The success of the beverage is reflected in the slogan for the product that appeared on its beer trays and posters: "Everybody's Drinking 'Yuengling Special' Now." Next, the brewery attempted to mirror its past success with its dark brew (porter) by introducing "Yuengling Por-tor." Here Yuengling followed the trend in the industry to promote its near beer as wholesome and healthful. The drink was advertised as "Pure, Wholesome, Refreshing, Satisfying," and "made from the Choicest Hops and Malt and Sparkling Mountain Spring Water, a Delicious and Healthful Drink."

A novel addition to the Yuengling lineup was "Yuengling Juvo" which, as opposed to a "near beer," was promoted as a "cereal beverage" and was suitable for children. The curious name reflects an industry trend. American brewers apparently saw some benefit in ending product names with "O" or "U." Some decided to utilize company or family names and initials. Pabst Brewing Company's near beer was called "Pablo." Schlitz produced "Famo," and if a customer called for a "Lux-o," it was a product of the Stroh's Brewing Company he wanted. Yuengling's ads for its cereal beverage generally depicted a family enjoying "Juvo" with a hearty meal. The slogans for Juvo proclaimed that "the taste tells" and that Juvo "adds to the enjoyment of a good meal." Customers were encouraged to "order it by the case." The brewery also produced another "non-intoxicating beverage" called "Alo." The label for the product encouraged the purchaser to "Serve Cold." The brewery also turned out a product that was available in drug stores. According to noted beer historian Will Anderson, Yuengling produced an "elixir" or "tonic" which contained 2 percent alcohol. The company, however, was "forbidden to sell more than five cases of it a week to any given retail druggist."[38]

With stable near-beer sales, the Yuengling Brewery echoed with the sound of moving bottling lines and rolling beer barrels as it had before and, while the company wasn't hiring any new workers, layoffs among its existing workforce were avoided. In 1918, the brewery's annual production reached the 100,000-barrel mark. Although specific figures for Yuengling's near-beer products are unavailable, one study estimates the brewery's output following the implementation of wartime prohibition fell to between 70,000 and 80,000, a surprisingly strong showing.[39] Remarkably, demand for Yuengling near beer increased in the late 1920s and early 1930s, because a new generation, which had never known real beer, was satisfied with the low-alcohol beverage. It was all they knew.

In addition to finding a near-beer recipe acceptable to the public, there's a basic reason why the Yuengling Brewery had some success with its near beer. It was one of the only breweries in the area producing the product. While Frank Yuengling was confident that he could produce a near beer that the public would accept, many other beer makers considered the taste of the area's beer lovers and did not even try. There is no evidence that the other Pottsville breweries—the Mount Carbon Brewery and the Rettig Brewing Company—made a serious attempt to market near beer. Other brewers also decided to close completely or marketed other products like soft drinks. Significantly, the Yuengling Brewery was one of the only breweries in the region to be *officially* licensed to brew malt beverages during Prohibition. It was issued license number 161.[40] One of the very few sources for the product, therefore, was at Fifth and Mahantongo streets. The brewery's long history in the community—approaching 100 years—also helped. Loyal customers who enjoyed Yuengling products decided to continue to do so, even if the beverage was near beer. The "tied-house system" also guaranteed the exclusive sale of Yuengling near beer in the taprooms owned by the brewery.

The Yuengling Brewery's official license to make near beer illustrates Frank Yuengling's determination to respect Prohibition laws.[41] Plenty of other individuals, including some brewers, did not approach the ban on alcohol with the same integrity. The initial hostility and disregard for Prohibition among the general public is rooted in the widespread perception that the Eighteenth Amendment was in reality class legislation. As January 17, 1920, approached, the poor could only sit and wait as plans were made to deprive them of their beer and saloons. The rich, on the other hand, had had a year to stockpile. One of the most notable examples was Republican Senator Boies Penrose of Philadelphia, one of the state's most vigorous opponents of Prohibition. The senator lived alone in a townhouse on Spruce Street. He died in 1921, shortly after the beginning of Prohibition. When his brother, Dr. Charles Penrose, began removing belongings from the house, he found $125,000 of liquor cached in the home. Prohibition could not stop the noted Pennsylvania legislator from sipping on his favorite whiskey.[42]

While Penrose's violation of the law seems innocuous, bear in mind the darker legacy of Prohibition, perhaps best expressed in Herbert Asbury's *The Great Illusion:*

> The American people had expected to be greeted, when the great day came, by a covey of angels bearing gifts of peace, happiness, prosperity and salvation, which they had been assured would be theirs when the rum demon had been scotched. Instead, they were met by a horde of bootleggers, moonshiners, rum-runners, hijackers, gangsters, racketeers, triggermen, venal judges, corrupt police, crooked politicians, and speakeasy operators.[43]

With organized crime turning out real beer from old breweries, Prohibition was turning into anarchy, and it seemed that little was being done about it. Certainly, enforcement of Prohibition laws was an expensive proposition for the federal government. Finding violators became the responsibility of federal agents, and there were never enough of them to adequately do the job. One estimate put the number of Prohibition agents in the country in 1920 at 1,526. If these agents had been distributed evenly throughout the country, each one would have had a territory of 2,340 square miles and a population of 70,000 to watch over.[44] On the federal level, the first two years of prohibition provided evidence that "enforcement was in danger of becoming a farce."[45] By 1923, "beating the feds" was the new national pastime. The position adopted by most states further weakened enforcement efforts: Prohibition was a federal matter, and it was up to Uncle Sam to track down the violators. Many Pennsylvania legislators clearly maintained this view.

Pennsylvania failed to provide any funding to enforce the Eighteenth Amendment, and it showed. The commonwealth probably had the nation's worst enforcement record, earning the dubious distinction as the "Gibraltar of the liquor traffic" among Anti-Saloon League officials. "When national prohibition came to Pennsylvania it stood on paper only," states Leland Bell. "Those who wanted a glass of beer, or a keg, or any quantity of booze, knew where to go and also knew the law would look the other way."[46] Eastern portions of the state, including Yuengling's major market, once again caused particular frustration for prohibitionists:

> The Pennsylvania League maintained there could be no "blacker" territory than the half of the state east of the Susquehanna river. In this territory stood just one dry county, Wyoming, and outside of it few townships or boroughs in eastern Pennsylvania were without saloons. Philadelphia, the Pennsylvania German counties, and the anthracite coal region were solid wet areas that formed the hard rock core of the "gibraltar of the liquor traffic.[47]

Less than two weeks after Prohibition went into effect, an official of the Pennsylvania Anti-Saloon League openly complained at the organization's annual meeting in Harrisburg. He noted that law enforcement officials in communities opposed to Prohibition simply ignored their obligation to enforce the law.[48] Indeed, in Pennsylvania, there were many instances in which federal agents seized liquor, only to have it restored to the owner by local police. Other Pennsylvanians circumvented the law by using alcohol under the loophole of "medicinal purposes." One study found that 40,000 gallons of alcohol were consumed in 1920 for "medicinal purposes" in a small town of 300 residents near Pittsburgh. By 1926, the public's disregard for Prohibition in Pennsylvania was so outrageous that Governor Gifford Pinchot (1865–1946), who was also an official of the Anti-Saloon League, was demanding a federal investigation.

Pennsylvania's beer lovers also had a variety of methods of getting beer with the same potency as in the pre–Prohibition days. One could violate the law and attempt to do the malting, mashing, hopping, fermenting and other beer-making tasks at home. Beer brewing, winemaking, and distilling in the basement became common. Early in Prohibition, there was little homebrew, or as Germans refer to it, heimgemacht, but this gradually changed, despite the fact that the product turned out by amateur brewers often tasted awful. By 1930, sales of beer ingredients like hops and equipment like hydrometers indicated that home brewing had become one of the nation's most popular hobbies.[49] In many communities, small stores, similar to the "head shops" that would prove popular generations later, sidestepped the law and sold all the ingredients, equipment, and recipes to make beer and other alcoholic beverages.[50] Northeastern Pennsylvanians also followed a trend of brewing and distilling at home, as a Senate committee investigating enforcement was to learn. A clergyman testifying before the committee called attention to the state's mining towns, where "prohibition had enormously increased drinking and introduced an illicit still 'into practically every other home.'"[51] Another alternative was to guzzle what became known as a "Miner's Highball"—a shot of illegal liquor or moonshine with a Yuengling Special as a chaser. Of course, beer lovers did not need to turn to homebrewing or illegal liquor. If people wanted it badly enough, real beer was available. In Pottsville, rumors circulated that one of Yuengling's old competitors in the city, the Rettig

Brewery at the 800 Block of Market Street, utilized its tunnels in the back of the brewery to make illegal beer for city residents.

When Prohibition began, the chief source of illegal beer was full-fledged breweries, which had supposedly switched to producing near beer. The process was surprisingly simple:

> The easiest method to obtain beer was to make a deal with either or both the workers and owners at a near-beer plant. By merely tapping the wrong storage tank a keg of near-beer could instead be a keg of fresh non-dealcoholized lager. Since brewing demands many large storage tanks, hiding such a scheme was much easier than one might suspect.[52]

In addition, brewmasters could easily turn off the de-alcoholizer for a period of time and let real beer flow. Infractions by licensed near-beer breweries were quite common in the early 1920s, with almost half of them reported for violations in 1921. In that year, revenue agents shut down Wilkes-Barre's Stegmaier Brewery and at least six other breweries in northeastern Pennsylvania. The action, at least at Stegmaier, was justified since it was generally acknowledged that the dealcoholizing unit at Stegmaier "was often turned off."[53]

Frank Yuengling never gave into the temptation to tap the wrong storage tank or turn off the distilling device and let real beer flow. True, the Yuengling Brewery had good reason to stay within the law. As one of the region's largest breweries, it was a prime target for federal agents looking for possible violations of the Volstead Act. A Yuengling brewmaster, N. Ray Norbert, also argued that the company's limited success with its near beer made "bootlegging" too risky. "If you were caught, that was the end of your brewing business," said Norbert. "With them [Yuengling] selling a fair amount of near beer, why bother? The key to the Yuengling Brewery was that they stayed away from shady characters. Mr. Yuengling wouldn't have anything to do with them. He was successful with near beer, because he had a very loyal following and they were not willing to take a chance either."[54] But this does not mean that Mahantongo Street wasn't a stop for federal agents. Early in the Prohibition era, the mountain tunnels that were created under the direction of D. G. Yuengling for the fermentation and storage of beer were closed. Prohibition laws limited the amount of near beer that a brewery could store and the feds, who were already short-staffed, sought to simplify their job by decreasing the brewer's storage space for near beer. Besides, Prohibition agents had enough to keep them occupied in other parts of Schuylkill County.

The man who earned a reputation as a Prohibition-era "beer baron" and the most renowned bootlegger in the lower anthracite region was Lamont "Monk" Miller of Ashland. His "business" was located just south of the northern Schuylkill County area in a valley near Fountain Springs. Beer trucks rolled out in the middle of the night from the "Mahanoy Manufacturing Company" and the "Fountain Springs Hotel." Reportedly, malt, hops, and water became beer at the "manufacturing company" and a 200-yard pipeline sent the beer to the "hotel," where it was racked. The operation was successful. Miller's operation was the source of most of the illegal beer in Schuylkill County, but newspaper reports also indicate that Schuylkill County was the source of much of the illegal beer being consumed in Philadelphia, possibly from Miller's "manufacturing plant." Miller made enough money brewing and distributing illegal booze to build a comfortable 24-room manor just outside of Ashland in Fountain Springs. Significantly, the chateau, complete with swimming pool, was constructed on a hill near the village and had a view that allowed the bootlegger to keep an eye on his business below.

"Monk" Miller faced little resistance from law enforcement officials locally, as one regional historian noted:

> The county was wide open. If you wanted a drink, you could find one in any town in the region. Monk placed money in the proper hands, state and local politicians, state and local police, judges, and county dignitaries. Because he took great care to touch all bases, he encountered no trouble distributing his illegal beer and moonshine throughout the area.[55]

Federal agents were less sympathetic and kept the bootlegging operation under surveillance. Miller somehow kept his brewery going, even after Repeal. Despite a personal vow to stay out of jail, Miller was convicted of defrauding the government of thousands of dollars in beer taxes in 1937 and was sentenced to a year and day in jail at the federal penitentiary in Lewisburg. After his release from prison, Miller once again found himself outside the law, operating a "black market" on goods that were in short supply during World War II — tires, gasoline, butter, and meat. In his final years, Miller operated a small grocery store in Ashland, where he gained a reputation for his generosity to those in need. Sadly, Miller's life ended in an act of criminal violence. Burglars broke into his home in Fountain Springs on June 3, 1969. Miller was tied up and beaten as the thieves sought to learn the location of a safe containing $1,200 and jewelry. The 72-year-old victim died hours later at a regional hospital. The murder of Ashland's notorious "beer baron" made headlines in newspapers across the state and produced wire stories in the Associated Press.

Most likely, some of "Monk" Miller's beer was enjoyed in Pottsville. Valuable insight into the city's attitude toward the "noble experiment" is provided by one of its most famous sons, accomplished short-story writer and novelist John O'Hara (1905–70). O'Hara, who gained fame with such novels as *Appointment in Samarra* (1934) and *Ten North Frederick* (1955), was familiar with the Yuengling family and was childhood friends with Frank Yuengling's daughter, Augusta. In fact, O'Hara was among the neighborhood children who took formal dance lessons with the Yuengling siblings inside the carriage house of the brewing family's home at 1440 Mahantongo St. O'Hara's father, a doctor, purchased Frederick Yuengling's townhouse at 606 Mahantongo Street in 1913, and the future bestselling author lived there until 1928. O'Hara recalled rumors that a two-block long tunnel connected the house of his youth with the brewery. "I never was able to find it," recalled O'Hara, "the cut-glass chandelier in the parlor was delicate and beautiful; the speaking tube from the third floor to the kitchen was a nice thing to pour a pitcher of water down; some of the stair landings were so dark you could stand in a corner of one of them and not be seen by a person a foot away."[56]

To his credit, O'Hara quit drinking when he was 48 and stayed sober the rest of his life. As his doctors pointed out to him in 1953, death was certain if he continued to drink. His stomach and liver wouldn't take it anymore.[57] Few would deny that John O'Hara enjoyed a drink now and then. "His drinking career was hectic, vicious, fearful, angry, driven by a mania for parties and escape into bistros," wrote one admirer of O'Hara's fiction. "In his flight from an Irish-Catholic background, he was scarred by hangovers of unbelievable spikelike intensity — paralyzing!"[58] Even when he was in his early teens, alcohol was the source of much bitterness between the future writer and his father. When Prohibition went into effect in the Pottsville of O'Hara's youth, there was clearly no shortage of booze in the city. O'Hara drew attention to the ethnic diversity of the area when he described the drinking at the parties he attended:

> [W]e drank everything we could lay a lip on, from boilo, which was a Polish whiskey that derived its name from the fact that we drank it while it was still-hot, to champagne that prudent men had laid down before Prohibition went into effect. We also drank a great deal of beer. The word would get around that some speak-easy was serving "good" beer and away we'd go before the Feds, those who were not taking graft, made their raid. In a section that was populated by German farming families who liked their beer, and Italian laboring families who liked their wine, and Irish and Slavic and English mining families who went for the hard stuff, Prohibition was in effect but ineffectual. We grew up in an atmosphere of complete contempt for the one law that affected the rich, the middle class, and the poor.[59]

That contempt showed as O'Hara and his friends took advantage of every opportunity to thumb their noses at the Eighteenth Amendment. "O'Hara's group called itself 'The Purity League,' six lads dedicated to circumventing the Volstead Act in every possible way," noted one of the biographers of the novelist. "The boys—two Bobs, a Beany, a Fred, a Deacon, and O'Hara (called 'Doc' in honor of his father, or 'Johno')—lived for practical jokes like piling bottles on the porch of Pottsville's foremost Methodist."[60]

Later, Pottsville's famous writer was particularly nostalgic about Christmas holidays when students attending prep school and colleges came home and got reacquainted. Making calls to homes usually involved wine, bootleg whiskey or even champagne. He recalled a specific incident on Mahantongo Street involving a bootlegger, a story that provides another illustration of the author's interest in themes of social class. On the morning after a party at the Schuylkill Country Club, O'Hara looked out on a silent, snowy Mahantongo Street. He then heard the noise of a loose tire chain in the distance: "Then it came a little faster ... and he saw an acquaintance pass by — Mort McDonald, a bootlegger who made an early delivery of champagne. As McDonald drove away, he expressed his opinion of Mahantongo Street customers by shouting: 'Merry Christmas, you stuck-up bastards! Merry Christmas from Mort McDonald!'"[61]

Another Schuylkill County community, Shenandoah, gained a reputation for lawlessness and the dubious distinction as "the only Western Town in the East" in the summer of 1930, when an incident involving one of the town's breweries and federal dry agents grabbed national headlines.[62] The Home Brewery owned a sta-ble-garage behind its main structure. Bootleggers used this location to produce nee-dle beer by "shooting" the kegs of near beer. On one occasion, they were tipped off that federal agents were in the area. When agents broke into the garage in search of the source of illegal beer, someone called the local police. Officer "Spookie" Dobrowolskie and another cop went to the scene, where they took the federal agents into custody for breaking and entering. The agents showed the officers their search warrant and other legal documentation, but Spookie refused to acknowledge them. The feds were placed in the borough lockup, giving bootleggers enough time to remove any evidence of the needle-beer operation.

In the neighboring community of Mahanoy City, the Kaier's Brewery shifted from a legitimate operation to a criminal front. Before the country went dry, Charles D. Kaier bought whiskey by the barrel and transferred it to quart or pint bottles for sale. The firm also had its own blend, "Kaier's Special 'A' Whiskey." Because it marketed both whiskey and beer, the Kaier family was particularly hard-hit by Prohibition and eventually disassociated themselves from the business. But the plant remained useful for some. Brewery historian Herman Ronnenberg points out that individuals involved in organized crime "'fronted' for legitimate brewery owners, but later they muscled in and took over via dummy corporations."[63] Such was the case with Kaier's, as two "front men" named Shalleck and Zack took over the operation of the brewery. The pair, like many other bootleggers, took several elaborate measures to move and disguise their operation. For example, a pipeline was constructed down Mahanoy Creek to a barn several streets away. Illegal high-alcohol beer then flowed down the pipeline to the barn, where kegs were filled and prepared for sale. Traditional beer that never made it to the distillation process was also stored in "secret walled-in cellars" in the brewery. As kegs were being filled with illegal beer, "spotters" were assigned to all the roads leading into Mahanoy City. Somehow, bootleggers were able to provide spotters with license plate num-bers and descriptions of cars driven by federal agents. If a federal agent's vehicle happened to be headed to town, a phone call from the spotter alerted those over-seeing the illegal keg-filling operation to assign workers to other tasks.

With bootleggers successfully providing plenty of illegal beer for the public, brewers who depended exclusively on near-beer sales were at risk. To turn a profit, branching out into other business ventures was essential. Schlitz made chocolate and candies. Anheuser-Busch found that part of its plant could be used for meat-packing, while another brewer tried to make money through the storage of furs. One brewer turned to the production of industrial alcohol, while another felt that the future rested in the production of spaghetti and macaroni. Locally, operators of the Kaier's Brewery made ginger ale, root beer and orange soda. Ice was also sold at the Mahanoy City plant. the F and S Brewery in Shamokin produced may-onnaise, vinegar, maraschino cherries, and bullion cubes. Others thought it might be possible to make a profit through the manufacture of malt syrup, malt extract and, perhaps one of the most popular alternatives, ice cream. Frank Yuengling clearly anticipated major changes in business conditions when he considered investing in the production of the rich, creamy treat in the summer of 1919, well before the full effect of Prohibition was in place:

> The latest rumor floated is that the Yuengling Brewery interests, when the beer business has received the kibosh, will be diverted in the direction of an enormous creamery. Color is given to this story by reason of the fact that the contract has been let to tear down the residences already owned by the family ... in close proximity to the brewery at Fifth and Mahantongo streets ... and that a Philadelphia architect is here preparing plans for a mammoth creamery to occupy their site.[64]

The rumor proved true a few months later when construction of the ice cream plant started in January, 1920. Area papers reported that the potential for success in the ice cream market was strong, since the closest ice cream plant was in Hamburg in Berks County. It wasn't a small investment:

> It is openly stated that the plans for this new industry, which Pottsville has acquired, call for possibly the biggest ice cream plant in the Middle States. Mr. Yuengling expects to be ready for the Spring and Summer trade ... the plant is now rapidly nearing the point where the wheels will be started turning and an ice cream product evolved that will be of a quality to drive other brands out of the territory.[65]

Perhaps Yuengling family ownership of a farm outside of Pottsville gave the company president insight into successful dairy farms in Schuylkill County, which could provide the creamery with an ample supply of milk for its ice cream. An article in the Pottsville *Republican* on December 5, 1933, noted that Yuengling was purchasing dairy products from 134 county farmers.

The dairy products from the Yuengling Creamery would develop a very strong reputation, particularly before the Great Depression. The dairy plant and the brewery eventually became separate companies, with one of Frank's sons, Frederick, leading the ice cream business and then a grandson, Frank Jr. Slow sales forced the Yuengling Creamery to close, but that would not be until 1985, proof that Frank Yuengling's prohibition venture was worthwhile. According to Carl Childs's study of the brewery during this period, the ice cream venture gave the brewery additional financial security at a time when it needed it most:

A Yuengling ice cream truck in later years. The Yuengling Creamery, located across the street from the brewery, was a key to the company's survival during Prohibition. (D. G. Yuengling and Son, Inc.)

By 1920, the first year of national Prohibition, the creamery had proven a remarkable success, thus alleviating the tremendous pressure for the brewery to market a popular near beer. Significantly, the success of the creamery may well have kept the Yuengling brewery from the temptations of producing illegal beer.[66]

Other new business ventures by Frank Yuengling brought handsome profits. While it appeared that alcohol would be banned, the government couldn't stop people from enjoying music and dancing. Jazz music was becoming increasingly popular and presented the opportunity for a lucrative investment. In 1918, the Pottsville brewer was approached by a Philadelphia businessman, Louis J. Brecker, to invest in a fashionable dance hall in the city.[67] Brecker, who was a student at the Wharton School of Business at the University of Pennsylvania, enjoyed dancing, but experience taught him that conditions in many of the jazz clubs in the city were very poor. He turned to Frank Yuengling, who invested $20,000 in a new Philadelphia ballroom, located in the downtown district at 12th and Chestnut Streets. The Philadelphia Roseland became highly popular, drawing crowds of whites who enjoyed jazz music performed by African-American entertainers.

One of the few problems with the Philadelphia location was that the city's blue laws forced the Roseland to close on Sundays. So Brecker's attention turned to New York City and, while on vacation in the Big Apple in 1918, he decided an even better business opportunity could be found there. This time, Frank Yuengling invested $40,000 in a New York Roseland, which was situated in an abandoned carriage house at 1658 Broadway and West 51st Street. The new ballroom was a huge success, attracting the top names in jazz and swing bands. Live radio broadcasts extended the reputation of the New York Roseland as one of the city's top clubs. In addition to the ballroom, the Pottsville brewer saw potential in other business ventures in New York as well, investing in several successful stage shows in the city. He also invested in a club closer to his hometown in Reading. One of Frank Yuengling's sons, David, recalled that his father was extremely busy during the Prohibition era: "In my youth I had always found it difficult to understand why my father stayed so long at his office and took so many business trips to New York and Philadelphia."[68]

Back in Pennsylvania, another valuable opportunity arose with the Sullivan County Electric Company, which was later sold for a handsome profit to Pennsylvania Power and Light Company. Closer to home, Frank Yuengling was president of the Pottsville Feed Company, a business formed in the 1930s and one that continued to supply area farmers until 1963. He also invested in gold mines, jewelry, railroads, and even a liquor store in Pottsville. All this was in addition to the businessman's position as president of the Pennsylvania National Bank and Trust Company. In addition to his business ventures, Yuengling was active in the Pottsville community. He was a member of the local executive committee for the Red Cross War Fund campaign during World War I. He was also active in the Trinity Episcopal Church and the Good Intent Hose Company.

The brewery marked its 100th anniversary in 1929. The occasion was probably more subdued than it normally would have been, since the Yuengling family and brewery employees could only celebrate with near beer. By this time, the debates over the merits of the "noble experiment" were intensifying. One problem was that some people were dying from the "seller's market" spurred by Prohibition. Not only were beverages diluted by bootleggers, but imbibers were drinking virtually anything. Beverages got their "kick" from questionable ingredients. In Chicago, people drank Yack Yack Bourbon, the main ingredient of which was iodine. In Philadelphia, a city that was a center for the production of industrial alcohol, Soda Pop Moon was packaged in soft drink bottles, and its intoxicant was rubbing alcohol. Other drinks contained industrial alcohol and antifreeze. In Atlanta, a woman arrested for public drunkenness confessed to drinking a cocktail of mothballs and gasoline. The beer that was made by bootleggers could be just as dangerous, a point that Eric Burns vividly makes:

> A government inspector found a brewery operating in a rundown barn somewhere in the Midwest; there were no cows or pigs or horses inside, no signs of any kind that the barn had recently been used for an agricultural purpose except for the hayloft overhead. But the hayloft was a cloud of pestilence. "Floating around on top of the ale in the vats," the inspector told his superiors, "were all sorts of refuse and filth — straw, hay, seed, mice, bugs, flies and other things not calculated to add to the portability of the ale. I found floating in one vat a large dead rat, almost as big as a fair-sized rabbit." Other foreign objects found by inspectors in impromptu breweries and distilleries include almost everything animal, vegetable, and mineral that was indigenous to the United States at the time.[69]

Major cities across the nation were also plagued with the violence bred by illegal trafficking in beer and whiskey. Gangland murders like the Saint Valentine's Day Massacre in 1929 (seven dead) added to the growing violence. Public disgust was heightened even further by reports of political corruption at high levels. Still, at least one person felt that Prohibition was working in Schuylkill County.

In a letter to the *New York Times* titled "Prohibition Aiding Miners," William Wilhelm of Pottsville provided an intriguing description of the changes in Schuylkill County in the 1920s. He concurred with previous assessments that Schuylkill was "the wettest county on earth." He then argued that Prohibition was a blessing to the region, noting in particular the changes to mining operations:

> Prior to prohibition mining operations were very much crippled from one to three days after every semi-monthly payday. Such a thing now is unknown.
> Prior to prohibition every Sunday morning in Shenandoah, especially after payday, there was a great line-up of wives and relatives to get husbands and brothers out of the lockup. That is now a thing of the past.[70]

Wilhelm also noted that Prohibition led to improved housing conditions and higher real estate values in the area. Brewers like Frank Yuengling, who owned valuable property thanks to the "tied house" system, benefited tremendously from the changes in the real estate market. According to Wilhelm's letter, "The breweries that owned so much choice property, especially corner sites, are selling the properties at three times the price they paid for them, and in some cases where they are still the landlords are getting double and triple the rent over and above the value when saloon keepers occupied the properties."[71]

Wilhelm's letter concluded by acknowledging the fundamental argument to repeal Prohibition — the flagrant lawlessness it spawned. He then attempted to refute the point by noting that the region had always had lawbreakers. Many Americans, however, viewed the rash of violent crime and political corruption as a far more serious problem. Not long after the Volstead Act went into effect, disgusted citizens began organizing to change the legislation. Significant organizations that sought to end prohibition included the Association Against the Prohibition Amendment, the Moderation League, and the Women's Organization for National Prohibition Reform, the Crusaders, and the American Hotel Association. The original goal of many of these groups was the modification of the Volstead Act; however, the Great Depression, while a disaster for the nation, provided the opportunity for total repeal.

Prohibition was at the head of the 1928 presidential election, and despite the fact that the dry Herbert Hoover defeated the wet Al Smith, the results gave those who favored Repeal some hope. As the country moved into the Great Depression, a dramatic drop in the number of breweries occurred. In 1929, 303 breweries were in operation. By 1930, the number would drop to 231, a decrease of nearly 25 percent. Deepening problems with the economy convinced some brewing industry insiders that real beer would return in the very near future. Jobs were needed, and the government would benefit from the revenue that could be generated from beer taxes. An illustration in the growing confidence that Prohibition would end is found in the Pabst Brewing Company's heavy investment in new brewing equipment as early as 1930. About two years later, the upgrade proved to be a wise business decision.

Franklin Delano Roosevelt, who favored Repeal, won the presidential election of 1932. Within a few weeks, hearings were held in Congress to modify the Volstead Act to bring it in line with the President-elect's campaign promise to allow the sale of light wines and beer. Those who testified noted that coopers (barrel makers), bottlers, malsters, hop-growers and other workers were needed to make beer and that thousands of jobs would be created if the brewing industry were reestablished. The hearings also focused on the percentage of alcohol allowed in beer, and 3.2 percent alcohol by weight was the final figure. After his inauguration, Roosevelt encouraged Congress to modify the Volstead Act as quickly as possible, and on March 23, 1933, the Cullen-Harrison Bill, or the Beer and Wine Revenue Act, was passed. The passage of the Twenty-First Amendment — which struck down the Eighteen Amendment (the only time that an amendment had been repealed) — would not come until December 5, 1933. But the Cullen-Harrison Bill allowed brewers to distribute traditional beer on April 7, 1933, at 12:01 a.m. Across the nation, brewers prepared.

Breweries that abandoned production altogether during Prohibition had much more work to do to start brewing again. In addition to the fact that beer takes time to age, they had to get rusty equipment up and running. Because it had been brew-

An ad sponsored by the Kaier's Brewery celebrating the return of real beer on "New Beer's Eve." (Courtesy of the Pottsville [PA.] *Republican & Herald.*)

ing near beer for over a decade, the Yuengling Brewery was much better prepared than most companies. The task of bringing back real beer back fell to Joseph Baus-beck, who had been retained as brewmaster in 1930. He simply turned off the de-alcoholizing device and let real beer flow again. At the retail level, future bar owners in Schuylkill County could not wait for the big day. In Pottsville, applications for retail licenses were received at the post office, and the lobby and hallways were crowded with applicants in the days leading up to April 7. The U.S. Department of Revenue reported that over 1,500 applications were received from throughout the county, giving beer lovers more places to imbibe than they had had in the pre-Prohibition days.[72]

Yuengling was among the many breweries that began preparing for "New Beer's Eve" by receiving an advance permit for production. Since breweries in many areas of the nation would not be ready to have beer on hand on April 7, the Yuengling Brewery was a key source for beer on the East Coast. Fifth and Mahan-tongo streets was the destination of truckers from not only northeastern Pennsyl-vania, but from other states as well. "Two of them were said to be from the Carolinas, while Virginia and other states south of the Mason Dixon line were rep-resented," reported the Pottsville *Republican*. "New York State and those further up the coast were also represented."[73] It was the busiest day in the brewery's his-tory. Starting at Fifth and Mahantongo Street, the line of trucks stretched for over two miles. Zero-hour for shipping real beer was 12:01 a.m. and, according to reports, a bright red Yuengling truck was loaded first. Then, trucks from out of the region were loaded with beer so they could get to their destinations in time for business on Friday. Anything with wheels was used to haul beer that day, from coal trucks to moving vans, from wheelbarrows to baby carriages. Yuengling beer was among the staggering 1.5 million barrels consumed by Americans within the first twenty-four hours of the return of legal beer.

The brewery entered the post-Prohibition era by producing its symbolically titled "Winner Beer," which was described in the Pottsville *Republican* as a "New Era Brew with Increased Strength." Several brewers, grateful to President Roo-sevelt for his actions on behalf of the industry, sent beer to the White House on New Beer's Day. August Busch's presidential delivery, a handsome beer wagon drawn by six Clydesdales, made the journey to the nation's capital without inci-dent. Such was not the case with Yuengling's shipment to Washington:

> Pottsville's first flush of the new beer was marked chiefly by the shipment from the brewery here of consignments that were understood to have reached 52,000 cases by noon Friday. When the brewery whistle blew at 12:00 o'clock, there was a general scurry of trucks, which continued until late this afternoon. Some 80 trucks were said to have left here ... the first truck to leave town being one consigned to Wash-ington D.C., where it arrived short 75 cases, purloined from the truck enroute. Thefts from the various trucks were reported on all sides Friday.[74]

The robbery of part of the Yuengling Brewery's gift to President Roosevelt was a crime that was never solved, but other breweries experienced similar robberies and were forced to hire armed guards to protect beer shipments in the days and weeks ahead, as demand continued to outweigh supply. At the White House, Roosevelt celebrated Repeal with a cocktail. The Yuengling beer that was sent was reportedly passed along to and enjoyed by the Washington press corps.

When legislators brought beer back, they also viewed it as a method of raising revenue, as the tax jumped from $1 to $5 a barrel. Each brewery also had to pay a $1,000 annual license fee. In addition to heavy taxation of beer, another legacy of Prohibition is tighter government regulation of the alcoholic beverage industry by the government. The exclusive sale of brands at brewery-owned saloons was abolished. Like other brewers, Yuengling circumvented the ban by legally separating the brewery from its properties in the area. The Yuengling Realty Corporation was formed in 1933; however, the company gradually pulled back on its real estate holdings in the decades ahead.

Winner beer was brewed by Yuengling to celebrate the end of Prohibition. A truckload of Yuengling's Winner Beer was sent to President Franklin Delano Roosevelt to mark the end of national Prohibition. (D. G. Yuengling and Son, Inc.)

For those entering bars and taverns, there were changes as well. For beer drinkers hoping that the return of real beer would bring back the "good old days," April 7 was a bit disappointing. The Great Depression, which reached its deepest point in 1933, helped temper the celebration. One difference that anyone entering a tavern would notice was the price of beer. In Pottsville, beer drinkers found that nickel beer was a thing of the past, and some taverns and restaurants were charging as much as 15 cents a bottle. Newspaper reports indicated that Pottsville residents "did not appear to be more than casually interested in the product.... The high cost of the beverage apparently was having its effect on the general sales." Oddly, many beer lovers found themselves longing for the beer they had drunk during Prohibition, because they found "the legally bottled goods flat in comparison with the bootleg product."[75]

After Repeal, each state could adopt its own system of alcoholic beverage control. In Pennsylvania, Governor Pinchot was elected on a dry platform in 1930. After national Prohibition was abolished, Pinchot called the Pennsylvania General Assembly into special session, where the regulations regarding the manufacture and sale of alcohol were debated. The result was the creation of the Pennsylvania Liquor Control Board (PLCB) and the state store system that is still in place today. Pennsylvania is one of only three states (Iowa and Utah being the other two) which has complete control over sales of liquor and wine. Over the years since its inception, critics of Pennsylvania's liquor laws argue that the present system reflects Pinchot's desire to "discourage the purchase of alcoholic beverages by making it as inconvenient and expensive as possible."[76]

Nationally, the business of brewing wasn't quite the same when it awoke in 1933. According to one industry historian, the businesses, in some cases, now passed to a new generation, one less "German":

> After Prohibition the breweries did not seem so German. They were merely American businesses with a long rugged history in this country behind them. The older executives, with their Teutonic backgrounds, were mostly gone; the new executives were second or more likely third generation German Americans and assimilation had overtaken them.[77]

Perhaps this point applies to Frank Yuengling as, through the decades, his varied business interests competed with his work at the brewery on Mahantongo Street. For example, in some newspaper accounts of his public service, Frank Yuengling's was referred to as bank president or "manufacturer," rather than "brewer." Still, the brewing tradition that had started in 1829 was very important to him. During Prohibition, he had demonstrated the same determination as his grandfather, and the family legacy continued, even if the glass was filled with near beer. The brewery, however, had little time to revel as it closed the Prohibition chapter of its history.

The seeds of the Yuengling Brewery's future challenges were sown more than a decade before Repeal. The obstacles were serious. The anthracite coal industry began its steep decline following World War I. Then came the crash on Wall Street in October of 1929. The Great Depression cut into demand for coal even further, and the large mining companies laid off thousands of miners.[78] Significantly, the unemployment did not necessarily mean that there was less alcohol consumed in the region. People who drink tend to consume more alcohol when they are out of work. One remark about coal miners in the 1930s presents a troubling image: "The incidence of alcoholism, an ever-present social danger in the coalfields, rose during the depression. Men who could not support their families sought refuge in drink and often took out their rage on wives and children."[79]

The depression brought bootlegging back to the area; however, it was bootlegging of another sort. Miners, who had limited skills beyond the collieries, decided to "bootleg" coal to heat their homes and make some money. They dug "coal holes" on company land, despite efforts by company police to stop them.

With "King Coal" dethroned, outmigration from the region began. Families were split, as some area residents, many who loved the region, were forced to look for work in automobile factories, steel mills and industries in Detroit, Buffalo, Pittsburgh, and Philadelphia. Most regional brewers would not survive northeastern Pennsylvania's weakening economy. The Yuengling Brewery had something other breweries did not have, however. In the face of serious challenges, the small family business on Mahantongo Street would slowly turn to its past to ensure its future.

Four

Surviving the "Shakedown"

"We were out of business. We just didn't know it."
— Richard "Dick" Yuengling Jr.

When taking a trip from Pottsville to Allentown, motorists drive past a brewery along Route 22 on the right-hand side of the road, one strikingly different in appearance from the one nestled against Sharp Mountain on Mahantongo Street. This plant has been operating not since 1829, but since 1972. The F. & M. Schaefer Brewing Company — New York City's most prominent beer makers and the nation's first large-scale lager producer — opted to construct a new plant on 149 acres of farmland in the Lehigh Valley. The company came to a decision that its old breweries in New York City, Baltimore, and Albany were too old and inefficient.[1] Modernization was the new priority, and the $46.5 million, "ultra-modern" Lehigh Valley plant was regarded as one of the world's best beer-making operations. By 1974, it was turning out 5,000,000 barrels annually. Yuengling, in a worrisome contrast, was producing about 75,000. Schaefer's bold move into eastern Pennsylvania illustrates not only Yuengling's vulnerability, but also symbolizes an industry trend. The New York-based brewer wasn't the only company creating facilities that looked more like petrochemical plants than time-honored breweries. Anheuser-Busch, Pabst, Schlitz, and Miller also curtailed upgrades on old plants and constructed more efficient breweries that were technological marvels. National breweries grew larger, and small, independent regional brewers like Yuengling were seriously threatened.

Skyrocketing beer sales could lead to an assumption that the decades following Repeal brought a dramatic increase in the number of breweries in the United States. Beer drinking did increase, but the trend in the industry was consolidation. The numbers are astonishing:

Year	*Breweries in the United States*	*Breweries in Pennsylvania*
1940	598	77
1950	407	57
1960	229	26
1970	142	19

133

An exhausted miner asleep on a case of Yuengling beer after a week-long rescue operation at
the Kocher Antracite Deep Mine near Tower City. On March 1, 1977, an inrush of water into
a gangway at the mine killed nine coal miners and injured three. (D. G. Yuengling and Son,
Inc.)

Pennsylvania and Wisconsin had the largest concentration of small breweries
during these decades, and the two states regularly slugged it out to take the prize
for the most breweries in the country. The Keystone State was able to maintain a
slim margin in most years. By 1980, the competition no longer mattered. Only 44
brewing companies operated in the entire country, and most beer was being produced in branch breweries managed by beer-making corporations. The reasons for
what beer historian Stanley Baron labeled the "shakedown" in the industry included
changes in financing, communications, public relations and promotion, and "an
increasing uniformity of taste."[2]

Few breweries in northeastern Pennsylvania survived the shakedown. As the
decades rolled on, beer lovers in many communities found that their favorite brand
could no longer be found across the bar. A partial list of closings included:

Tamaqua's Liberty Brewing Company (1934)
Fountain Springs Brewing Company (1934)
Frackville Brewing Company (bought out by Kaier's Brewery) (1936)

Ashland Brewery (formerly the Schuylkill Home Brewing Co.) (1941)

Hazleton Pilsner Brewing Company (1954)

Mauch Chunk Brewery (1968)

Columbia Brewery (1968)

Kaier's Brewery (1968)

Stegmaier (1974)

Fuhrmann and Schmidt (1976)

Mount Carbon Brewery (1976)

Richard L. Yuengling, Sr. (1915–1999). (D. G. Yuengling and Son, Inc.)

How did the Yuengling Brewery escape the same fate? Part of the answer rests in Frank Yuengling's early decision to upgrade equipment.

In the decade following Repeal, many breweries failed to improve production potential and modernize their packaging equipment. When the brewing industry awoke from its slumber in 1933, it found that bottling technology had advanced, thanks in large part to a new competitor — the soft drink industry. For several decades, Americans had enjoyed root beer, ginger ale, and various colas, and now beer producers were forced to take the threat of companies like Coca-Cola seriously. On the technological side, the growth of the soft drink industry led to improvements in machinery that made the bottling process speedier and more efficient. Brewers wanted to take advantage of the advancements.[3] Yuengling's bottling shop had remained essentially the same since Frederick Yuengling had opened it in 1895. In 1936, Frank Yuengling invested in a new, larger shop to enhance bottling capacity. In an indication of the continuing changes in bottling technology, the bottle shop would be upgraded with all new equipment again in 1952.

No sooner had the updated bottling plant been completed than Frank Yuengling had to address another major change rippling through the brewing industry — the emergence of canned beer. Efforts to market beer in cans had been underway for many years, but they had failed for two major reasons. Beer's high carbonation creates great internal pressure. In addition, beer is highly sensitive to metal and requires some form of insulation between the beer and the metal container. The American Can Company (Canco) had been working on these problems since 1931 and marketed its solution in 1934 with a flattop can with a special enamel lining. The packaging firm approached the Krueger Brewing Company of Newark, New Jersey, with a request to give the can a trial run. The brewery agreed, and, on June 24, 1935, the canned beer was test marketed in the same city where David Yuengling Jr. had operated his brewery after the Civil War — Richmond, Virginia. The public apparently liked it. Other breweries followed Krueger's lead quickly. Pabst introduced its "Export Beer" in its "TapaCan" in Cedar Rapids, Iowa, in early July of the same year.

One problem with the new cans was that an opener was required to get to the beer. Schlitz's entry in the canned beer wars, the "Cap-Sealed" can, didn't need an opener, a feature that appealed to beer lovers who had a tendency occasionally to misplace things. "Cap-sealing" also offered an advantage in the packaging process that was particularly attractive to small brewers like Yuengling. Because it resembled a bottle, the new can could be filled with the same equipment, making an investment in new and expensive canning equipment unnecessary. Yuengling did not hesitate in joining other small breweries on the "Cap-Sealed" bandwagon. The Pottsville brewery first canned beer in the summer of 1938.

Yuengling's relatively early decision to package beer in cans was popular with local consumers and bolstered future beer sales. Thanks to national Prohibition, beer drinkers lost their propensity to visit the local tavern or saloon, and, after Repeal, consumers were no longer limited to purchasing beer in draft form from the local tavern. Modern electric refrigerators, which began entering American homes on a modest scale in the 1920s and 1930s, moved into mass production in the 1940s. Now, Americans could bring beer home and keep it cold, an alternative that steadily increased in popularity. In 1935, most beer was sold in kegs, and canned or bottled beer comprised only about 30 percent of the industry's output. Sales of beer by the case were clearly on the rise by 1938, as more beer drinkers could avoid the trip to the tavern entirely. Improvements continued to be made in the packaging of beer in cans and bottles and, as early as 1940, packaged beer outsold draft for the first time ever. By 1959 packaged beer would account for a whopping 80.2 percent of total production. Canned beer continued to grow in popularity, and, by 1969, it would outsell bottled beer.

F. Dohrman Yuengling (1913–1971). (D. G. Yuengling and Son, Inc.)

Breweries would not be satisfied with simply having the technology to package beer. Methods of shipping and distributing beer are also important. In order to compete with other breweries, a dependable fleet of delivery trucks was necessary. In this regard, the Yuengling Brewery was in better shape than its competitors, largely due to its business ventures during Prohibition. Freshness is crucial to both beer and ice cream. In the 1920s, Yuengling needed to deliver its products over a large area and do so quickly. As the 1930s approached, the company, perhaps in anticipation of the end of the noble experiment, invested more heavily in delivery trucks for both its near beer and ice cream.[4] To maximize the efficiency of the new vehicles, the shipping department was also mod-

New technology at the brewery in the 1950s. (D. G. Yuengling and Son, Inc. / Chuck Hogan and Ray Reu.)

ernized with the construction of new loading and unloading facilities, as well as a parking and service garage.

The trucks used for the delivery of beer in the aftermath of Prohibition were much smaller than vehicles used today, often not much bigger than a pickup truck. Yuengling made arrangements with distributors to paint their trucks with signs to advertise its brand. The colorful vehicles helped keep the company's name before beer drinkers in both small towns and large cities throughout Pennsylvania. The smaller trucks had to be loaded and unloaded by hand which was a time-consuming process. Gradually, the brewery shifted to delivering beer by tractor-trailer, with forklifts lifting "palletized" beer. The larger trucks, however, had a more difficult time making their way along the narrow streets leading to the brewery on Mahantongo Street, much to the frustration of motorists. In addition to improvements in transportation, several other upgrades at the brewery were made. The brewery's old-fashioned, hand-fired boilers were replaced by a new boiler house. A new brew house, with a lauder tub, was constructed. More space was added to the hop-storage room.

Any improvements in technology and transportation were greatly impacted when America entered World War II. The thirst of American soldiers made the 1940s one of the great boom periods for the American brewing industry. Remarkably, World War II reduced the availability of materials crucial to the business, things like bottles, bottle caps and tin for cans. Beer delivery became more problematic with the scarcity of tires and gasoline. The federal government, however, felt that beer could fortify the morale of the troops. The War Food Administration even saw fit to order that every brewery earmark 15 percent of its production

An early example of a Yuengling truck in Philadelphia. Yuengling kept up with transportation advances following Prohibition. (D. G. Yuengling and Son, Inc.)

for troops fighting the war. American soldiers apparently appreciated the government's action — even those dispatched overseas. In the last year of the war, for example, over 50 million cases were shipped to soldiers serving across the globe. War spending also improved the economy on the homefront, resulting in some banner years for the brewing industry. From 1942 to 1945, sales records for beer were shattered. In contrast to World War I, when brewers faced anti-German sentiment and the threat of prohibition, brewing became an essential industry in the war effort. But while the upswing in the industry aided area breweries in the short term, World War II led to a shift in consumer taste that would seriously weaken regional brewers in the long term. This shift can be traced to the early 1940s.

While wartime restrictions limited the availability of cans in the United States, a dull, military-olive can was used to ship beer overseas. When beer was transported to the battlefronts in its camouflage cans, it wasn't Yuengling that was quenching the thirst and calming the nerves of the servicemen. Government contracts for beer were big and went to national brewers like Schlitz, Pabst, and Anheuser-Busch, which could fill the orders. One factor that prevented Yuengling from getting government contracts was its rural location and declining rail access. Still, *some* Yuengling beer was making its way overseas during the war, as one Pottsville-area World War II veteran recalled:

> There is one incident I will never forget during World War II. I was going down a big hill in Belgium. It was a very hot day. My helper and I had to deliver a 20-ton load of ammo to a forward position. There were two Sherman tanks in front of us. They pulled into a field to let me go by.
> I spotted a small eating place, so I pulled off the road and went in. Two women

were serving small sandwiches and drinks. Well, I got a big surprise when the women spoke English. They asked me what I wanted to drink. I asked, "Do you have beer?" She said yes and she pulled out a bottle of Yuengling. My eyes popped.

I told the women that I was from the same city the beer came from. I didn't ask them how they got it.

This is a true story. It was unbelievable.[5]

Despite the astonishing sale of a few bottles of the Yuengling brand at the small café in Belgium, it was still the national brewers who scored a promotional bonanza as they helped quench the thirst of off duty servicemen far from home. Many soldiers, who were normally satisfied with the beer from their local, regional brewery before Pearl Harbor, didn't mind the taste of the brews produced by the major breweries.

The national beer makers seized this opportunity. When soldiers returned home, the big brewers redoubled efforts to increase the availability of their product. Their goal was to make their brand available to any veteran, no matter where the beer drinker lived in America.[6] Some larger regional brewers did gain in popularity during the war. Coors, for example, developed a mystique among soldiers, who got a taste of the brand as they prepared for duty at the nation's military camps. Demand for the brand did rise outside its traditional market in the West. Smaller regional brewers like Yuengling were not as fortunate, and the rise in consumption of the national beers continued to hurt the company.

To fend off the anti-German American prejudice that had gripped the country and damaged brewers during World War I, the brewing industry took exceptional measures to help the World War II effort. In some cases, brewers encouraged employees to enlist in the Armed Forces. Frank Yuengling's son, Dick, who would later take over the brewery, enlisted and served in the U.S. Army Corps as a staff sergeant with the 1060th AAF Base Unit. And another significant figure in Yuengling's history, future brewmaster N. Ray Norbert, who joined the brewery in 1942, was only on the job for a few months before he enlisted and served in the 8th Army Air Corps.

In northeastern Pennsylvania, World War II temporarily eased the downward spiral of the anthracite coal industry, and unemployment in the regional also dropped as residents went off to serve their country. In fact, demand for coal became so high during the war that mineworkers were offered draft deferments. Six-day work weeks at the collieries became common.[7] Hard times returned, however, following the end of the war, and by 1950 the industry was in ruins. Anthracite coal began to lose to bituminous coal in industrial markets. In addition, anthracite's use for home heating declined steadily, thanks to alternative sources of energy like fuel oil, natural gas, and electricity. Even in northeastern Pennsylvania, coal trucks with their long chutes made deliveries to fewer and fewer homes. Why put up with the ashes from the coal? The declining job market prompted an exodus of people from the region by the late 1940s, and within a few years emigration intensified to troubling levels.[8] In the Wilkes-Barre-Hazleton area, for example, emigration slashed the population by 8 percent between 1950 and 1957. Northeastern Pennsylvania breweries soon began to feel the business crunch.

Miners relaxing with a few beers. They were a dying breed. In the 1940s, deep coal mining in the region began to be replaced by strip mining, which was less costly. Following World War II, the anthracite mining industry slowly collapsed leading to high unemployment and migration from the region. (Courtesy of George Harvan Collection, National Canal Museum, Easton.)

Pottsville and the Yuengling Brewery were not immune to the region's economic decline. At one time, if Pottsville-area residents needed to catch a train to Philadelphia, they could do so at nine different times during the day. Eventually, there would be no rail link between Pottsville and the City of Brotherly Love. The reason? Pottsville had experienced an upsurge in population from 14,117 residents in 1890 to 24,530 in 1940, but since that time, the population of the city, like Wilkes-Barre, dropped by approximately 8 percent each decade. Between 1940 and 2000, Pottsville's population dropped a total of 36.6 percent to 15,549. For Yuengling, the city's population decline was bad enough, but the group leading the charge from the region was also significant. Many of them were young, working-class men, the cornerstone of the beer market.

Not only did Yuengling have to struggle with a decline in its customer base, but local competition also remained surprisingly strong. Several other breweries tenaciously stayed in the fight for remaining beer drinkers until the mid-1970s. The Stegmaier Brewery appeared to be in the best position to survive. In the tough times, Stegmaier was forced to request concessions from its unionized employees and only received them "[p]robably because many of the workers were simply happy to have a job, when so many area residents did not."[9] Still, Stegmaier had a 60-truck fleet and rail services to cover a distribution area along the East Coast from Maine to Florida. The Wilkes-Barre facility's output reached a half-million barrels by 1940 and hovered around that point for many years afterword. The brand could be found in many bars in northeastern Pennsylvania, including those in Yuengling's home county. Sales figures from 1951 placed the Yuengling Brewery right in the middle of familiar coal-region brands:

> Stegmaier (Wilkes-Barre)—500,000 barrels
> Kaier's (Mahanoy City)—183,500 barrels
> Old Reading (Reading)—173,500 barrels
> Gibbons (Wilkes-Barre)—173,500 barrels
> Yuengling (Pottsville)—115,000 barrels
> Sunshine (Reading)—108,000 barrels
> F & S (Shamokin)—114,500 barrels
> Mount Carbon (near Pottsville)—less than 80,000 barrels
> Columbia (Shenandoah)—less than 60,000 barrels

Some of the brewery's chief competitors would even score some significant successes during the 1950s. For example, the figures for Yuengling's nearest competitor, geographically speaking, the Mount Carbon Brewery, would improve, as one of its brands, Mount Carbon's Bavarian Beer, would become extremely popular in the Pottsville area. Surprisingly, the Mount Carbon Brewery would surpass Yuengling in sales by a considerable margin from the 1950s through the mid-1970s. Yuengling would ultimately outlast the Mount Carbon Brewery, as the latter closed in 1976; however, as a further indication of the popularity of the Bavarian brand, Yuengling purchased the recipe, along with the Mount Carbon Brewery's cases, bottles, and kegs, and brewed that beer for about another decade. In northern Schuylkill County, the figures for the Kaier Brewery indicate that the company was enjoying some of its peak years. In fact, in 1951 Kaier's beer captured the prestigious Star of Excellence in Brussels, Belgium, for the best American-Canadian beer. However, the forecast for the future of these breweries would dim, especially when the national brewers skillfully promoted their names through modern advertising mediums.

Even in the age of radio and television, Yuengling continued to be satisfied with its reputation as a "discovery brand." Its approach to advertising was still conservative, based on the belief that people discover brands by sampling them. Emphasis was placed on point-of-sale promotional work as well, and Yuengling used newspaper advertising and billboards sparingly. The brewery could never depend on these promotional techniques exclusively, however. It has remained fully aware of national trends in beer advertising, and this held true with the advent of radio and television. The company first used local radio advertising to remind

Yuengling employees and their children at a company picnic. (D. G. Yuengling and Son, Inc.)

area beer drinkers about the brand. On May 9, 1946, WPPA, or AM 13, signed on the air in Pottsville, becoming Schuylkill County's first radio station. Two years later, WPPA's FM sister station, WAVT FM 102 (named for the owner of both stations, A.V. Tidmore of Pottsville), signed on the air. The company also advertised on radio stations in Philadelphia. And just as the company was utilizing radio ads, a powerful new medium was starting to flicker.

In 1945, television advertised beer for the first time. It was only natural that the milestone occurred during the broadcast of a baseball game, when the small Narragansett Brewing Company of Cranston, Rhode Island, sponsored a Boston Red Sox game. Surprisingly, regional brewers led the way in television advertising in the early days because ads were inexpensive. However, television gradually became a stronger force for the brewing industry as more televisions became available on the mass market. The national breweries, which had the money to advertise the most, were soon sponsoring regular television programs. Pabst, for example, was among the advertisers that sponsored the first color television program on June 25, 1951.

Brewers in northeastern Pennsylvania first appeared to be immune from the threat of national advertising campaigns. The first television stations in New York City and Philadelphia had difficulty getting their signals into the mountainous region. However, John Walson Sr., a Schuylkill County resident, solved the problem. Walson, who owned an appliance store in Mahanoy City, tried to sell televisions as they became increasingly available in 1947, which was the same year that networks began broadcasting national programs. Only people in communities like Frackville and Hazleton could be convinced to spend money on the new technology, since their homes were located on the tops of mountains. The businessman realized that he needed to improve reception to boost sales, so he erected an antenna on top of a nearby mountain and ran a strand of cable to an adjoining shed, where he connected the cable to several television receivers.

Walson initially had to take people up the mountain to convince the skeptics that the new technology worked. Later, in 1948, he ran used army-surplus wire to carry the signals from the antenna on New Boston Mountain to his warehouse. In the late spring and early summer of that year, he made additional improvements to the system, stringing lines from the mountain to his appliance store, and he hooked up lines to several homes along the way. The incredible response to television sets in his store window, where people gathered to watch channels 3, 6, or 10 out of Philadelphia, convinced

A Yuengling ad from the 1950s. (D. G. Yuengling and Son, Inc.)

Walson that there was a real business opportunity here. Reception was no longer a problem, and cable television was born.[10] A prime target of Walson's system was Pottsville. In its first year alone, Walson's cable system extended to 1,200 homes, and some bars, too. Even though the medium was in its infancy, sets could easily be found in bars and taverns across the country by 1947. Tavern owners almost immediately noticed a correlation between a television set behind the bar and the quantity of beer flowing through the taps. Beer advertisements on television mattered.

As the years went by, the expense of television advertising left smaller brewers at a distinct disadvantage, but they scored some successes in countering the promotional efforts of the nation's major brewers. One northeastern Pennsylvania brewer was particularly successful in its attempt to attract customers through television advertising. Stegmaier used television advertising as early 1951 in an attempt to crack the Philadelphia beer market. The brewery "sponsored a Bing Crosby production, 'TV Playhouse,' which aired on Philadelphia's Channel 6, and launched a large-scale newspaper advertising campaign coordinated with the television program. The television ads helped spread Stegmaier's popular slogans such as "Cold and Gold from the Poconos" and "Ring-A-Ding-Ding, Do the Stegmaier Thing, Any Time at All.'"[11]

A Yuengling Porter poster from the 1950s. (D. G. Yuengling and Son, Inc.)

Yuengling management decided to turn to television advertising as well. The earliest example is a commercial produced at a Lancaster-area television station in the early 1960s.[12] Since then, television crews have regularly come to Mahantongo Street to film both inside and outside the brewery or to interview the president of the firm. Some commercials have featured images of the brewery's crowded Rathskeller, where tourists enjoy samples of their favorite beer. Others emphasized the brewery's family tradition and included pictures of the five generations of the Yuengling family that led the company. Commercials for Yuengling air periodically on television stations based in Philadelphia and the Wilkes-Barre-Scranton area.

Despite the advertising efforts of the smaller breweries, customer loyalty, which had been rock solid in northeastern Pennsylvania in the past, continued to weaken in the 1950s and 1960s, a result of television campaigns launched by the large, corporate beer makers. Big brands became hip. Worse yet, Americans slowly came to believe that the only style of beer on the market was light lager. This was particularly bad news for brewers like Yuengling, which had always prided itself on offering a portfolio of beers that included porter and ale. Regional brewers became increasingly perceived as makers of a sub-premium product, and sales plummeted.

By the early 1960s, the combination of emigration from the area and national trends in the industry ultimately proved devastating to regional breweries. Most simply yielded to the changing times and closed. In some cases, larger breweries took over smaller ones and continued to keep the brand name alive, at least temporarily. In 1966, Kaier's Brewery was sold to the Henry F. Ortlieb Brewing Company of Philadelphia for $500,000. The Philadelphia brewer was only able to keep

Dick Yuengling Sr. sampling some of his brew at the Bavarian Summer Festival. (D. G. Yuengling and Son, Inc.)

the Mahanoy City plant in operation until 1968. Ortlieb then attempted to keep the Kaier's brand name in circulation through its Fuhrmann and Schmidt subsidiary in Shamokin. F & S, however, stopped brewing in 1976 and worked on plans to re-organize. Any plans to bring the old brewery back went up in flames a short time later when the plant was gutted by fire.

Another acquisition came in 1974, when the Stegmaier Brewing Company, which employed 300 workers at an annual payroll of $1.3 million, was acquired by Lion, Inc., a cross-town rival and the brewer of Gibbons beer. Lion, Inc., continues to brew and market the Stegmaier brand. When Edward R. Maier, the great-grandson of Charles Stegmaier, made the surprising announcement about the acquisition of the Wilkes-Barre brewery, Dick Yuengling Sr. must have wondered if he would be forced to make a similar announcement in the very near future. While Stegmaier was bigger, the two companies were similar. Like Yuengling, Stegmaier was a family-run business that had lasted four-generations. Stegmaier also had loyal employees, many of whose parents or grandparents had been dedicated workers at the brewery. Sadly, 150 Stegmaier workers lost their jobs under the acquisition. The firm was admired as a respectable business by brewing industry insiders, and its closing seemed like the end of an era.[13]

The sound of barrels of beer being filled and loaded still echoed on Mahantongo Street, despite the ominous news about other breweries. Of course, the closing of competing regional breweries helped Yuengling sales. In some cases, Kaier's, Stegmaier, or F & S drinkers simply shifted their allegiance to the closest regional brewery. The increase in sales, however, was minuscule, due to the growing popularity of national brands. There were attempts to give the area (and local breweries) a boost. One was the development of the Bavarian Summer Festival, at Lakewood Park, in Barnesville, Pennsylvania, in 1969. The festival was the brainchild of Kermit Dietrich, a former salesman for Reading's Sunshine Brewing Company, who decided the Schuylkill County region needed an "economic and psychological boost." Billed as "Octoberfest in July," the event attracted over 100,000 in its first year and became "one of the largest and most successful Germanic Festivals in the country."[14] The festival would survive for many years, but it would eventually fade. The Yuengling Brewery also had high hopes of gaining publicity in the late-1960s, when Paramount Pictures filmed Martin Ritt's highly expensive epic, *The Molly Maguires*, in the coal region. The film producers, in a bid for authenticity, needed the name of an old brewery to be featured in the bar scenes. "It shall be at the discretion of Paramount Pictures to utilize every and all poster, advertisements, labels, etc. as Paramount finds it necessary to do so in its production of *The Molly Maguires*," Len Jacobs, a production assistant for the studio, wrote to Dick Yuengling Sr. The brewery granted permission to have its name appear in the film.[15]

While added publicity helped boost sales a bit, it was Yuengling's position as a family-operated business that helped considerably during the lean years. One generation continued to prepare the next to manage the brewery. Frank Yuengling's able leadership of the brewery, which had started in 1899, was coming to a close. He resigned as president in 1960. He stayed on as chairman of the board until January 29, 1963, when he passed away at Pottsville Hospital after suffering a hip fracture in a fall. But before his death, two of his sons—Richard Sr. and F. Dohrman—were already prepared to operate the brewery. Both men had received extensive training in beer making. After purchasing the interest of the other heirs of the brewery, the sibling management of the brewery worked well for several years, with Richard Sr. handling most of the matters related to sales. F. Dohrman worked to keep the production end of the business running smoothly until his untimely death in 1971.

Once when asked the secret of Yuengling's longevity, Dick Sr. replied, "Good local support, family tradition, good product, and reasonable prices."[16] The brewery president might have added "hard work." Dick Sr. followed a path similar to the one followed by the Yuengling boys of earlier generations. He had begun working at the brewery at the age of 15, doing the most menial work in the plant. In fact, Dick Sr. worked at the brewery all his life with only two brief exceptions: his years in the military during World War II as a member of the Army Air Corps in England, and the time he had spent earning a degree from the United States Brewers Academy in New York City. The Yuengling Brewery has generally had a small administrative staff, and Dick Sr. oversaw several functions at the facility, in addition to managing personnel and sales. He would open the facility at 7 a.m. each day and personally answer letters from business associates, beer can collectors, and history buffs. He also handled marketing and advertising, helped conduct

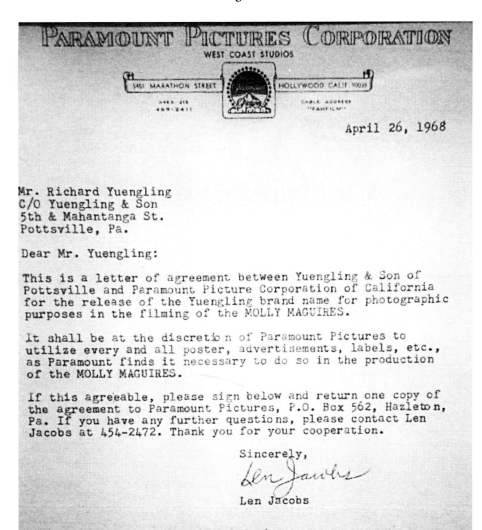

A permissions letter from Paramount Pictures to Dick Yuengling Sr. The studio sought to use the Yuengling brand name during the filming of *The Molly Maguires* in 1968. (D. G. Yuengling and Son, Inc.)

tests of beer, and often served as bartender at the Rathskeller after tours were completed.

Yet the hard work of Dick Sr. and the employees at the brewery could not quell concerns that the brewery was in the final chapter of its history. In some years, production fell to about 75,000 barrels, or 40 percent of capacity. The company just barely managed to meet payroll a few times, and each year appeared to be the last. Under a very tight budget, brewery managers looked for any opportu-

A Yuengling horsehead beer tray. (D. G. Yuengling and Son, Inc.)

nity to pinch pennies or boost sales. While national breweries were closing old plants and building modern facilities with the latest technology, Yuengling had to work to squeeze the most out of the equipment it had. In the 1960s, the plant was still running on outdated direct-current (DC) electrical power. As late as 1964, a nineteenth-century steam-driven ice machine was still in operation, and attracted people interested in seeing how it worked. In the 1960s, wooden fermenters were still used to produce the brewery's ale and porters.

Yuengling still did its best to modernize, just as it had in the past; however, it now needed to find creative ways to cut costs on equipment. In this way, the demise of other breweries in northeastern Pennsylvania helped. Why let abandoned brewery equipment go to waste? While Yuengling supervisors were concerned and even saddened by the closing of so many regional breweries in northeastern Pennsylvania in the 1960s, they did not let an opportunity to scavenge good equipment go to waste. For example, when the Lebanon Brewery closed in 1959, Yuengling obtained more beer trucks.

Another key factor was Pennsylvania's system of direct case sales through retail beer distributors. At the end of the Prohibition era, legislators revamped the beer laws. Legislation prevented brewers from resurrecting the tied-house system that gave them control over retail outlets, but it also included policies that protected Pennsylvania's rich brewing culture from competitors. For example, the beer industry in the state has operated under a three-tier system since 1934: brewer, wholesaler, and retailer (beer distributor). This system benefits regional brewers because distributors also work under a legislative oddity known as the case law.[17] Under Article IV, Section 441, of the Pennsylvania Liquor Code, the state's beer distributors are the *only* outlet for the sale of beer by the case or the keg. Perhaps most importantly, selling beer in grocery or convenience stores is against the law. For this reason, beer distributors account for 70 percent of the state's beer sales. Consumers in the Keystone State can purchase two six-packs or one twelve-pack, but they suffer sticker shock from the marked-up prices and are reminded to stop off at the beer distributor the next time they want to take beer home.

The 16-ounce returnable bottle, a key weapon for regional brewers in the fight against national beer makers. (D. G. Yuengling and Son, Inc./Chuck Hogan and Ray Reu.)

Meanwhile, in other states, sales of beer in grocery stores, convenience stores and liquor stores enabled national brewers—with their high volume, deeply-discounted beer — to squeeze regional brewers off the shelves. In Pennsylvania, however, tighter laws on beer sales helped Yuengling and the state's other regional breweries to stay competitive with national brands on price. Cases of 16-ounce returnable bottles provide a significant example. Thrifty beer lovers in Yuengling's market considered the 16-ouncers to be quite a bargain for just a few additional bucks. Local brewers liked the packaging, too. The larger, returnable bottle was much easier for the local brands to provide to the state's beer distributor, and the returnable bottle was an inconvenience for remote national brewers. The 16-ounce bottle played a very significant role in keeping the Yuengling Brewery afloat in times of languishing sales.

In dealing with the dark times, the Yuengling Brewery benefited from the assistance of a skilled brewmaster, who would play an increasingly important role in the company: N. Ray Norbert. Brewing was part of Norbert's family tradition in Schuylkill County. His father, Zigmunt A. Norbert was brewmaster at Shenandoah's Columbia Brewery. Norbert's background reflects the level of training and experience that is necessary to become a brewmaster. He served an apprenticeship at the Columbia Brewery after he graduated from the West Mahanoy Township High School at the age of 16. While at work at the Shenandoah brewery, he expanded his knowledge of engineering, chemistry, and biology by taking classes at an area college. He then attended the United States Brewers Academy in Manhattan, where he attained his brewmaster diploma. He also did post-graduate work at the school, focusing on brewing chemistry and bottleshop operation.

Norbert started work at Yuengling in 1942, but his career at the brewery was briefly interrupted when he served in the military during World War II. When he returned to Schuylkill County after the war, he went back to the Pottsville brewery as assistant brewmaster. Significantly, Norbert had the opportunity to take the reins as brewmaster in the late 1940s, when brewmaster Joseph Bausback died suddenly of a heart attack. Norbert was only 26 at the time, and his father advised him not to take the position until he had more experience. William Sherk, who had served in the United States Army as a lieutenant, then followed Bausback as brewmaster and worked in the post for approximately ten years until he left to work at another brewery. By 1960, Norbert had gained vast experience in brewing and, when he was offered the brewmaster's post that year, he accepted. Despite the benefits of a skilled brewmaster who was turning out a quality product, sales continued to decline.

The surest sign of instability at the brewery was a somewhat strained relationship between Dick Yuengling Sr. and his son, Dick Jr. In his youth, Dick Jr. wasn't quite comfortable with his family's reputation as one of Pottsville's leading families. Much to the chagrin of his father, Dick Jr., like most teenagers, had a streak of defiance and rebelliousness.[18] Nothing illustrates this point more than the father's plans for his son's education. With the brewery continuing to perform worse each year and small breweries throughout the area continuing to close, Dick Sr. encouraged his son to stay away from the brewing business. There was clearly no future in it. Dick Jr., however, had other ideas, and it wasn't the only time he ignored his father's advice.

N. Ray Norbert, a key figure in the development of popular beers at the Yuengling Brewery. (D. G. Yuengling and Son, Inc.)

Dick Sr. and his father, Frank, had both attended Hill School, a prestigious private school in Pottstown, about 60 miles from the brewery and

Pottsville.[19] The choice of the school had been accepted without question, but times change. When Dick Jr. turned 13, his father felt the school would be right for his son as well. The problem was that Dick Jr. wanted to attend Pottsville High School. According to Dick Jr., the conflict culminated when his father took him to Hill School for the admissions interview:

> The admissions officer asked me to explain why I wanted to attend the school. I thought, 'It's now or never.' I told him I didn't want to attend that school at all.
> That was it. They weren't going to accept anybody who didn't want to go. My father was furious. The 90-minute trip back from Pottstown seemed to last eight hours.[20]

But Pottsville High School did seem to be the right fit for Dick Jr. He established lasting friendships at the school and pursued his love of sports, playing baseball and basketball. On the academic side, things didn't work out quite as well. He tried a year at Lycoming College but later admitted that he "wasn't much of a student."[21] A college degree didn't appear to be particularly important though. He already was working in his chosen profession in his hometown.

Even before he graduated from Pottsville High School, Dick Jr. had taken the path followed by the men in the earlier generations of the family. He had started working at the brewery at an early age. By 15, he was already lifting and stacking cases and barrels of beer around the brewery. He also helped with the maintenance of taverns and hotels in which the brewery maintained an interest. As Dick Jr. approached his 30s, he had his own ideas about running the brewery and wanted the company to make larger capital investments to modernize. It was his father, however, who was responsible for keeping the brewery in the black. Decades later, after years as the head of the brewery, Dick

A menu cover produced by Yuengling in the 1950s. (D. G. Yuengling and Son, Inc.)

Jr. would say that he understood his father's cautious approach to the brewery's finances. But in the early 1970s, the generation gap at the company could not be healed. The headstrong son decided in 1973 to strike out on his own. He became manager of Wholesale Beverage at Westwood Road in Pottsville.

Another sign of change for the Yuengling family occurred a few years later with the death of Augusta (Roseberry) Yuengling on June 6, 1975, at the age of 92. Mahantongo Street would never be the same as generations faded with time. It seemed that an era had passed. One of her sons, David, wrote a letter in 1978 to a member of the household staff whom he admired. While accepting recent changes, he became nostalgic about the times at the home in his youth:

> I go back to Pottsville about twice a year, and when I do I stay in the old house at Fifteenth Street and Mahantongo. Everything is gone now. All of the furnishings have been either been distributed among us or have been sold. In the silence I often wander from room to room. The house stands empty there.
>
> We can never go back to that which was in the days when the house was vibrant and alive and we all congregated on the side porch for cocktails before Sunday dinner; we can now only observe those times with a backward glance. Perhaps it is just as well. All of us change with time, and what was suitable for us a half century ago is not always that which is suitable for us now. We are a different people from those who lived in that house those many years ago, different but still the same. Time has a tendency for change and, with time, so have we.
>
> Dad and Mother and Dohrman are gone now. Augusta and Frederick and Dick and I have all proceeded along our separate ways. This is as it should be.[22]

In 1979, the heirs of Augusta Yuengling donated the home to the Schuylkill County Council of the Arts for use as a cultural center. The Yuengling name received more recognition for its rich history when the family home was also named to the National Register of Historic Places.

As the 1970s passed into the Reagan era, Dick Yuengling Jr. continued working at the beer distributorship in an attempt to prove that he could establish a successful business on his own.[23] His business carried a wide variety of beers, in addition to the brand that carried the family name. The businessman gained insight into the beer business from a distributor's perspective, and he learned about the rapid changes that can take place in the industry. Indeed, new styles and packaging were invading the stacks of cases at beer distributorships in the 1970s and 1980s. One style of beer could even help Americans shed a few pounds. In 1967, Rheingold introduced a reduced-calorie beer for the first time. Named "Gablinger's" for the Swiss doctor who founded the formula, the brand was "spectacularly awful" and never really caught on.[24] Not long after Rheingold's innovation, Chicago-based Meister Brau produced a Meister Brau Lite that tasted a bit better and recorded somewhat better sales. The public, however, wasn't quite ready for a health-conscious beer. This would change when the Miller Brewing Company got involved and bought the rights to the Meister Brau name and its reduced-calorie recipe. Miller's brewers fiddled with the process and introduced their new brand: Lite Beer from Miller. The beer industry would never be the same.[25] Through its "Tastes great ... Less filling" advertising campaign, Miller made the drinking of reduced-

Installation of cereal cooker in 1985. (D. G. Yuengling and Son, Inc.)

calorie beers fashionable. Demand grew, and other large breweries were jumping on the light-beer bandwagon.

For Yuengling, what appeared to be a fad presented a problem. Unlike larger national brewers, capacity limitations made it difficult for the Pottsville beer maker to simply turn around and produce a newfangled brew. Besides, the concept of a light beer seemed out of place in Yuengling's home market, where coal miners had preferred more potent brews. The evolution of light beer, in a sense, was a setback that seemed to put the old brewery further out of step with the beer-drinking public. Still, in the volatile brewing industry, the market changes quickly. Amazingly,

Installation of cereal cooker in 1985. The brewery on Mahantongo Street would undergo exten-sive renovations and improvements for the remainder of the century. (D. G. Yuengling and Son, Inc.)

after decades of decline and just when business conditions seemed to be at their worst, the pendulum started to move in the Pottsville brewery's favor. The key year was 1976.

As America prepared for its bicentennial, a deeper interest in the past came along with it. The brewery's status as America's oldest had received little notice before. In 1976, however, it was placed on the National Register of Historic Places and the Pennsylvania Inventory of Historic Places. The nomination for the National Register noted D. G. Yuengling and Son, Inc., as "the best remaining example in Pennsylvania of the small local brewery representative of the historical origins of this important industry."[26] The emphasis on history returned a few years later when the brewery marked its 150th anniversary in 1979. CBS did a segment on the brew-ery to mark the 150th anniversary celebration.

The brewery's 150th anniversary and state and national recognition of the brewery's historical status led to an upswing in local support for the company. There was a clear lesson in the recognition for historical status: After years of poor sales, the brewery saw its first upturn in sales in decades. In Schuylkill County, it once again became fashionable "to support your local brewery." The renewed popularity of the Yuengling brand was bolstered by a color, commemo-rative beer can that featured a colorful portrait of the brewery in the late nine-teenth century, when the brewery had been headed by Frederick Yuengling. The labels on Yuengling's beer bottles featured a portrait of the brewery as it had

A Yuengling poster emphasizing the brewery's recognition as America's oldest. (D. G. Yuengling and Son, Inc.)

appeared in the 1840s. Within a few years, the brewery was updating equipment to keep up with demand.

Perhaps the most significant factor in this turnaround had occurred many years earlier and far from Pottsville. It would have a tremendous impact on the Yuengling Brewery. There had been a brewery on West 2nd Street in South Boston called the Boston Beer Company. (The company is not affiliated with Jim Koch's current Samuel Adams operation.) It had opened in 1828. In 1956, the Boston Beer Company went out of business after brewing beer for 128 years.[27] Yuengling became "America's Oldest Brewery," and the company began using the phrase on its beer products and related novelty items.

Just as it received a boost from its historical recognition in the 1970s, the Yuengling Brewery's status as "America's oldest" would become an increasingly "bankable quality" as the company moved into the last two decades of the twentieth century.[28]

Five

Getting Bigger in the Micro Boom

"More than anything, though, beer is a badge."
— Philip Van Munching, *Beer Blast* (1997)

The lead article in the local section of the Pottsville *Republican* on July 24, 1985, announced, "5th-generation Yuengling Runs Brewery."[1] After operating the beer distributorship for more than a dozen years, Richard "Dick" Yuengling Jr. came home. He bought the brewery from his father, whose declining health made it difficult for him to keep up with the demands of operating the brewery. In the newspaper report, the 42-year-old brewery president indicated that dramatic changes weren't on the horizon. There was nothing to get excited about. In retrospect, Yuengling's subdued comments might seem overly humble. Whether he realized it at the time or not, the company was on the threshold of the largest expansion in its history. The brand would become available in more states and re-enter urban markets it had abandoned for decades. But would the company remain faithful to its heritage as a small-town, family brewery?

As many people grow older, they develop a deeper appreciation for their family heritage. Dick Yuengling Jr. is not tremendously sentimental about the history that permeates the brewery. Yet he knows the key place the brewery holds in American brewing history and, increasingly, he speaks with pride about the importance of the company, as well as its potential. "As America's oldest brewery, I thought we stood a chance," Yuengling once said. "I knew we made good beer, and I knew we could make it."[2] In his initial years as at the helm, Yuengling also came to understand that the old brewery was at a crossroads, facing a challenge as serious as Prohibition. The business owner recalls how his father and uncle warned him that regional breweries were dying. He agreed, and the growing number of vacant storefronts in Pottsville and other communities throughout Schuylkill County told him that the regional economy would not keep the brewery going for much longer. He knew that stagnation resulted in business failure in a climate dominated by corporations. "We could say we're just going to remain small and operate here," Yuengling said. "But my feeling is, sooner or later, it would all start to slip away."

If the family business was looking at long-term survival, it had no choice but to expand. Fortunately, business conditions could not have been better for a brewery like Yuengling to move into markets outside its regional core.

Dick Yuengling based many of his business decisions on a significant transformation in the industry — one that had its roots in the West in the 1960s. In the summer of 1965, 27-year-old Fritz Maytag used a portion of his family's washing-machine fortune to buy the historic Anchor Brewery in San Francisco and continue producing the distinct Anchor Steam brand. Maytag's business decision put smaller, regional breweries on the comeback trail. Finally, beer drinkers were ready for change and started seeking alternatives to the national brands. In the mid-1970s, Jack

Dick Yuengling, Jr. (D. G. Yuengling and Son, Inc.)

McAuliffe served the first ale at his very tiny (two-barrel) New Albion Brewery in the California wine-country community of Sonoma. The tapping of the new suds distinguished McAuliffe's operation as America's first "Micro Brewery" or "Craft Brewery." A year later, President Jimmy Carter approved the repeal of a law that placed federal restrictions on homebrewing. Beer lovers could experiment and learn to make their own beers, ales and porters at home. Soon some homebrewers were going into production and the "microboom" was ignited. The first brewpub was opened in an old opera house in Yakima, Washington, in 1982. One brewing industry historian, in describing the dramatic spike in the number of breweries, compared the state of the industry to the days when D. G. Yuengling arrived in the United States. Brewing history appeared to be repeating itself:

> From west to east — and in between, too — there's something really exciting going on: small breweries are popping up all across the country. Called boutique or micro-breweries, there are over 30 in operation now, with a new one seemingly blossoming every few months or so.
>
> Output is low, from 300 to 30,000 barrels a year — but quality and variety are high, with most brewing a hearty ale, a dark lager, perhaps a porter or stout. It's almost like the very beginnings of commercial brewing in America in the early 1800's ... small brewers, local distribution, distinctive brews.[3]

The Keystone State was quickly caught in the wave as small craft brewing moved eastward. Beginning with the development of Dock Street Amber Beer, Philadelphia recalled its roots as a beer-producing center and witnessed a brewing renaissance. In Pittsburgh, a brewpub was opened in 1989 by the Pennsylvania Brewing

Company, the first such establishment in the state since pre-Prohibition days. Throughout the state, men and women bored with their careers turned to their love for beer and became entrepreneurs, opening microbreweries and brewpubs. New ales, lagers and porters were being crafted by companies in communities large and small. At least 50 new beer makers entered the market in Pennsylvania including such names as the Franconia Brewing Company in Mount Pocono, John Harvard's Brew House in Wayne, the Stoudt's Brewing Company in Adamstown, Tröegs Brewing Company in Harrisburg, and the Whitetail Brewing Company in Carlisle. The trend brought Pennsylvania back to its brewing roots.[4]

The microbrewery craze was not the only change in the market. Beginning in the 1970s, the nation experienced a wave of beer immigration, with a notable increase in the sale of imports like Heineken from Holland, Guinness from Ireland, Corona from Mexico, and Foster's from Australia. American consumers began equating imported beer with "class and sophistication," traits that America's national brands seemed to lack. Adventurous American brewers were soon "asking themselves if the traits that made foreign beers sell couldn't be replicated here in the states."[5] Examples of upstarts who ventured into the "super-premium" beer market and worked to throw out the foreign brands include Jim Koch's Boston Beer Company, with its Samuel Adams Boston Lager, and Pete Slosberg, with his Pete's Wicked Ale. These more expensive brands soon became part of the fastest growing segment of the industry. Big was no longer hip, and "mass-produced" once again became a "synonym for lousy."[6] The national brands, so popular in the 1960s and 1970s, fell out of fashion just as other sudsmakers stumbled upon a formula for success: "smaller = authentic, authentic = snob appeal, snob appeal = $."[7]

Koch, with the Sam Adams brand in his arsenal, eventually dominated the microboom. How did he do it? The company president changed the name of his family beer from Louis Koch Lager to Samuel Adams *Boston* Lager in recognition of the brewing tradition in his company's home city. Consumers were impressed, but knowledgeable industry insiders and beer historians knew the name was problematic. Samuel Adams Boston Lager was contract-brewed in several locations, most notably at the Iron City Brewery in Pittsburgh, Pennsylvania. The brewery's decision to connect its beer to one of the nation's Founding Fathers, Samuel Adams, raised another flag. The name and label of the brand emphasized patriotism, featuring a portrait of Sam Adams above the words "Brewer" and "Patriot." The emphasis on patriotism was a marketing ploy that fit in nicely with the spirit of the country during the Reagan-Bush era.[8] There's no doubt that Samuel Adams was patriotic. He was, after all, a key figure in the fight against British colonial rule and a signer of the Declaration of Independence. However, the historical authenticity of the title "brewer" was a stretch. According to an article in *Boston* magazine, Sam Adams did not drink lager and, technically, he was not a brewer. The noted patriot was "a malster, a soaker and drier of barley, and not a very eager or adept one at that, according to every colonial record. Sam inherited the malting house from his father and rode it straight into collapse, for times staving off receivership only by bullying creditors with fast talk."[9] Despite charges that he had fabricated a link between the brewery and the historical figure of Sam Adams, Koch won praise for turning out a quality product. Few could deny that his brand was a hit.

Dick Yuengling, a friend of Jim Koch and admirer of the Boston brewer's work, drew an important lesson from the bluster behind the Samuel Adams brand and its use of regionalism and history in marketing. His brewery had a true historical link that stretched back almost as far as the eighteenth century. The company had made beer since 1829, and federal and state agencies documented it as America's oldest brewery. If a dose of historical fiction could help make Samuel Adams popular with consumers, what about a brewery with an authentic historical tradition behind it? Couldn't his brewery market its products just as successfully? After all, the brewery had gained some momentum in 1976 when it had begun reminding potential customers of its long brewing tradition. The colorful, commemorative beer cans and bottles from that period, featuring portraits of the brewery in the nineteenth century, proved to be surprisingly popular and increased sales.

Yuengling also realized that the Samuel Adams brand successfully played to the patriotic fervor of the late 1980s. America's oldest brewery could easily appeal to the patriotic sentiments of consumers. After all, what could be more patriotic than the image in the brewery's original title — the *Eagle* Brewery? In the decades following prohibition, the eagle logo had become harder to find on the company's bottles and cans—if it was there at all. The packaging was highlighted by a superimposed "Y and S" logo, the Yuengling name in bold, modern script and a simple color scheme. But just as the portrait of Samuel Adams dominated the label of Jim Koch's popular brand, couldn't the American eagle — the symbol of the nation — make an equally impressive statement? Clearly, the spirit of the times presented the brewery with an opportunity to emphasize its rich brewing tradition, shake off its second-rate, sub-premium image, and regain the respectability that had eroded after Repeal. Most importantly, the brewery could expand its market and increase sales. Of course, it would take a great deal of work — but that was something familiar to Dick Yuengling Jr.

"The Beer Baron of Pottsville," as one reporter referred to him, has an energetic, aggressive spirit and takes a hands-on management approach at the brewery. He describes himself as a "worker," and the trait is reflected in the clothes he wears. Rather than the suit and tie of a company president, Yuengling is noted for his casual garb — blue jeans and a plaid shirt. "I don't dress this way as some kind of costume but because when I come to the brewery, I work," he once stated. The brewery president is regularly among the first to arrive in the morning and is often the last to leave. He is not one to hide behind his desk. Instead, he might be found on the loading docks as he jockeys a forklift among the pallets of beer. As his tenure lengthened, Yuengling himself would be surprised at the amount of his product being loaded into tractor-trailers.

The Yuengling Brewery, technically, is too large to be labeled a microbrewer, even in the 1980s. The trend, however, did put the brewery in a much better position than both the national breweries and the upstart microbreweries. The "big boys" of the industry like Anheuser-Busch, Miller, and Coors were threatened by the craze and scrambled to develop brands aimed at this market. Their success was limited, however. As for the new craft microbreweries, Yuengling had a clear advantage. Because the Pottsville company had produced and delivered beer since Andrew Jackson's presidency, it had the infrastructure to offer beer at a lower price than most microbrews. The first clue that Yuengling's reputation was on the upswing came with the rising sales of one its oldest styles of beer.

Yuengling has traditionally offered a variety of beers, and its lineup has changed several times over the decades. Just a few of the beers that have been introduced and discontinued include Old German, Yuengling Bock Beer, Winner Beer, Yuengling Pale Ale, and Yuengling Cream Ale. In the cost cutting measures following the lean years following World War II, the brewery concentrated mainly on three brands: Pottsville Porter, Lord Chesterfield Ale (Yuengling is among the last of the large brewers to have ale in its portfolio), and Yuengling Premium Lager, a Pottsville favorite. The brewery's bestseller was its Premium brand which, as a "price" or "discount" brand, appealed mainly to a shrinking blue-collar market. The microbrew revolution, however, encouraged people to experiment with different beers, like porter. At the time, few breweries made the dark, rich beer, and if they did, they could not offer it at a price comparable to Yuengling, a company that had been proudly producing porter since 1829. In the late 1980s, Yuengling's porter brand gained in popularity among beer connoisseurs and people in their 30s. The brewery, however, could not rest on the sales of its dark brew alone.

Dick Yuengling realized that his brewery's existing portfolio of beers was falling out of step with the market. He also understood the unique advantages of operating a family-owned business. One major plus is the ability to avoid bureaucratic red tape. A family-owned company also has more flexibility and can develop new products quickly. In a bold move that provided a hint of things to come, Yuengling decided to produce a style of beer made increasingly popular by the national brewers. Light beer had been on the market for over a decade and, clearly, it was not going to fade away. Brewers across the nation knew that Miller Lite ads infiltrating television screens in the 1970s and 1980s were a marketing success. The calorie-conscious crowd was growing, and even beer drinkers in the coal region, who usually preferred more potent brews, were looking for a light beer. Yuengling also felt it wouldn't hurt the

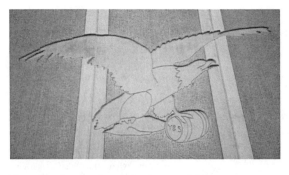

Yuengling's classic eagle logo, which serves as a reminder of the original Eagle Brewery established by D. G. Yuengling, is embedded boldly in the concrete of the new brewery at Mill Creek. (D. G. Yuengling and Son, Inc.)

region's beer lovers to shed a few pounds, and he wasted little time in discussing the idea with his experienced brewmaster, Ray Norbert. Dick Yuengling Jr. had always drawn on the experience of others, particularly in his initial years as president; however, he probably wasn't pleased with his brewmaster's initial response to his idea. Norbert had some reservations about adding a light beer to the brewery's portfolio. His first concern was the brewery's limited capacity. It would be difficult to turn out four brands of beer. The older, experienced craftsman also tended to view light as a "cut-rate" beer. Still, the experienced brewmaster knew the brewery had to keep up with the times, so he went to work on Yuengling Light.

In developing the new product, Norbert aimed to produce a better light beer than the national brands by keeping the beer in the brew house for a longer period.

Yuengling Premium Light. First brewed by the company in 1986, the brand signaled that Yuengling would aggressively work to satisfy customer demand under Dick Yuengling Jr. (D. G. Yuengling and Son, Inc./Chuck Hogan and Ray Reu.)

This meant more expense, but the brewery president agreed to his brewmaster's plan. The result was a 98-calorie beer that satisfied Norbert, who commented, "Our light beer doesn't taste like water. It has some character to it."[10] Production of Yuengling Light began on June 25, 1986. The promotion for the new brand showed that the company would be more aggressive under its new president. In contrast to the emphasis on word of mouth in decades past, the company made sure that readers of state and regional newspapers were aware of Yuengling Light through feature stories and a vigorous ad campaign. The possibility of television commercials in the Wilkes-Barre and Scranton market was also explored. Yuengling Light showed that the brewery would not be complacent in the face of industry trends.

In another attempt to satisfy the changing taste of consumers and take advantage of the microbrewery craze, Yuengling decided to further differentiate the company from the national brands by producing a beer that, in a sense, took beer drinkers back to the days of the brewery's founder — Traditional Amber Lager. The new brand was developed slowly and with great care. For a model, Brewmaster Norbert looked to the past and the lagers that had developed in Czechoslovakia during the first half of the nineteenth century. Traditional Lager is different from the clear, lighter standard American beer. It has an amber hue and contains more hops and a darker, carmel malt. A key ingredient is special hops grown to Yuengling's specifications in Washington State. The brand hit the market on November 1, 1987.

Finally, the brewery rounded out its portfolio of beers with a brand that the *public* had been producing for years. In Schuylkill and Berks counties, creative Yuengling drinkers had been mixing Yuengling Porter with Yuengling Premium or Lord Chesterfield for years—a homemade black and tan that can be mixed to suit any taste. Pete Cammarano, owner of one of the most popular beer bars in Reading—the Northeast Taproom—had one day contacted the brewery in Pottsville and requested a pre-mixed barrel of half Porter, half Lord Chesterfield. The brewery was more than happy to satisfy the request, and the bar owner sold it as "Molesterfield" (although it was more formally known as "Half and Half.") Soon after, other tavern owners had asked for half and half, too. So much of it had been sold in Reading that Yuengling recognized that it could add another brand to his portfolio. Norbert told him that 60 percent porter and 40 percent premium made a much better blend, and Black and Tan was first made in 1986. The company later marketed it more aggressively in the early 1990s in an attractive black 16-ounce can.

The company's updated portfolio of beers received high marks. It was enjoyed by the regular "Joe Six Pack" crowd. Some beer connoisseurs, who were aware of the company's history and heritage, also admired the quality of both the old and new brands. Unfortunately, the customer base familiar with the Yuengling name was limited. The quality of the beer made on Mahantongo Street was regarded as "Pottsville's little secret," but Dick Yuengling was anxious to spread the word. He realized, however, that his product did not have the right image and that his marketing strategies needed to be improved. He also knew he was not the right person to do the job. Marketing and sales were not one of his strengths. Just as he had leaned on the advice of his brewmaster, Yuengling also recognized that he needed help promoting his product. "I know when to bring in people to do the things I don't know how to do," he admitted. Wholesalers and distributors also encouraged Yuengling to hire a marketing and sales director, and he followed that advice in 1990 with the hiring of David Casinelli. Casinelli brought a strong background in beer marketing to Pottsville. The son of the sales manager of L and M in Philadelphia, he had at least eight years experience working with All Brand Importers. All Brand was noted for remaking the image of one of its brands, Australia's Foster's Lager, in 1980. The importer's successful effort to convince the Australian brewer to shift from a squat, snub-nosed bottle to a large, noticeable twenty-five-ounce can proved to be a hit with beer drinkers.[11] Similarly, Casinelli would find himself charged with remaking a brand image and giving the company's business sensibility a modern style. The marketing strategies implemented by the company's new executive were bold.

Casinelli believed the brewery's long-term survival hinged on its ability to compete with national brands in metropolitan markets. With this in mind, he encouraged Dick Yuengling to revamp the packaging of the beer immediately. For decades, Yuengling's cans and labels had not changed much. Their block script, plain graphics, and simple logos took the consumer back to the Eisenhower Administration. More importantly, they served as a reminder of the times when the brewery was saddled with a lackluster image. As the new products were introduced in the late 1980s, some minor changes in packaging design were also made. Still, a major weakness in the look of Yuengling products was a lack of uniformity, a significant problem for those trying to market the beer. Beer industry expert Philip Van Munching assessed the beer market during the Reagan-Bush years and came to the conclusion that "beer is a badge." As Van Munching explains, "No one can tell how much you paid for your beer when it's in a glass— you're counting on that bottle on the bar in front of you to show you've got taste … and maybe to show that you've got bucks as well."[12]

Casinelli believed that Yuengling Brewery needed a "badge" to represent both its rich history and the quality inside the bottle. The new sales manager suggested to the company president that the brewery shift to a "gourmet beer image" that gave the packaging a more mature look. In addition to changing the packaging, the new sales manager also suggested that display materials at the point of sale should be upgraded to reflect the changes made to the label. The sweeping changes to the brewery's image would be expensive. Casinelli hoped to retain one of Manhattan's top firms— D'Addario Design Associates— to handle the project. The high cost caused Yuengling to balk at first. It was, after all, only the *outside* of the bottle and can. It's what's *inside* that counts, thought Yuengling. After resisting the change for several months, Yuengling finally went along with Casinelli's strategy.

An intriguing challenge awaited D'Addario Design Associates. Casinelli and Yuengling were looking for a new, contemporary look to attract new customers in an expanded market. Yet the businessmen realized that beer drinkers do not like radical change, and they did not want to alienate the brewery's faithful, established fans. With this in mind, they charged the design company to emphasize the company's long family heritage and history as the main reference point for the new design. Three features highlight the new imagery: the impressive keg-clutching eagle logo (harkening back to D. G. Yuengling's original name of the company, the Eagle Brewery), the brewery name in a traditional, classic script, and the words "America's Oldest Brewery." To bring about the uniformity that the packaging had lacked, designers found a way to bring the portfolio of Yuengling beers under a "family product line," with each label essentially the same but individualized by a color scheme (porter is distinguished by a red label, Premium by gold, Yuengling Light by white, etc.). In the end, brewery officials were very pleased with the efforts by the design company and the new labeling it produced. In fact, since the new design has been accepted, Yuengling's marketers have made it a point to make sure that every label, box, and point-of-sale item contains the eagle logo, the Yuengling script, and the phrase, "America's Oldest Brewery."

Yuengling's expanded portfolio had already started to attract more regular customers in its local market. Now, with the packaging and point-of-sale changes in place, preparations were made to boost sales in the city that had maintained close connections to the Yuengling family generations earlier — Philadelphia. Casinelli, who knew the area well, linked Yuengling with larger, more aggressive wholesalers. It was a move that Dick Yuengling Jr., who views wholesalers as the key to the industry and "partners" in the business, fully supported. Casinelli also encouraged what has been labeled the "micromarketing" of the brand. Unable to afford large television campaigns like the national brewers, Yuengling promoted itself heavily at "point of sale" contacts, local events, trade shows, and product samplings. Soon Yuengling could be found at places it had never been before. Casinelli promoted the brand "at high-end on-premise accounts in such places as Philadelphia's Historic District and Penn's Landing area which gained the beer more cachet."[13] In Pottsville, it was being ordered in upscale restaurants like the Greystone. And it was showing up at professional football and baseball games at the former Veteran Stadium in Philadelphia. Of course, the Yuengling brand was just as expensive as other brands of beer at the ballpark—$5.75 for a 12-ounce cup. But high prices do not necessarily drive consumers away.

Premium pricing had not stopped brands like Samuel Adams from posting high sales figures. Consumers often believe that if you have to pay more, the product must be better. And, as Van Munching notes, the growing beer market in the late 1980s and 1990s was made up of people "who were aware of what things cost and were not immune to the need to impress."[14] Many people will spend more for a case of beer to avoid the "cheap bastard" tag. So, in some areas, the price of the Yuengling brand was raised to above-premium levels. Locally, the price of the beer remained reasonable. At a small neighborhood bar in Minersville, a customer could order a Yuengling and be charged about 40 cents. Order the same beer at Eli's on Penn's Landing in Philadelphia and the wallet was lightened by around $2.50.[15]

As Yuengling beer became available in more locations, interest grew. It developed a "mystique" or attained what some would consider a "cult status" that cut across class lines. Not only were urban professionals discovering the brand in fashionable clubs, but coal-region residents continued to be faithful to the regional brewery, as the beer showed up regularly at events like block parties, graduation parties, or weekend jam sessions. Like members of the perennial band that formed in the 1960s, the Grateful Dead, the Yuengling Brewery had more than a touch of gray, but it was hip. Yuengling took advantage of every opportunity to create even more interest in the brand. The company president welcomed publicity and frequently shared time with reporters in the company office while workers interrupted interviews with questions concerning truck routes and delivery schedules. Magazines and newspapers provided most of the coverage of events at the brewery; however, as demand for the Pottsville product grew, television and radio crews also made the pilgrimage up Mahantongo Street to document "America's Oldest Brewery."

A notable example of media attention can be found in a segment on the brewing industry on the History Channel's *Empires of Industry* series. The crew from the documentary's producers, Jupiter Entertainment of Knoxville, Tennessee, visited the brewery in January 1997, and the program aired in October of the same year. In the documentary, the Yuengling Brewery was cited as a primary example of the small, family-operated breweries that had sprung up across the country in the nineteenth century. Appropriately, the company's segment in the documentary came well before the program's discussion of macrobrewers—Anheuser-Busch, Miller, and Coors. Exterior shots of the brewery appeared as the narrator described the company's distinction as "America's Oldest Brewery." The brewery president was included in the segment, proudly standing before the old brewery tunnels as he shared his knowledge of the company's important place in brewing history. In another documentary venture, James Bartolomeo, a filmmaker from New York City, came to the brewery to make *Yuengling from Pottsville: The Story of America's Oldest Brewery*. Bartolomeo, an assistant cameraman at Home Box Office who had developed a taste for Yuengling Porter when it was available in New York, made the documentary for $14,000.[16] National Public Radio reporter Jack Speer came to the brewery in the summer of 2000 to conduct interviews for a three-minute segment on the brewery. The company also reached more potential customers when it launched a website in 1996. A few enthusiastic fans also launched their own sites, which included photographs from tours of the plant.

Tours of the brewery are regarded as an important promotional device. For decades, Yuengling management has welcomed visitors. Other beer makers offer to show people around the plant, but visitors are usually kept far away from the action. Those who write about beer for a living agree that there is something special about visiting the Pottsville facility. "This is without a doubt one of the best brewery tours in the country," observes Lew Bryson. "Others may be more polished and intimate, but few take you right down onto the floor of a hard-working sizable brewery."[17] In 1991, the tour was expanded to include a brewery museum and gift shop. The idea for the museum was conceived by Dick Yuengling who, in the late 1980s, continued to come across historical treasures around the company offices. In the dusty company safes, file cabinets, desks, and cabinets he would find old documents, photographs, notebooks, beer collectibles. Some of the relics had been haphazardly stored away and forgotten for generations. Yuengling recognized the importance of his findings and felt the material from the family archives should be shared with the public. He wasn't quite sure how to go about it, so he sought the assistance of a family friend with a deep interest in the history of the brewery. Cleo Logothetides, who would become curator of the museum, helped identify and catalog the historical items. She then designed shelves, cabinets and display cases for the items the company president had found. In a particularly creative touch, wood from old barrels at the brewery was used to build some of the display cases. Also on display are old coasters, beer cans, trays, mugs, glasses, labels and other breweriana. The museum, located in a room next to the Rathskeller, shares space with the gift shop and its souvenir items like clothing, hats, posters, mugs and glasses. The museum-gift shop developed into a popular exclamation point to the brewery tour.

Casinelli's marketing strategy, coupled with extensive media attention, resulted in success. The three new brands were a clearly a hit, and, remarkably, they did not undercut sales of Yuengling Premium, Pottsville Porter, and Lord Chesterfield Ale. Yuengling Light performed well in the market, and Black and Tan did even better. The brewery even had problems keeping up with the demand for its mix of Porter and Premium, and many beer distributors had to disappoint customers looking for Black and Tan. The uniqueness of the brand helped spread the brew-

Yuengling's Traditional Amber Lager. Re-introduced in 1987, the style of beer proved to be tremendously popular and posted astonishing sales figures. It is now Yuengling's flagship brand. (D. G. Yuengling and Son, Inc.)

ery's name along the East Coast. Proof of its popularity is found in the fact that the brand was "copycatted." Several breweries put out their own Black and Tans not long after Yuengling's appeared on the market. However, the Yuengling Black and Tan and Yuengling Light did not come close to having the impact that another new beer had on the brewery's sales.

Like a runaway beer truck, there was nothing stopping Traditional Amber Lager. Shortly after its introduction, it made up 20 percent of Yuengling's sales and became the company's flagship brand. Within ten years, Amber Lager would account for 60 percent of the brewery's trade.[18] In what has been described as one of the greatest upsets in brewing history, Amber Lager began outselling Budweiser in Philadelphia in 1998. If patrons entered a bar or tavern in the City of Brotherly Love and ordered a lager, the generic term stood for Yuengling Amber Lager. The keys to its success were good consistency and taste, as well as a reasonable price. But even those who could afford higher-priced brands sought out Yuengling's Traditional Amber Lager. Famous personalities like Jack Palance and Arnold Palmer became fans of the brew, and it has even attracted attention in Europe, thanks to high praise for the beer from one of Pottsville's most famous native sons— General George A. Joulwan, NATO supreme allied commander in Brussels, Belgium. "It's made this company what it is today," Yuengling told a reporter for the *Republican.* "It's developed a reputation for this company that we didn't have before ... as a good craft brewer.... It has made the consumer realize there's a good little brewery here in Pottsville." Traditional Lager proved so successful that it led to a spin-off brand, Yuengling Lager Light, in early 2002.

Sales figures in the 1990s, anchored by Traditional Amber Lager, were astounding, increasing from 15 to 35 percent each year. Through the decade, the total sales increases were estimated at about 400 percent. In early 2000, authorities on American brewing were amazed at Yuengling's sales figures. In an interview for *Modern Brewery Age* in the spring of 2000, a former Anheuser-Busch executive and industry analyst, Robert S. Weinberg, commented, "The guy who has me amazed is Yuengling. All of what he has done so far, he has done essentially in Pennsylvania. I thought the numbers couldn't be authentic, but they are authentic. He has done something extraordinary." Such dramatic growth did present problems, however.

In the early 1990s, as the "little secret" about the beer being made in Pottsville was spreading, Yuengling stretched well beyond its Pennsylvania-New Jersey-Delaware core market to include other states like Maryland, New York, Washington, D.C., and pockets of Virginia. On a limited scale, the brand could be found in other states from Maine to the Carolinas. The brewery probably moved too hastily, because before long there was evidence the brewery had overextended itself. With the capacity at the old Mahantongo Street brewery limited, it became impossible to keep up with demand. In a period of generally flat growth in the beer industry, this was a problem that other brewers would have loved to have. But it was still a problem.

The first signs of trouble surfaced locally. Shortages occurred among distributors in Yuengling's core market in Eastern Pennsylvania. For a short time, a sense of betrayal gripped older Yuengling drinkers who had stuck by the brewery in the hard times. According to the *Wall Street Journal*, some Schuylkill County beer distributors posted signs bitterly blaming the export of Yuengling to other states as the reason for the shortage. Beer retailers and bartenders called the local newspapers to complain about the scarcity of "Vitamin Y." The situation became particularly acute during the peak summer months of July and August. Some business owners felt compelled to voice their frustration with Dick Yuengling directly. The brewery president understood the frustration of wholesalers, retailers, and the consumers. As the head of the small family business, Yuengling, in contrast to the heads of large corporations, personally handled as many complaints as possible. He sympathized with beer distributors who were watching prospective customers walk out the door empty-handed because no Yuengling lager was available. Shifts were added in an attempt to keep up with demand, and employees were brewing, packaging, and transporting beer virtually around the clock. Demand still outweighed supply, however. What could be done about the shortage?

Yuengling realized the importance of the regional market and implemented a policy of retrenchment. Satisfying local demand became a priority. In the early 1990s it pulled out of New England, New York, Maryland, Washington, D.C., North Carolina and much of Virginia. In 1994 and 1995, it even withdrew from Pittsburgh so it could supply Eastern Pennsylvania consumers. The brewer also made sure that Yuengling beer retained its original, lower price in its home county. Of course, scaling back the size of the market was only a temporary measure. Somehow, more beer had to be squeezed out of the Mahantongo Street brewery, a difficult proposition for a plant that was recognized as a nineteenth-century landmark.[19]

When D. G. Yuengling was preparing to hand over the reigns of the brewery to his sons not long after the Civil War, his brewery was producing about 15,000 barrels of beer annually. Of course, expansion projects by subsequent generations have increased capacity. After sales started to pick up in 1976, the company allotted a large percentage of its earnings to updating and expanding equipment. The brewery also gained financial assistance for projects through state tax credits. The fact that the brewery was listed on the National Register of Historic Places and the State Register of Historic Places made projects more complex, however.

Because of these historic designations, the architecture had to retain its old form, and any improvements required that the building be returned to its original state. In 1980, for example, the brewery's 100-year-old copper brewing kettle was replaced by a stainless steel one. Installation required the dismantling of the brewhouse's stained-glass ceiling, followed by its restoration once the new equipment was in place. A few years later, in 1985, brewery management purchased a 10,000-pound steel cereal cooker to replace the cast-iron one which had been used since 1907. Once again, historical status proved to be a curse rather than a blessing. To get the equipment in place on the upper floor, a wall had to be ripped out to get it inside. Brewery management considered installing a stained glass window where the wall was removed; however, as an historic site, the building had to retain its old form, and the wall had be rebuilt exactly as it was before. The installation of the new equipment inside the brewery's existing structure helped bring the brewery's annual capacity to approximately 180,000 barrels by 1990. Interior space continued to be a source of frustration as the years rolled by:

> I've got a 1952 bottle washer here that I'd like to get rid of, but how the hell am I going to get it out of here? But we've got a 1952 walking beam pasteurizer that works just fine. And we've got a 40-spout can filler that does about 520 cans a minute, installed in 1991. We added a Krone's labeler two or three years ago, and that's been nice. But we had to knock a hole in the wall to get it in here, and get permission from the church next door to bring a crane in. Everything is so jammed in.... We have to replace equipment, but we can't shut down to do it.[20]

As he worked to increase capacity, Yuengling started to consider areas around the existing property, but there was really no space left.

The Yuengling Brewery's location at 5th and Mahantongo streets had its advantages in the nineteenth century, supplying D. G. Yuengling with the cold caverns to age his lager. As the millennium approached, the landlocked location against a hillside was a roadblock. Still, there was some available ground around the premises — primarily a parcel of land behind the plant at Howard Avenue and Fifth Street. Dick Yuengling decided to use it. In 1992, the brewery launched its most ambitious expansion project to date. Construction workers shoehorned new storage and holding tanks behind the brewery. The expansion also included increasing refrigeration and updating the electrical system. When the first phase was completed, annual capacity increased to 270,000 barrels. Four years later, when another phase of renovation was completed, the capacity of the small brewery on Mahantongo Street reached over 300,000 barrels.

The projects Yuengling supervised in the 1990s demonstrate that he shared at least one notoriously German characteristic practiced by earlier generations of his family—thrift. It was estimated that Yuengling saved many thousands of dollars on the expansion project by finding and purchasing secondhand tanks, bottlers, and labelers. If it worked well and did not sacrifice quality, why not? Profiles of Dick Yuengling often note that he is a "cautious" businessman. His prudence with a dollar is perhaps rooted in his experiences during the lean decades when the brewery was just managing to meet payroll. A biographical essay in a national business magazine provides insight into Yuengling's business philosophy. "A man with old-fashioned values, Yuengling is wary of debt; his firm is virtually debt-free," noted *Forbes* magazine. "He pinches pennies, too. He's always on the prowl for used equipment, and has on occasion gotten irate when he spots mail with a 32-cent stamp destined for a wholesaler. Why couldn't one of his drivers drop the letter off when delivering beer?"[21]

Another example of Yuengling's tightfistedness came in 1989. In response to increased media attention to the problem of alcohol abuse, the 1980s were marked by a rise in the number of organizations calling for more careful monitoring of the use of alcoholic beverages.[22] The government, in response to public pressure, required a warning label under the Right to Know Act about the dangers of alcohol for pregnant women and people who drink and drive. Yuengling agreed with the message that the label contained. But there was a drawback. Even though the label requirement became law in 1988 as part of the Anti-Drug Abuse Act, many breweries had huge stocks of labels. Many of the labels would have to be discarded after November 18, 1989. At the Yuengling Brewery cartons and cartons of labels had to be thrown out. "It's been quite costly," Yuengling said. "Quite a few thousand dollars." The brewer doubted that legislators were aware of the complicated process of labeling when they passed the law. He also expressed doubts about the effectiveness of labels. Yuengling, who enjoys a cigarette every now and then, argued that warnings have been on cigarette packages since the early 1960s but that people still continue to smoke. It would be a mistake, however, to place too great an emphasis on Yuengling's thriftiness and his cautiousness as a businessman. In contrast to these characteristics, the measures the brewer took to keep up with demand would show that he was more than capable of taking risks and investing heavily in his company.

In the continuing effort to ease the burden on the old brewery, Yuengling reluctantly decided to turn to a technique that other breweries utilized: contract brewing. It is not unusual for a brewery to turn to another beer-making facility to increase capacity.[23] Yuengling turned to contract brewing as a last resort. When sales of the Traditional Amber lager skyrocketed, the company had no choice but to turn to the former Schaefer Brewery in Fogelsville, near Allentown (then owned by another family brewing dynasty, the Stroh Brewery of Detroit), to make its Black and Tan.[24] Before committing to a deal, Dick Yuengling had to be satisfied that Stroh could produce "a good flavor match." About one-tenth of the brewery's volume was being produced at the Stroh's Brewery after contract brewing started in June, 1996.

Contract brewing was not the ultimate answer to easing the pressure on the old brewery. During the 1990s, rumors had been circulating that the brewer would construct a new facility. The deal with Stroh stopped the buzz about a new brewery, but not for long. In the late 1990s, a committee of Yuengling executives held meetings to plan the future. A variety of options went around the table. Committee members considered doing nothing and continuing operations as usual, but this put the future of the brewery at risk. Expanding the level of contract brewing was another option. Another consideration was more investment in upgrading the Mahantongo Street location; however, space limitations made this impractical. Selling to a national brewer was another idea that surfaced but was quickly dismissed. Companies like Anheuser-Busch or Miller would in all probability have considered buying the brewery and then phasing out the Yuengling brand. Another alternative was to acquire another brewery. Or what about the most expensive alternative, the one that had been rumored for years: Could a new brewing facility be in Yuengling's future?

Personnel decisions provided a clue of what the future might hold. In 1997, Yuengling hired James L. Helmke, a senior faculty member at Siebel Institute of Technology, Chicago, and a former employee of Labatt. Helmke assumed the position of vice president of operations. A post was also offered to Helmke's wife, Bronwyn A. Tulloch, who had a brewmaster's diploma. If a new brewery were planned, Helmke and Tulloch would fit in nicely. Tulloch had experience overseeing large brewing operations. She had been director of brewing for the Coors brewery in Memphis, Tennessee. A highlight of Helmke's resume included the construction of a brewery in Vietnam. The pair would have an opportunity to put their experience to use.

On Thursday, May 8, 1998, Yuengling made an important, unofficial announcement to a gathering of representatives from 62 beer wholesalers at the Valley Forge Convention Center near Philadelphia. He confirmed rumors that had been circulating. Yuengling would indeed construct a new $50 million brewery in the Pottsville area. The official announcement of the plant came the following day, when a large number of Yuengling fans, politicians, and reporters squeezed into the brewery's museum. As Yuengling explained, the company had to grow if it was to survive in an increasingly competitive market. The new brewery would give the company the capacity to expand its markets. At times, Dick Yuengling was uncharacteristically emotional as he made the announcement, striking a note which emphasized the rich tradition of the brewery, recalling his great-great-grandfather and subsequent generations of the family. "I'm sure old D. G. would be very proud of this," he said, with his daughters gathered around him. "He's looking down on us as are the others who've run this brewery."[25] The company president also recognized the dedication of the brewery employees over the generations for playing

Yuengling announces plans for new $50 million brewery

Yuengling's NEW BREWERY

INSIDE
- Wholesalers briefed in Valley Forge Thursday reacted with glee.
  Details, Page 8

INFO CONNECT
828-6000 453-1000
462-3000 647-7575
889-5200 362-4000
773-2211 345-3200

- Hear excerpts from remarks at this morning's press conference:

Lt. Gov. Mark S. Schweiker — Selection 1351
Brewery owner Dick Yuengling — Selection 1352
State Sen. James J. Rhoades — Selection 1353
State Rep. Bob Allen — Selection 1354
U.S. Rep. T. Timothy Holden — Selection 1354

WHAT DO YOU THINK?
...about hosting America's newest brewery.
Selection 1350

Schuylkill online
http://www.pottsville.com

Fifth-generation brewery owner Richard L. Yuengling Jr. smiles broadly as David A. Casinelli, D.G. Yuengling & Son executive vice president, announces plans for a new $50 million plant to wholesalers meeting in Valley Forge Thursday.

BEN MORRISON/Staff Photo

100 jobs planned at Mill Creek site

Newspaper headlines announcing the construction of the new brewery. (Courtesy of the Pottsville [PA.] *Republican & Herald*.)

a key role in bringing the family business to one of the most important days in its history. In a later interview, he emphasized "a family commitment, passed on from his 'forefathers,' to 'keep this place alive'" as a key factor in the decision to construct a new brewery.

Maintaining operations in Pottsville was also of primary importance to Yuengling's management. Company officials recognized that Yuengling's image as a small regional brewer was the key to its success, so maintaining operations in the Pottsville area was essential. "America's Newest Brewery" would be located on a 16-acre site owned by the Schuylkill Economic Development Corporation along Mill Creek Road, near the Saint Clair Industrial Park. Just as D. G. Yuengling made access to quality water a key factor in the decision to locate in Pottsville, the location of the new brewery was based in part on access to its existing water source, the Schuylkill County Municipal Authority.

The new facility was only one part of a "double-barreled" expansion, and for good reason. A new brewery takes years to build, and 2001 was a modest estimate for the completion of Yuengling's new plant. What could be done? When plans for the new facility were announced, the brewery was still having problems keeping

The Tampa, Florida, brewery. The facility puts the brewery in a better position to gain customers in markets in the South. (D. G. Yuengling and Son, Inc. / Chuck Hogan and Ray Reu.)

up with high demand. Another bold move was necessary, and this measure was reminiscent of the mid-nineteenth century when the sons of D. G. Yuengling expanded the family's operations to other states. This time, however, the family brewing tradition would reach further south than David Yuengling Jr.'s venture in Richmond, Virginia.

Yuengling purchased a 485-acre brewery in Tampa, Florida, a facility located just around the corner from the famous Busch Gardens, where both Anheuser-Busch and, later, Stroh, brewed beer. The announcement of the purchase came in April 1999. Consumer demand had created the need to purchase a medium-sized brewery somewhere. "I can't get through another summer without another facility somewhere," the company president said in a press release, "and that's why the Tampa plant came into play." As was the case with the contract brewing in Allentown, Dick emphasized that it was important for the brewery to have a "flavor match." This would be a bit more of a challenge, since environmental conditions were so different in Florida.[26] Charged with finding the flavor match was the new manager of the Tampa plant, master brewer Otto Wiesneth.

The portfolio of Yuengling beers in the 1990s. (D. G. Yuengling and Son, Inc.)

The official opening of the Tampa facility came on August 12, 1999, and brewery officials once again emphasized the rich history of the company. At the entrance to the new plant, a portrait of D. G. Yuengling was on display, as well as several company posters and signs. The gift store was already well stocked with Yuengling clothing and merchandise. The Florida brewery had the capacity that Yuengling felt was just right to meet the demands of its customers—1.5 million barrels per year. In addition to helping Yuengling supply its core market. The Tampa plant also put the brewery in a position to sell plenty of beer in Florida. Sales manager Casinelli acknowledged that Yuengling planned to go after consumers in the Sunshine State once the company's capacity problems stabilized. The Yuengling Brewery followed through on this promise. By the summer of 2000, Yuengling beer was available to Florida distributors, and Yuengling plaques and vinyl banners were popping up in bars in Gainesville. Slowly, the company expanded to distributorships in other states in the South, including North Carolina and Alabama. The brewery's sales force approaches states in a contiguous, domino fashion.

Significantly, Yuengling first started to attract attention in college towns in the South. Not long after the purchase of the Tampa plant, the Yuengling portfolio of beers was available at stores near the University of Florida at Gainesville and also at the University of Alabama at Tuscaloosa, which is described in the school newspaper as "a football town with a drinking problem." Like other brewers, Yuengling saw sales potential among college students.[27] Yuengling consistently scores high grades from undergraduates in Pennsylvania, outselling Budweiser 4–1. The beer is enjoyed at Penn State's main campus, as well as at Philadelphia universities like Penn, Villanova, Temple, and LaSalle. According to Dick Yuengling, the popularity of his brand reflects a distaste for large corporations among nonconformist students. They respect Yuengling's longevity and the fact that the brewery is family owned and operated. In 2002, Yuengling made a considerable investment to switch to the Sankey (ball-tap), replacing the old Hoff-Stevens (two-prong) tap. Dick Yuengling, who recalls filling wooden kegs and whole barrels in his youth, said the barrel upgrade was motivated, in part, by the growing popularity of the Yuengling brand at college frat houses.

Slowly, larger breweries were looking at Yuengling's growing popularity and noticed the negative impact the regional brewery was having on their own sales. They would see if something could be done about their competition in Pottsville. There's one sure way to eliminate a business rival — buy it. Would Dick Yuengling be interested in selling? In the late 1990s, while the company was exploring its options to have its beers contract brewed, Anheuser-Busch and Miller were contacted about bottling the Yuengling brand at their plants. Yuengling's business inquiries prompted the larger brewers to explore and investigate what was going on in Pottsville. "They climbed D. G. Yuengling & Son's mountainside brewery, America's oldest," wrote a reporter for the Associated Press. "They tasted the old Porter, the newfangled Lager and the popular Black and Tan. And then they offered to buy the whole place. Fifth-generation owner Richard L. Yuengling Jr. politely declined."[28] The brewery president later explained that his decision not to sell was based on his thoughts about the four previous generations that had worked to build the company and keep it going. He felt that they would have wanted him to keep it in the family. Spurning the offer from the macrobrewers was an easy, quick decision; however, challenges against Yuengling were made that were more threatening. One very significant legal matter was initiated by another major brewer, Molson. A claim made by the Canadian firm struck at the heart of Pottsville company's recent marketing success, but it was more personal, too. For Yuengling found itself fighting for a treasured part of its heritage as the legality of the company's title as "America's Oldest Brewery" went before the courts. It would be a time-consuming case.

Since 1956, the phrase "America's Oldest Brewery" had appeared on Yuengling's products and novelty items. In 1993, perhaps spurred by its growth, Yuengling sought to register the phrase as its legal trademark by filing an application with the U.S. Patent and Trademark Office (PTO). In 1994, the PTO published the trademark in its Official Gazette.[29] It sounded like a rather simple step. But there was an objection. In 1995, the giant Molson Breweries of Toronto, Canada, objected and filed a trademark challenge. The cases of both firms went before the Trademark Trial and Appeal Board. The dispute hinged on the word "America." Molson had opened its first brewery in 1786, well before the birth of David Gottlieb Yuengling. Attorneys for Molson argued that Yuengling's use of the slogan "America's Oldest Brewery" was "deceptively misdescriptive" because "America is synonymous with North America." Molson's legal team cited *Webster's New Geographical Dictionary* definition of America as "either continent of the Western Hemisphere (North America or South America), often, specifically, the United States of America." As part of its evidence, Jeffery Kellar, the director of marketing for Molson Breweries U.S.A., testified and introduced copies of Molson television and radio spots that stressed Molson's standing as "North America's oldest brewery."

Yuengling stood by its claim that it was America's oldest brewery, and consumers were not being deceived. Dick Jr. provided a deposition for the case and was called to Philadelphia to testify. He pointed out the designation of the brewery as "America's oldest" by the Pennsylvania Inventory of Historic Places and the National Register of Historic Places. He also provided a variety of exhibits to illustrate the company's use of the mark since the late-1950s on its labels and promotional materials, as well as on items sold in the brewery's gift shop. In addition to the company president's testimony, the Yuengling legal team further noted that "Molson's own advertising recognizes a distinction between Canada and America with its strong emphasis on the Canadian origin of its product."

In the end, on November 11, 1998, after almost five years of legal debate, a panel of three administrative trademark judges agreed with Yuengling's position. The opinion stated that Molson "has failed to produce any evidence that the purchasing public in the United States would equate the term 'America' with North America, rather than the United States of America." The Pottsville *Republican* hailed the legal victory for the local brewery. "It is a victory worthy of David's triumph over Goliath," read an editorial. "Molson is one of the giants of the industry, sold all across the continent, and with a huge arena bearing its name in Montreal. Yet Yuengling … battled Molson for the right to call itself what it truly is and won."[30] The fifth-generation owner of the Yuengling Brewery, while always confident the case would be won, expressed delight when the decision finally came down. "There was no question in my mind that we couldn't use the slogan," he said. "We really are America's oldest brewery." The important legal victory brought 1998 to a happy close, but the following year would be marked by changes that symbolized the close of a chapter in the brewery's history.

Brewmaster Ray Norbert, whose tenure at the brewery had extended through three generations of the Yuengling family, retired in January, 1999. High praise marked Norbert's retirement reception in the brewery's Rathskeller barroom. Dick Yuengling credited Norbert for leadership that had helped the brewery through the lean years. Norbert's skills as a brewmaster were a key to the brewery's later success, and expansion projects at the brewery would not have been possible without him. Similarly, Norbert had kind words for the Yuengling family and the staff he had worked with during his 57-year career. "I have great admiration and respect for all of the employees and assistant brewmasters that worked with me," he said. "Without their effort and cooperation, it would be impossible to attain our goals."[31] James P. Buehler, a 27-year employee at the brewery, took over the helm as brewmaster in February, 1999.

In a sharp contrast to the celebration of Norbert's work at the brewery, sad news came to the brewery a few months later of the passing of Dick Yuengling Sr. on March 27, 1999, at the age of 83. Praise poured in for the former brewery president who had guided the company through adverse times. Pottsville Mayor Ter-

New brewery at Mill Creek. The new brewery helped give the company the capacity it needed to meet demand. (Courtesy of the Pottsville [(PA.] *Republican & Herald.*)

ence P. Reiley described Dick Sr. as an asset to the city, a man who was pleasant and accommodating. Brewmaster Beuhler described Yuengling as a "good man" and "a great person to work for," noting that he would be missed by many friends.[32]

Dick Jr. continued to struggle to keep up with demand as the new millennium drew closer. The increased capacity at the Mahantongo Street location and the purchase of the brewery in Tampa helped ease shortages. Still, Yuengling would be in a much better position when the Mill Creek brewery was completed. The company projected a May 2000 opening. Predicting the completion date of any large construction projects is an art, not a science, as Dick Yuengling would learn. Deadlines are rarely met. Actual work on the 272,000-square-foot facility began a few months after the announcement of the project. In contrast to the Mahantongo Street brewery's hillside location, the setting of the new facility was a flat surface with easy access—perfect for producing plenty of beer. In September 1998, construction crews began the process of clearing the land at the 16-acre site. Work on the drainage system and assembly of the steel framework followed. By the following spring, in May 1999, the walls were in place, with the concrete proudly emblazoned with the company's familiar eagle logo. The warehouse portion of the structure was finished by late summer, and the entire facility was largely completed by the end of 1999. Then the tedious phase of the project began in 2000 — the installation of equipment and hookups.

Any visitor can see that the new brewery is clearly geared for high production. It accommodates forty 1,000-barrel storage tanks, a 5,625-square-foot brew house, and a three-story, 32,250-square-foot-per-floor stock house. Two packaging lines move bottles along a conveyor belt through a shared pasteurizer. About 1,000 bottles per minute are filled. Kegs are filled by machines with "racking guns." The old brewery has four "racking guns," while the new brewery features eight and is capable of filling 1,800 barrels per day. The historic brewery has a 10,000-square-foot warehouse and distribution center. In contrast, the same facility at the new brewery measures 100,000 square feet. Loading docks are easy for trucks to access.

Even though the building was new, the equipment that was installed in 2000 was not. Much of it was recycled from other facilities. In October 2001, the facility was finally producing beer on a limited scale. By February 2002, the new facility, essentially completed, was operating at about 50 percent capacity. The brewery was supposed, initially, to open at 500,000- to 700,000-barrel capacity, until Yuengling could build its reputation in expanded markets. The new brewery, however, remained at half capacity longer than anticipated. In its late stages, the project hit a snag that had the potential to undermine years of effort.

The new Yuengling Brewery was constructed on what had once been a thriving railroad yard, where millions of tons of anthracite coal moved on its way around and out of Schuylkill County. At one time, the site had been loaded with acres and acres of rail cars. The decline of the coal industry, however, had left rusting railroad lines. When construction of the new brewery began there was, ironically, not a railroad or rail car in sight. Yuengling's new plant needed rail access to bring products from throughout the country. Corn comes from Minnesota, and malted barley comes from Wisconsin, for example. As the project continued, Yuengling began work to connect the brewery to the nearby Reading, Blue Mountain & Northern Railroad Company. It was a slow process, too slow for a brewery president anxious to increase production. In Pottsville's neighboring community of Port Carbon, council members were concerned about the safety of residents living near the railroad tracks, particularly in the vicinity of the Jackson Street crossing. Time went by without the council acting on the necessary permits. In the summer of 2002, tension between Yuengling and the borough mounted as the deadline for the rail line application to the Public Utility Commission drew near. Council continued to have concerns about rights of way and road crossings. Yuengling accused the borough of stonewalling for almost two years and estimated that the council's failure to act on a rights of way agreement had cost the brewery between $200,000 and $300,000. He pointed out that insufficient grain was making it to the new brewery. The railroad needed to be completed and soon.

By October 2002, thanks to the intervention of county economic development officials, a compromise was reached on all sides. In the end, the blueprints for the rail project were redrawn to include more track and space. As a result, the switching of rail cars could take place farther away from borough streets. Work on the railroad could finally move to completion. On Thursday, January 16, a small gathering of brewery officials and reporters at the new brewery braced against the cold and watched a locomotive pulling two train cars full of brewers' malt break through a large Yuengling banner. It was probably the closest that the new brew-

The new Yuengling Brewery, completed in 2000. (D. G. Yuengling and Son, Inc.)

ery came to an official opening. The arrival of the diesel engine and its freight symbolized the completion of the project. Finally, the new brewery had all the pieces in place to run at capacity and run smoothly. The rail cars had the capacity to carry 190,000 pounds of grain. Regular delivery of materials put the company in the position to produce 1 million barrels per year at the location, twice the amount of beer the old brewery could produce. The historic plant in Pottsville, combined with the new plant and the Tampa addition, gave Yuengling a highly respectable 3 million-barrel capacity. After struggling for years to meet demand, the brewery finally had the capacity it wanted. This might have been mistaken as time to relax, but the company still faced many headaches.

In the years just before the burden was taken off the Mahantongo Street brewery, the strain may have been a bit too much for equipment at the old plant. The facility was keeping up with the pressure of its 300,000-barrel capacity; however, more industrial wastewater was being discharged from the facility — a fact that didn't go unnoticed by the Environmental Protection Agency. The discharge from the brewery, an estimated 150,000 gallons daily, reportedly overloaded the capability of the Pottsville's sewer treatment plant. Water that is treated at the sewer plant in Pottsville then makes its way into the Schuylkill River at a point upstream from drinking water outlets for other communities. If the water isn't treated properly, the discharge from the sewer plant pollutes the river. EPA industrial wastewater permits seek to protect sewer treatment facilities. The agency requires companies to maintain permissible pH levels in their wastewater, as well as acceptable levels of copper, lead, nickel, and zinc. Yuengling had its industrial pre-treatment wastewater permit in place and felt it was complying with its permits. But the EPA didn't see it that way. In an ironic twist, the brewery, which prides itself on the pure water used to make its beer, was charged with violating the Clean Water Act. In 2000, the brewery was fined $137,500 for alleged violations. A

$110,000 fine for having illegal amounts of metals and acid in its waste followed in 2002.

The operators of the city's sewer treatment plant, the Greater Pottsville Area Sewer Authority, and the EPA continued to pressure the brewery to install pollution-control equipment and meters. Private businesses, particularly family-owned businesses, do not appreciate being told what to do. The company expressed a willingness to comply and replaced an old pasteurization machine with a new one in hopes of correcting the problem and satisfying the EPA. At the same time, brewery managers continued to raise questions about the fairness of some of the demands made by the agencies, particularly the development of a holding system for the wastewater. Yuengling's attorney, former state Senator Fred Hobbs, sought to ease the tension between the brewery and the EPA through meetings with agency officials in Philadelphia. "Dick was caught in a real supply demand squeeze," the lawyer told a reporter for the Pottsville *Republican.* "That's why he had to build on the old brewery and put a strain on it. Yuengling was in an impossible situation when the brewery was really producing over capacity in the late 1990s." Later, the company requested an extension of time to bring itself into compliance with the environmental agencies, noting that the age of the brewery presented some obstacles. Dick Yuengling told reporters that brewery management wanted to upgrade; however, the age and location of the plant made it a slow, difficult process. The company planned to have the meters requested by the EPA in place before the close of 2004. Attorney Hobbs suggested that part of the problem could be rooted in a failure by the sewer plant to upgrade and modernize so it could absorb and treat runoff with higher levels of metals and acids. The situation was alleviated with the completion of the new brewery in Mill Creek. With the new plant on line, wastewater from the old brewery deemed problematic by the EPA was reportedly reduced by two-thirds.

In 2004, Yuengling Brewery reached its 175th anniversary and planned special promotional campaigns to mark the occasion. Some of Yuengling's competitors were apparently not in the mood for celebrating, however. The Miller Brewing Company, for example, voiced objection to state tax credits received by the Pottsville beer maker and several of the other larger Pennsylvania brewers, including Pittsburgh Brewing Company, Latrobe Brewing Company (makers of Rolling Rock), and Lion Brewing Company, Wilkes-Barre. Under Pennsylvania's 2004 budget, brewers producing less than 1.5 million barrels are eligible to for up to $200,000 in tax credits for the purchase of capital equipment used for manufacturing. The tax breaks were first established in the 1970s and subsequently grew even larger, but in 1989 the credits were scaled back to cover only breweries making fewer than 300,000 barrels a year. The expansion of the barrel limit in the 2004 budget to 1.5 million brought Yuengling, which produces about 1.2 million barrels per year, and the Latrobe Brewing Company under the umbrella of eligibility for the tax credits. The lobbying effort to expand brewery tax credits, however, had been initiated by the Pittsburgh Brewing Company, the maker of Iron City, I.C. Light, and Augustiner beers. The president of the Pittsburgh Brewing Company, Joseph Pic-

Dick Yuengling Jr. explains the brewery's new robotic keg-filling operation to members of the Pennsylvania's House Liquor Control Committee who toured the new Port Carbon brewery. The new robotic system required the Yuengling Brewery to purchase 400,000 new kegs, some which can be seen in the background. (Pottsville [PA] *Republican & Herald*.)

cirilli, said he sought the help of local legislators as he planned improvement projects at his 260-employee facility.

The Miller Brewing Company argued that the tax credits should only be available to "true small Pennsylvania brewers," in other words, the smaller microbreweries. A Miller attorney drafted a letter to the Pennsylvania State Brewers Association to support repeal of the measure and suggested that legal action would lead to the elimination of the entire tax credit. A representative of the Coors Brewing Company also objected. However, the tax credit remained attractive to Pennsylvania brewers considering adding new brewing tanks or installing new packaging equipment. Few brewers in the state, including Yuengling, appeared willing to pass on the generosity of the Pennsylvania legislature.

The Pennsylvania Liquor Code and Pennsylvania Liquor Control Board (PLCB) regulations that had benefited regional brewers like Yuengling have come under attack as well.[33] A group, Modernize Our Beer Laws (MOBL), formed in 2004 and began pushing for changes in the way beer is sold in Pennsylvania. Members of MOBL include the Pennsylvania Beer Wholesalers Association as well as Anheuser-Busch, Miller and Coors. The group began encouraging the elimination of the state's ban on Sunday sales by beer distributors. The organization also wants Pennsylvania to allow the sale of 12-packs at beer distributors, arguing that the measure would help drive down price and stop consumers from going out of state to buy their beer (despite the fact that cross-border sales of alcohol are against the law). Sales of 12-packs at beer distributors, according to those favoring the change, would encourage consumers to experiment with the more expensive craft beers produced by local independent brewers. Dick Yuengling has adopted the position that any change would bring the commonwealth a step closer to beer sales in convenience stores and supermarket chains like Wal-Mart. Such action, according to the brewery president, would make Pennsylvania's small brewers, beer distributors, and wholesalers vulnerable to the discounting tactics of the macrobreweries.

Many beer industry insiders indicate that Pennsylvania's law makers are beginning to favor change and significant revisions in Pennsylvania's beer laws are on the horizon. If so, the Yuengling Brewery would again be forced to adapt. Critical business decisions will need to be made to stay in the fight for customers. Fortunately, the family bond that helped in generations past still exists. Amid the brewery's recent flurry of expansion, construction, and acquisition, something almost went unnoticed. As the 1990s rolled on, Dick Yuengling was no longer the only family member working to keep the family brewing tradition alive. The sixth generation was standing at his side.

Epilogue

Something to Be Proud Of

I would endeavor to say that yours is more than a business. One would
not be exaggerating to postulate that yours is an American institution.
— Philip P. Heilman in letter to
Dick Yuengling Jr. in 1985

The former Eagle Brewery on Mahantongo Street is now getting a little more rest.

With the completion of the new brewery in Pottsville and the acquisition of the Stroh facility in Florida, D. G. Yuengling and Son has the capacity it needs to meet demand. Sadly, the old red brick building at 5th and Mahantongo streets has been referred to by some as a "subsidiary operation" of the company. It will never be completely put out to pasture, however. There's too much history behind it.

The anthracite mining industry that lured David Gottlieb Yuengling to Pottsville still has a pulse. Coal is still being dug by mammoth machines in strip mining operations. There are still some underground mines, and they invite comparison with the Yuengling Brewery. The underground mines in Schuylkill County are small, family operations. Young men — and women — are still taken down mine shafts as kids, and their family history has entered their blood. Despite being hounded and threatened by federal mine inspectors, some parents still hope their children will keep the tradition alive.[1] These small mines could endure for many more generations. But the days of the large coal companies and thousands of beer-loving coal miners are gone. Evidence of the days of "King Coal," such as the large piles of culm (the coal waste by-product) are gradually being eliminated. Mine reclamation projects and co-generation plants, which convert coal waste by-products into steam heat and electricity, are changing the landscape. Birch trees are springing up in areas once blighted by tons and tons of coal waste. Efforts to fill dangerous strip mining pits continue, too, as the industrial scars continue to heal.

The region is turning to its historic past to help its economy. Projects like the Pennsylvania State and Historical Museum Commission's anthracite museum complex in Ashland, Eckley, and Scranton attract thousands of visitors each year. Yuengling also plans to use tourism as a big part of its marketing plan, and the historic brewery is the centerpiece. The Schuylkill County Visitors Bureau describes the brewery as the biggest draw in the county, attracting over 30,000 tourists. They

The historic Yuengling Brewery.

Dick Yuengling with his daughters. From left, Jennifer Yuengling, Sheryl Yuengling, Wendy Yuengling Baker, and Debbie Yuengling Ferhat. (D. G. Yuengling and Son, Inc.)

come from throughout the United States, Europe, Asia, Africa, and South America. Of course, as visitors come through the brewery, they expect beer to be made there, and so it will be. But at a slower pace. The strain won't nearly be as strong as the mid-1990s, when the brewery was attempting to squeeze as much as possible out of the plant.

Still hovering over the region and particularly Schuylkill County is the drink-loving reputation that was established even before the Civil War. For example, recent statistics continue to indicate that the number of retail liquor licenses issued in Schuylkill County is well above the statewide average.[2] Numbers shed little light on whether citizens in the county drink more than the rest of the nation or the state. The legend, however, lives on. And in the spirit of reformers and prohibitionists of old, efforts continue to curb problems related to alcohol abuse in the coal region. One of the current areas of concern among county and state health officials is underage drinking. In Pennsylvania, it is illegal for anyone under 21 to drink alcohol. It is also illegal for anyone to buy or provide alcohol to anyone under 21. To raise awareness of the issue, Pottsville area high school students participated in the Pennsylvania Liquor Control Board's "Project Sticker Shock" at a local beer distributorship. Students affixed stickers reminding adults of Pennsylvania law regarding alcohol and minors to cases of beer, with the hometown brew probably among them. Yuengling's management is not threatened by the campaign or others like it. Those within the brewing and distilling industries are arguably the biggest advocates of responsible drinking. Well before recent campaigns by national brewers to curb alcohol abuse, a Yuengling advertisement from the 1950s read, "Drink the best, but not to excess."

Yuengling plans to continue to enter new territories in the years ahead, with the aim of covering the East Coast. Georgia and South Carolina are targeted next. As the company enters new markets, area residents' pride in the brewery grows. When they find Yuengling in Florida, Delaware, New York, Alabama and North Carolina, they are reminded of home and point out that the product from "America's Oldest Brewery" is *their* beer. And former area residents remember Yuengling's reputation. If they return to Pennsylvania from their homes in Texas, California, Missouri, Kentucky, or Tennessee, they'll often place a case or two of Yuengling in the trunk before heading back home. Or if they know someone is visiting the Keystone State, they'll ask them to bring some of the "Pride of Pottsville" back.

Family Business magazine, in a recent ranking, listed the Yuengling Brewery as 31st among the nation's oldest family companies. Higher on the list were mostly New England family farms and funeral homes that have passed from generation to generation. The key to longevity for the oldest surviving family firms rests in abiding by four major rules:

1. Stay small.
2. Don't go public.
3. Avoid big cities.
4. Keep it in the family.

There are, of course, exceptions to rules. Yuengling's ultimately unsuccessful ventures in the New York market in the late nineteenth century violated the first and third rules, but the brewing tradition survived. Is history now repeating itself? Possibly. Only time will tell if D. G. Yuengling and Son, Inc., has taken on more than it can handle in its recent expansion. While it only claims a small percentage of the beer market compared to national brewers, Yuengling can no longer be regarded as small, and the brand is sold in major urban markets. It regularly ranks among the nation's top ten beer producers. Yuengling is a significant employer as well. About 200 workers keep the beer flowing at Yuengling's three brewing operations. Many of the jobs are among the area's highest paying and include an attractive benefits package, thanks in part to a contract with the Teamsters union. This is good news for economically hard-hit Schuylkill County.

On an afternoon in August of 2002, at Pottsville's JFK pool complex, the city's Bicentennial Committee gathered to announce plans for festivities in 2006. This included the announcement that D. G. Yuengling & Son would donate its pump house site at 1000 Mahantongo Street to the city as a park for the celebration. What was known as "Yuengling's Private Mountain Reservoir" will be known as Yuengling Bicentennial Park and will be developed into the perfect location for festivities surrounding the 200th anniversary celebration, with a gazebo, benches, and gardens. Significantly, it was not the company president speaking on behalf of the brewery at this meeting. Two of his four daughters, Jennifer L. Yuengling and Sheryl L. Yuengling, discussed the contribution of the pump-house site, valued at

$145,000, with the local media. It was becoming clear that the sixth-generation is getting ready to enter the business.

When Dick Jr. considered the substantial debt entailed in the construction of a new facility and buying a brewery in Florida, he looked ahead and thought of the future role his four daughters would take in the company. If the daughters were not willing to get involved in the family business, the new brewery and the company's expansion was in doubt. The oldest daughter, Jennifer L. Yuengling, recalls an important family meeting:

> [M]y dad pulled myself and my three sisters aside and said: "You know, things are getting really busy here and I'm going to need some help and I'd really like it if you four would be interested in coming back. If you are interested, I have a place for you. If you're not, that's OK too." I think that's when my decision was made. He reached out and said, "I need some help."[3]

The daughters' involvement in the once male-dominated brewing industry is actually part of an industry trend. In contrast to the nineteenth century, when brewers gave little consideration to women taking an active role in the day-to-day operation of beer making, women are taking important positions in the brewing and marketing of beer. At the Yuengling Brewery, gender has not been an issue. As Jennifer explained, "I really haven't had a problem with it. My relationship with the men that work here has been fine. I mean, I respect them and in turn I think they've given me respect as well." Women brewers are really nothing new. Brewing has traditionally been a women's job. In the Middle Ages, ale was brewed by women, and the tradition continued. Today, examples of women involved in brewing on the East Coast abound. The best example at the Yuengling Brewery is Bronwyn Tulloch, who, prior to working at Yuengling, helped direct a four-million barrel plant for Coors. Voicing an opinion that his great-great grandfather evidently didn't share, Dick Yuengling Jr. once stated, "I haven't read anywhere that a woman can't run a brewery."

The daughters have already started to prove their father's point. They have followed the pattern that men in earlier generations followed. When they were old enough, their father encouraged them to work at the brewery, so they could learn about the brewing business from the bottom up. All four started working at the brewery when they were in school and took on a variety of duties, first learning about retail in the gift shop. Later, they moved on to giving tours of the brewery and learned more about its history at the same time. Their father did not impress the family legacy on his daughters, and he acquiesced as each pursued separate career paths and went off to expand their education after graduating from high school. The daughters reconsidered their role in the family business when the company expanded at record levels in the 1990s and their father contemplated major expansion projects.

In a fortunate turn, the Yuengling sisters have backgrounds suited for separate aspects of the brewing business. Jennifer earned a business degree from Bucknell University in 1993 and a master's degree in counseling psychology from Lehigh

Dick Yuengling reviews plans for the new Yuengling Brewery at Mill Creek with his daughters Jennifer, left, and Deborah. (Courtesy of the Pottsville [PA] *Republican & Herald*.)

University, Bethlehem, in 1996. When she decided to take up the family tradition, she underwent a rigorous training program at the brewery to learn about fermentation, storage, and packaging. She then went to Chicago to attend the Siebel Institute, earning a brewing technology certificate in 1997. Upon her return to Pottsville, she gained more experience alongside the master brewer of the company. Deborah Yuengling Ferhat is a certified public accountant, having earned an accounting degree from Moravian College, Bethlehem. In 1996, she began working full-time in the brewery's business office, handling payroll and accounting. The youngest daughter, Sheryl, received a bachelor's degree in consumer science from the University of Alabama and returned to Pottsville to work in shipping and distribution at the family brewery. Another daughter, Wendy Yuengling Baker, has credentials that could easily be applied to the marketing and advertising side of the brewing business. In 2004, after gaining experience as a production artist for an advertising firm in Maryland, Wendy joined her sisters as a full-time member of the brewery staff.

Jennifer and Deborah are also working mothers. They both have two children, raising speculation about a seventh generation to take up the tradition. But that's looking too far into the future. Formal succession plans are not even in place yet. Dick Jr. continues to be passionate about the brewery and undoubtedly has additional plans to strengthen the company. When he does retire, however, the brewery will not be given to his daughters. They will follow the pattern of earlier generations and buy it, and the women will face the same pressure to carry on the Yuengling tradition that their father felt. According to Deborah Yuengling, the brewery now has the capacity that it needs but faces the challenge of utilizing it properly. It will be important that demand for Yuengling beer remain high. She is optimistic. "People like the taste of Yuengling beer and the history behind the brewery," Deborah stated. "So as long as the customer continues to demand it, we'll continue to brew it."

Working at the Yuengling Brewery provides daily reminders of its historic past, and experience has already given the Yuengling sisters the inspiration to confidently face the future. As Jennifer has said, "There were struggles at times, and I'm seeing what they went through. When I was younger, I took it for granted. Now it's really something to be proud of."[4]

Those are words that David Gottlieb Yuengling — who started brewing beer in Pottsville, Pennsylvania, way back in 1829 — would have been delighted to hear.

Appendix A
Yuengling Chronology

1806   D. G. Yuengling born in Aldingen, Germany, on March 22.

1823   D. G. Yuengling's second wife, Elizabeth Betz, born.

1825   Schuylkill Canal completed linking Pottsville and Philadelphia.

1828   D. G. Yuengling emigrates from Württemberg, Germany.

1829   D. G. Yuengling settles in Pottsville and establishes Eagle Brewery at North Centre Street location.

1831   Fire destroys brewery. D. G. Yuengling rebuilds brewery at the Mahantongo Street location.

1841   D. G. Yuengling marries Elizabeth Betz on February 14.

1842   David G. Yuengling Jr. born.

1848   Frederick G. Yuengling born on January 26.

1855   Plane engineering opens rail access to northern Schuylkill County, shifting the center of coal production from southern to northern Schuylkill County.

1860   David Yuengling Jr. accepts position as foreman at John Frederick Betz's brewing operation in New York City.

1862   William, the youngest of the ten Yuengling children, born.

1866   David G. Yuengling Jr. manages construction of a five-story brick brewery in Richmond, Virginia.

1867   John Frederick Betz ventures into Philadelphia market by leasing William Gaul's Brewery at 401–421 Newmarket and Callowhill.

1871   David Yuengling Jr., while continuing to operate the Richmond brewery, turns his attention to the brewing market in New York City. He begins operation of an ale brewery at 5th Avenue and 128th Street.

1873   Company adopts official name of D. G. Yuengling and Son. Frederick Yuengling appointed as father's partner. Brewery produces 23,000 barrels. Frederick and Minna Dohrman of Brooklyn, New York, exchange wedding vows on April 3.

1875   David Yuengling Jr. purchases a second brewery in New York City, at 10th Avenue and 128th Street, for making lager. Known as Yuengling and Company-Manhattan Brewery, the facility produced a brand known as New York Lager Beer.

1876   Frank D. Yuengling, son of Frederick and Minna Yuengling, born on September 27.

1877   D. G. Yuengling passes away in September at the age of 70. Telephone connects brewery office with the plant, making Yuengling Pottsville's first continuous telephone subscriber.

1878   Yuengling family sells interest in the Richmond, Virginia, operations.

1881   Copper kettle with a capacity of 320 barrels installed in brewhouse. Stained-glass ceiling also installed in brewhouse.

1882   Augusta Roseberry, future wife of Frank Yuengling, born on September 29.

1893   On August 16, Charles Guetling and his dog, Prince, complete trip from Pottsville to the Columbian Exposition in Chicago (almost 900 miles) with a barrel of Yuengling brown stout in a wheelbarrow. The journey began on July 19.

1894   Elizabeth (Betz) Yuengling passes away at the age of 71 on January 9 at 501 Mahantongo Street.

1895   Brewery begins operation of bottling plant.

1898   William Yuengling passes away on August 7 at the age of 36.

1899   Frederick Yuengling passes away on January 2 at the age of 51.

1901   Brewery production reaches 65,000-barrel mark.

1906   Nicholas Dennebaum appointed brewmaster.

1907   Frank Yuengling marries Augusta Roseberry in April. New cereal cooker, with a capacity of 150 barrels, is installed at brewery.

1912   Minna Yuengling, wife of Frederick D. Yuengling, passes away on February 6 at her home at 606 Mahantongo Street.

1913   Frank Yuengling home at 1440 Mahantongo Street completed and family moves in. F. Dohrman Yuengling born on December 16.

1914   Frank D. Yuengling officially named president of D. G. Yuengling and Son, Inc. The Yuengling home adjacent to the brewery becomes the site of the present company office.

1915   Richard Yuengling Sr. born on August 16.

1918   Frank Yuengling invests $20,000 in the first Philadelphia Roseland Ball room at 12th and Chestnut St. Brewery annual production reaches the 100,000-barrel mark.

1919   Roseland Ballroom at 1658 Broadway at the corner of 51st Street opens on New Year's Eve, aided by $40,000 investment from Frank Yuengling.

1920   National Prohibition takes effect on January 17. Construction of Yuengling Ice Cream plant begins the same month.

1929   Brewery making "near bear" on its 100th anniversary.

1930   Joseph Bausback appointed brewmaster.

1933   National Prohibition ends. On April 7, Yuengling begins production and distribution of beer with 3.2 percent alcohol by weight.

1936   Brewery modernizes bottle shop to upgrade production potential.

1938   In the summer, Yuengling beer packaged in cans for the first time.

1942   N. Ray Norbert, future Yuengling brewmaster starts working at the brewery.

1943   Richard Yuengling Jr. born on March 10.

1949   Brewmaster Joseph Bausback passes away. William Sherk appointed to the post.

1954   Yuengling marks 125th anniversary.

1956   The Boston Beer Company, which had brewed beer since 1828, goes out of business. Yuengling is now "America's Oldest Brewery."

1960   Frank Yuengling resigns as brewery president.

1963   Frank Yuengling passes away on January 29.

1971   F. Dohrman Yuengling passes away.

1975   Augusta Yuengling, wife of Frank Yuengling, passes away on June 6.

1976   Brewery placed on the National Register of Historic Places and the Pennsylvania Inventory of Historic Places. The Mount Carbon Brewery, Yuengling's last competitor in the Pottsville area, closes. Yuengling purchases the Mount Carbon firm's recipe for its popular Bavarian brand.

1978   Heirs of the estate of the late Augusta Yuengling convey the Frank D. Yuengling Mansion at 1440 Mahantongo Street to the Schuylkill County Council for the Arts (SCCA), the SCCA to use the home as a cultural and education center.

1979   Brewery gains additional publicity as it marks its 150th anniversary and produces a colorful commemorative can to mark the occasion. The Frank D. Yuengling Mansion is entered on the National Register of Historic Places in Washington, D.C.

1980   Brewery's 100-year-old copper brewing kettle replaced by a stainless steel kettle.

1985   Brewery installs a 10,000-pound cereal cooker, replacing the cast-iron one used since 1907. Pottsville *Republican* announces that Dick Yuengling Jr. has purchased the brewery and becomes the fifth-generation owner. Yuengling Creamery closes, bringing an end to production of Yuengling Ice Cream, which had started during the Prohibition era.

1986   Production of Yuengling Light begins on June 25. Brewery also introduces Black and Tan.

1987   Yuengling Traditional Amber Lager introduced on November 1.

1990   David Casinelli hired as sales manager. The company also retains D'Addario Associates to design new labels.

1992   In November, the brewery launches expansion project at its Mahantongo Street plant in order to keep up with the increase in demand for the brand.

1996   Yuengling goes on line at www.yuengling.com. Yuengling "contract brews" Black and Tan at Stroh's Brewing Company in Allentown. Marjorie H. "Marge" (Hood) Yuengling, wife of Dick Yuengling Sr. and mother of Dick Yuengling Jr., passes away at her home.

1998   On May 8 Yuengling announces construction of a new $50-million brewery on a 16-acre site along Mill Creek Road near the Saint Clair Industrial Park; Yuengling wins "Molson Case" and retains legal rights to slogan "America's Oldest Brewery."

1999   Dick Yuengling Sr. passes away on March 27; brewmaster N. Ray Norbert retires in January; James P. Buehler named brewmaster in February; in April, Yuengling announces purchase of former Stroh Brewery in Tampa, Florida.

2001   Retired Yuengling brewmaster N. Raymond Norbert passes away in October.

2002   New brewery on Mill Creek Road begins production of Yuengling beer in February. Yuengling introduces Yuengling Lager Light early in the year, the brewery's first new product since 1987. Yuengling family donates the brewery's former pump-house prloperty on Mahantongo Street to the city to become Yuengling Bicentennial Park.

2003   Rail line to new brewery opens on Thursday, January 16.

2004   Brewery marks 175th anniversary.

Notes

Introduction

1. Kenneth Lyle Kann, "Working Class Culture and the Labor Movement in Nineteenth Century Chicago" (Ph.D. diss., University of California, Berkeley, 1977), 127.

2. Max Rudin, "Beer and America," *American Heritage* 53.3 (2002): 28–38.

Chapter 1

1. Information about D. G. Yuengling's death and funeral are drawn from reports in the Pottsville *Miners' Journal*, October 3, 1877.

2. According to church records from Aldingen, Germany, acquired by the company, D. G. Yuengling had at least one sister, Maria Christiana, who was born on August 12, 1812.

3. Document of the Historical Society of Schuylkill County.

4. Other notable American brewers who learned their craft in Württemberg include Charles Stegmaier of Wilkes-Barre, Pennsylvania, Christian Schmidt, Philadelphia, and Samuel Liebmann, founder of the Rheingold Breweries, New York.

5. A notable example of a brewer who learned as an apprentice in Germany was the founder of the Coors Brewing Company, Adolph Joseph Coors. Both of Coors' parents died when he was only 15, and before the young man immigrated to America he signed a three-year article of apprenticeship with the Henry Wenker Brewery. Insight into the skills and equipment needed to brew beer in the nineteenth century are provided in Part Two of *One Hundred Years of Brewing* (New York: Arno, 1974).

6. Document of D. G. Yuengling and Son, Inc.

7. Rich details about the Americanization of Pennsylvania Germans in the Early Republic are featured in Stephen Holt, *Foreigners in Their Own Land* (University Park: The Pennsylvania State University Press, 2002). German immigration to the American colonies, particularly Pennsylvania, is studied in great detail in Marianne S. Wokeck, *Trade In Strangers: The Beginnings of Mass Migration to North America* (University Park: The Pennsylvania State University Press, 1999).

8. Wokeck, 1.

9. *Ibid.*, 26.

10. Quotations from immigrant letters are found in Wokeck, 29.

11. Some sources place the year of D. G. Yuengling's journey to America at 1827. However, a copy of D. G. Yuengling's naturalization papers at the Historical Society of Schuylkill County, signed by the brewer himself, states that he immigrated in 1828. In addition, his sister, Maria Christiana, who, according to church records also immigrated to America, may have accompanied Yuengling on the journey. The year she immigrated is yet to be documented, however.

12. Chapter 4 of Wokeck, *Trade in Strangers*, "The Ordeal of Relocation," graphically describes the hazards faced by German immigrants during the transatlantic voyage to America. While Wokeck's study focuses on eighteenth century Germans, the chapter offers insight into conditions at sea faced by immigrants like D. G. Yuengling in 1828.

13. Details about the early history of brewing in the United States are drawn from a classic study originally published in 1903, *One Hundred Years of Brewing* (New York: Arno, 1974). Another very helpful study is Gregg Smith, *Beer in America: The Early Years 1587–1840* (Boulder, Colorado: Siris, 1998). Smith's study includes a concise overview of D. G. Yuengling's significance as a pioneer brewer in America, 170–171.

14. Taverns and hotels played such an important role in the developing nation that many

communities are named after them. The Schuylkill County village of Hometown, for example,
is named after the Home Sweet Home Hotel operated by a pair of Pennsylvania German farmers, William and John Kaup. See William Cissna,
"A Tradition Brewing," *Pennsylvania Heritage* XI
(Fall 1985), 26–31.

15. The importance of the tavern in America's early history is detailed in Peter Thompson,
*Rum Punch & Revolution: Taverngoing and Pub-
lic Life in Eighteenth-Century Philadelphia*
(Philadelphia: University of Pennsylvania Press,
1999). In addition to drinking, taverngoing provided the opportunity to meet friends, conduct
business, and gossip. During the Revolutionary
War, the taverns were the setting for political discussion and intrigue, earning the label "hotbeds
of sedition" by the British. Indeed, Thomas
Jefferson penned the Declaration of Independence in Philadelphia's Indian Queen Tavern.

16. The struggles of early American commer-
cial breweries are described in detail in Peter
Park, "The Supply Side of Drinking: Alcohol
Production and Consumption in the United
States before Prohibition," *Contemporary Drug
Problems* 12 (1985) 473–509.

17. An enjoyable study of historical trends in
alcohol consumption is Mark Lender and James
Martin, *Drinking in America: A History* (New
York: Free Press, 1982). A more focused study of
drinking habits in the United States prior to the
Civil War is W. J. Rorabaugh, *The Alcoholic Republic* (New York: Oxford University Press,
1979). Other very helpful studies are Eric Burns,
*The Spirits of America: A Social History of Alco-
hol* (Philadelphia: Temple University Press,
2004), and Susanna Barrows and Robin Room,
eds., *Drinking: Behavior and Belief in Modern
History* (Berkeley: University of California Press,
1991).

18. The quotations from Herancourt's diary
are taken from Stanley Baron, *Brewed in America:
A History of Beer and Ale in the United States*
(Boston: Little, Brown, 1962), 182.

19. Sources conflict regarding the length of
D. G. Yuengling's stay in Baltimore. Most sources
indicate that he wasted little time moving to
Pennsylvania. One biographical sketch of the
brewer, however, claims that he remained in Baltimore for two years. See Adolf Schalck and Hon.
D.C. Henning, eds., *History of Schuylkill County*
(Madison, Wisconsin: State Historical Association, 1907), 545.

20. Cissna, 27–28. Cissna's article provides a
fine overview of the early history of brewing in
Pennsylvania. A brewery was established in
Reading as early as 1763 by Henry Eckert. Brew

houses were established in Pittsburgh not long
after the Revolutionary War in 1782.

21. Rich Dochter and Rich Wagner, "Brewerytown, U.S.A.," *Pennsylvania Heritage* 17.3
(1991), 24–31. Another text with helpful information about the number of breweries is Frederick William Salem's groundbreaking book on
the beer industry, *Beer, Its History and Its Economic Value as a National Beverage* (Hartford,
Conn.: F. W. Salem and Co., 1880). The book
provides an appendix that lists the number of
brewers in the United States, a list developed
from the statistics of the United States Brewers'
Association. The association's study, apparently
conducted in response to a request by the federal
government, ranks Pennsylvania second in the
number of breweries — 317, not far behind New
York's 365. Cissna's "A Tradition Brewing" puts
the total number of breweries in Pennsylvania's
history at an astounding 865.

22. In 1810, only 129 breweries were operating in the United States, and the Lancaster region
could boast nine. For rich details about the brewing industry in Lancaster County, see Charles
Lynch and John Loose, "A History of Brewing in
Lancaster County, Legal and Otherwise," in *Journal of the Lancaster County Historical Society* 70.
1 (1966), 1–99.

23. The Lauer Brewery was founded by
George Lauer in Womelsdorf, Pennsylvania in
1823, then relocated to nearby Reading in 1826.
The Lauer name is very significant in American
brewing history. George Lauer's son, Frederick,
took over the brewery and, in 1844, became the
country's first major lager producer, earning him
the title, "father of the American brewing industry." Frederick Lauer was also the first president of the United States Brewers Association
starting in 1865. Prior to his death in 1883, at the
age of 74, Frederick Lauer passed ownership of
the Reading brewing operation to his sons, Frank
P. and George F. Lauer brewing operations would
later extend into Schuylkill County in the mid-
nineteenth century. For additional details about
Lauer, see Frederick William Salem, *Beer, Its History and Its Economic Value as a National Beverage*, 178–180. For insight into the operations of
the brewery in the 1870s, see Rich Wagner,
"Lauer Brewery, Circa 1874," *Zymurgy* (Summer
1983), 24–27. Another noteworthy business in
Reading during D. G. Yuengling's visit to the city
was a brewery managed by Georg Michel Brobst
from 1814 to 1832.

24. Historian and folklorist George Korson's
book, *Black Rock: Mining Folklore of the Pennsylvania Dutch* (Baltimore: Johns Hopkins University Press, 1960), is one of the very few studies

that offer insight in the role played by Germans in the development of the anthracite coal region. Korson describes the canal as, for the most part, "a Pennsylvania Dutch enterprise. It was dug through Pennsylvania Dutch farms. Pennsylvania Dutch dollars contributed to its financing. Pennsylvania Dutch brains and brawn participated in its construction" (112). For details about Korson's career, see Angus Gillespie, *Folklorist of the Coal Fields: George Korson's Life and Work* (University Park: The Pennsylvania State University Press, 1980).

25. One of the most detailed studies of the early history of the anthracite coal industry is Alfred Chandler, "Anthracite Coal and the Beginnings of the Industrial Revolution in the United States," *Business History Review* 46 (Summer 1972), 141–181. Important books on the subject include Edward J. Davies, *The Anthracite Aristocracy: Leadership and Social Change in the Hard Coal Regions of northeastern Pennsylvania, 1800–1930* (DeKalb, Ill.: Northern Illinois University Press, 1985); William Gudelunas and William Shade, *Before the Molly Maguires: The Emergence of the Ethno-Religious Factor in the Politics of the Lower Anthracite Region, 1844–1872* (New York: Arno, 1976); and Grace Palladino, *Another Civil War: Labor, Capital, and the State in the Anthracite Regions of Pennsylvania, 1840–68* (Urbana, Ill.: University of Illinois Press, 1990). One of the strongest general treatments of the entire history of the region is Donald Miller and William Sharpless, *The Kingdom of Coal: Work, Enterprise, and Ethnic Communities in the Mine Fields* (Philadelphia: University of Pennsylvania Press, 1985).

26. Korson, *Black Rock*, 110.

27. For more on the early uses of anthracite coal, see Frederick Binder, "Anthracite Enters the American Home," *Pennsylvania Magazine of History and Biography* 82.1 (1958), 82–99.

28. A booklet marking the brewery's 125th anniversary notes that coal from "nearby collieries" is used by the company. The publication features a photograph of "the most modern" automatic coal stoker and its caption states, "From the beginning Yuengling's has taken advantage of the economy and efficiency of hard Pennsylvania anthracite."

29. Details about the early development of Pottsville and its dependence on the Schuylkill Canal are drawn from Ronald Filippelli, "Pottsville: Boomtown," *Historical Review of Berks County* 35.4 (1970), 126ff. The subject is also addressed in J. Bennett Nolan, *The Schuylkill* (New Brunswick, New Jersey: Rutgers University Press, 1951.), a book that includes helpful details about significant communities along the river's banks.

30. Miller and Sharpless, 47.

31. Joseph Neal, quoted in Korson, *Black Rock*, 99.

32. Variations on the eagle image could be found in many places in the early nineteenth century. For additional details on the importance of the image of the eagle in American culture, see Philip Isaacson, *The American Eagle* (Boston: New York Graphic Society, 1975) and Clarence Pearson Hornung, *The American Eagle in Art and Design: 321 Examples* (New York: Dover, 1981).

33. Zerbey's *History, Pottsville and Schuylkill County, Penna.*, notes that the Eagle Hotel first featured a sign with the slogan, "Don't Give Up the Ship," the dying words of Captain James Lawrence during a naval battle in the War of 1812. Subsequent proprietors of the establishment replaced the sign with one that depicted an American eagle.

34. Dale P. Van Wieren, *American Breweries II* (West Point, Pa.: East Coast Breweriana Association, 1995). Subsequent references to opening and closing dates for breweries are drawn from this book.

35. Donna Baker, *Vintage Anheuser Busch: An Unofficial Collector's Guide* (Atglen, Pa.: Schiffer, 1995).

36. Testimony to the importance of the image can also be found inside the Mahantongo Street brewery, where a large, hand-carved walnut eagle can be found in the Rathskeller. The carving has had a home at the brewery since the 1890s and nested in the company office before moving to the taproom.

37. Turner, George Kibbe. "Beer and the City Liquor Problem," *McClure's* 33 (1909), 531.

38. *Miners' Journal*, May 22, 1847.

39. Anthony F.C. Wallace, *Saint Clair: A Nineteenth-Century Coal Town's Experience with a Disaster-Prone Industry* (New York: Knopf, 1987), 167. A brief discussion of drinking establishments in the anthracite region in the mid-nineteenth century is found in Wallace's study, 164–67. For additional information about the emergence of the saloon, see Madelon Powers, *Faces Along the Bar: Lore and Order in the Workingman's Saloon, 1870–1920* (Chicago: University of Chicago Press, 1998), 13–18.

40. Edith Yuengling speculates that some records could have been destroyed in fires. See Edith Yuengling, "The Story of the Yuengling Brewery," *Publications of the Historical Society of Schuylkill County* 9.1 (1989), 43.

41. *New York Times*, September 8, 1888.

42. Research yielded no details about the 1831 fire; the blaze is noted in company records and in Joseph H. Zerbey's *History, Pottsville and*

Schuylkill County, Penna. The latter states that the fire occurred (probably incorrectly) in 1832.

43. The planning and construction of the present Saint Patrick's Cathedral took place from about 1833 to 1839. According Pottsville historian Iona Grier, a 12-foot-wide vein of anthracite coal has been discovered under the church. The cornerstone of the cathedral was laid on September 24, 1837. The Yuengling Brewery and Saint Patrick's Church have traditionally had a good relationship.

44. Samuel Wiley, *Biographical and Portrait Cyclopedia of Schuylkill County, Pennsylvania.* (Philadelphia: Rush West and Co., 1893), 741.

45. Document of the D. G. Yuengling and Son Brewery, Pottsville, Pennsylvania. In the 1960s, a decreasing flow at the spring prompted the company to switch to filtered municipal water.

46. Pennsylvania beer historian Richard Wagner — no relation to Johann — worked for several years to see that an historical marker was placed on the site in Philadelphia. His efforts paid off with the dedication of a marker by the Pennsylvania Historical and Museum Commission in December 2001.

47. The temperature factor and the need for ice prompted many nineteenth-century brewers like Yuengling to follow a traditional Bavarian brewing season — from Michaelmas on September 29 to Saint George's Day on April 23. In the summer months, many brewers limited their production to ale or were forced to turn to another occupation until the brewing season returned. For more on caves and early efforts to keep beer cold, see Stanley Baron, *Brewed in America: A History of Beer and Ale in the United States* (Boston: Little, Brown and Company, 1962), 230–231. World famous beer critic Michael Jackson, writing about the birth of lager beer, once noted the Yuengling Brewery as a key example of the caves used in the nineteenth century beer-making process: "I have seen several natural cellars in many of today's Bavarian breweries, for example, at the Yuengling Brewery established in the Delaware Valley by a family from Baden-Württemberg."

48. At least two sources place Yuengling among the earlier producers of the popular type of beer. John Siebel and Anton Schwartz, in *A History of the Brewing Industry and Brewing Science* in *America* (Chicago: G. L. Peterson, 1933), note that "D. G. Yuengling began to brew lager beer at an early date." Joseph H. Zerbey's *History, Pottsville and Schuylkill County* (Pottsville: Pottsville Republican, 1933–35), also notes that D. G. Yuengling was "among the first to make lager beer." The name Yuengling can probably be placed ahead of other familiar American lager producers — Frederick Miller, Joseph Schlitz, Adolph Coors, Frederick Pabst, and Adolphus Busch — who mark the pages of brewing history well after the early 1840s.

49. William Warren Sweet, *The Story of Religion in America* (New York: Harper and Bros., 1950), 334.

50. Dives, Pomeroy and Stewart, *History of the County of Schuylkill: In Honor of the County's Centenary.*

51. Davies, 129–130.

52. For a discussion of German mining pioneers, see Korson, *Black Rock*, 102–8.

53. Investigations of the Molly Maguire episodes following the Civil War have led to some detailed studies of Irish immigration in the anthracite region. See, for example, Kevin Kenny, *Making Sense of the Molly Maguires* (New York: Oxford, 1998), 24–27. Other notable books on the Molly Maguires include Wayne Broehl, *The Molly Maguires* (Cambridge: Harvard University Press, 1964), Anthony Bimba, *The Molly Maguires.* (New York: International Publishers, 1932), and James Walter Coleman, *The Molly Maguire Riots: Industrial Conflict in the Pennsylvania Coal Region* (Richmond: Garrett and Massie, 1936).

54. For more on the relationship between the Molly Maguires and tavern-keeping, see Kenny's *Making Sense of the Molly Maguires*, 196.

55. Powers, 175–176.

56. Lender and Martin, 60. In addition to Lender and Martin's analysis of Irish drinking habits, a classic study of the subject is Richard Stivers' *Hair of the Dog: Irish Drinking and Its American Stereotype* (New York: Continuum, 2000).

57. Quoted in Earl C. Kaylor Jr., "The Prohibition Movement in Pennsylvania, 1865–1920" (dissertation, Pennsylvania State University, 1963).

58. Saint Patrick's Brewery is described in Edith Yuengling's "The Story of the Yuengling Brewery" and Joseph Henry Zerbey, ed., *History of Pottsville and Schuylkill County, Pennsylvania* (Pottsville, Pennsylvania: *Pottsville Republican*, 1933–1935), 187–88.

59. Preface, Dale P. Van Wieren, American Breweries II (West Point, PA: Eastern Coast Breweriana Association, 1995), vi.

60. Edith Yuengling, "The Story of the Yuengling Brewery," 51.

61. George Lauer and Orchard Brewery employees were among those who attended the funeral of D. G. Yuengling in 1877. The Orchard Brewery changed ownership several more times

before it eventually closed as the Mount Carbon Brewery in 1976.

62. This trend would continue as Pennsylvania attained the status of the nation's leading beer maker in the nineteenth century. There are plenty of examples of breweries in communities surrounding Pottsville. In Schuylkill Haven, Michael Kirkslager produced beer at Saint John and Union Street. Minersville's earliest brewery was established in 1868 at Sunbury and North Front streets and operated by Ernest C. Nickol. Unfortunately, it stayed in business less than a year. The F. J. Kear Company didn't have much more success, operating from 1879 to 1880. More enduring Minersville breweries included the Diamond Brewery, operated by Charles Zapf and Company. Charles Zapf, an immigrant from Baden, Germany, worked at several Pottsville breweries, including Yuengling, before starting his own brewery at Laurel near Third Street in Minersville. The brewery stayed in business for about 50 years. The porter brewed at the Diamond Brewery was particularly popular around the turn of the century. The Miners Brewing Co. (later Union Brewing Co.) produced beer from 1890 to 1907. In Tamaqua, Joseph Adams opened a brewery on Broad Street in 1860 that would change ownership several times until Prohibition. Other early Tamaqua brewers include an operation by Conrad Ifland on Rowe Street in 1868. Henry Kalb, Joseph Haefner, and George Sinzer also brewed beer in Tamaqua during the Gilded Age.

63. Powers, 53.

64. Photographs of beer deliveries to factories and workers enjoying beer during their breaks can be found in George Kibbe Turner's article in McClure's magazine, "Beer and the City Liquor Problem."

65. "Rushing the growler" is discussed in great detail in Madelon Power, *Faces Along the Bar: Lore and Order in the Workingman's Saloon, 1870–1920* (Chicago: University of Chicago Press, 1998), 120–27.

66. Miller and Sharpless, *The Kingdom of Coal*, 128. Chapter 4 of this text, "Working in the Black Hell," provides extensive details about the duties performed by anthracite coal miners and the dangers they faced.

67. Quoted in Wallace, *Saint Clair*, 164.

68. Martin, 214.

69. Quoted in Kaylor, 378–79.

70. Joanne Ciulla, *The Working Life: The Promise and Betrayal of Modern Work* (New York: Random, 2000), 198.

71. *Ibid.*

72. Miller and Sharpless, 133–34.

73. Raymond Calkins, *Substitutes for the Saloon* (Boston: Houghton Mifflin, 1901), 3.

74. Miller and Sharpless, 147.

75. Burns, 55.

76. Information about the prohibition movement in Pennsylvania is drawn largely from Earl Kaylor Jr.'s two-volume dissertation, "The Prohibition Movement in Pennsylvania" and Leland Bell's master's thesis, "The Anti-Saloon League in Pennsylvania." Both scholars completed their projects as graduate students at Pennsylvania State University. Another key source is Asa Earl Martin, "The Temperance Movement in Pennsylvania Prior to the Civil War," *Pennsylvania Magazine of History and Biography* 49 (1925), 195–230.

77. Martin, 218.

78. Christian Keller, "Germans in Civil War-Era Pennsylvania: Ethnic Identity and the Problem of Americanization" (unpublished dissertation, Pennsylvania State University, 2001), 34.

79. *Ibid.*, 47.

80. Zerbey, 753.

81. Quoted in Grace Palladino's *Another Civil War: Labor, Capital, and the State in the Anthracite Regions of Pennsylvania, 1840–68* (Urbana: University of Illinois Press, 1990), 75. In addition to Palladino's study, Bannan is discussed in detail in books and articles focused on the Molly Maguires. Very helpful discussions of the editor of the *Miners' Journal* include William Gudelunas Jr., "Nativism and the Demise of Schuylkill County Whiggery: Anti-Slavery or Anti-Catholicism," *Pennsylvania History* (1978), 225–36, and Kevin Kenny, "Nativism, Labor and Slavery: The Political Odyssey of Benjamin Bannan" *Pennsylvania Magazine of History and Biography* 118.4 (October 1994), 325–361.

82. *Miners' Journal*, June 25, 1853.

83. Martin, 208–209.

84. For highlights of the Yuengling Brewery's architectural significance, see Susan Hanna and Michael J. O'Malley's "America's Oldest Brewery: A Pictorial History," *Pennsylvania Heritage* (Spring 1980), 25–30.

85. Miller, 51.

86. *Miners' Journal*, September 28, 1877.

87. Davies, 139–140.

88. D. G. Yuengling was married twice. His first wife, Margaretha (Langhardt), was born in 1794 and passed away in 1839. Information about D. G. Yuengling's first wife is drawn from cemetery records at the Historical Society of Schuylkill County.

89. Adolph Schalck and Hon. D.C. Henning, eds. *History of Schuylkill County Pennsylvania …*

(Madison, Wisconsin: Wisconsin State Historical Association, 1907).

90. *Miners' Journal*, September 28, 1877.

Chapter 2

1. In his article "Beer and the City Liquor Problem," George Kibbe Turner describes the growth in beer consumption: "In 1860 the sale of beer in the United States was 3.22 gallons a head; in 1908 it was 21 gallons—two thirds of a barrel" (528).

2. Advances in refrigeration are so important in America's brewing history that an entire chapter is devoted to the subject in *One Hundred Years of Brewing*, 121–34.

3. Ronald Plavachan, *A History of Anheuser-Busch 1852–1933* (New York: Arno, 1976), 69.

4. An informative sketch of Frederick Yuengling is contained in Samuel Wiley's *Biographical and Portrait Cyclopedia of Schuylkill County, Pennsylvania* (Philadelphia: Rush West and Co., 1893), 740–743.

5. The Bergner and Engle Brewing Company reached third place in production among American breweries in 1877, aided considerably by a sizable German immigrant population in Philadelphia. For more on the Bergner and Engle Brewing Company, see Gregg Smith, *Beer in America: The Early Years: 1587–1840* (Boulder, Colorado: Siris, 1998), 166–170.

6. Roland Berthoff, "The Social Order of the Anthracite Region, 1825–1902," *Pennsylvania Magazine of History and Biography* 89 (1965), 261–91.

7. *Ibid.*

8. *Ibid.*

9. Geoffrey Wolff, *The Art of Burning Bridges: A Life of John O'Hara* (New York: Knopf, 2003), 6.

10. Finis Farr, *O'Hara: An Autobiography* (Boston: Little, Brown and Company, 1973), 28.

11. According to Frederick William Salem, *Beer, Its History and Its Economic Value as a National Beverage*, Yuengling sold 15,265 barrels in fiscal year 1877, 13,404 in fiscal year 1878, and 13,688 in fiscal year 1879.

12. [Munsell and Co.], *History of Schuylkill County* (New York: W.W. Munsell Co., 1881).

13. *Pottsville Republican*, January 2, 1899, 1.

14. The early twentieth century lithograph of the Yuengling Brewery was used on a Yuengling can in the 1970s to mark the 150th anniversary of the company. More recently, it was developed into a popular poster.

15. Pamela Walker Laird, *Advertising Progress: American Business and the Rise of Consumer Marketing* (Baltimore: Johns Hopkins University Press, 1998), 122.

16. Adolf Schalck and Hon. D.C. Henning, eds., *History of Schuylkill County Pennsylvania* (Madison, Wisconsin: State Historical Association, 1907), 547.

17. Edith Yuengling, "The History of the Yuengling Brewery" (1957), 45.

18. According to Edith Yuengling, "[a] personal relationship based on mutual respect developed between the owners of the Perot and Yuengling businesses" (41). For more on the Perot malting operations, see *One Hundred Years of Brewing* (170–173).

19. The first brewery to establish coast-to-coast shipping by rail was the William J. Lemp Western Brewery based in Saint Louis. The brewery owned approximately 500 refrigerated railroad cars and operated its own railroad, the Western Cable Railway Company.

20. Plavachan, 88–89.

21. In what is a sign of the importance of D. G. Yuengling and Son at this time, the brewery is the first business listed on the organization's documents. Other members of the brewers association were Chas. Rettig and Son, L. Schmidt, Chas. D. Kaier Co., Home Brewing Company, Columbia Brewing Company, Anthracite Brewing Company, Furhman and Schmidt, Engle and Smith, Chas. Zapf and Co., Lykens Brewing Company, Lauer Brewing Company, and P. Barbey and Son.

22. Munsell's *History of Schuylkill County* provides profiles of the chief burgesses in Mahanoy City, including a John Weber who was born in Bavaria in 1831 and came to America in 1853. After residing in Saint Clair for a time, Weber "came to Mahanoy City and for years has represented the brewery firm of D. G. Yuengling and Co. in this vicinity." Similarly, there may have been a Yuengling branch office in Hazleton. The *New York Times*, in a story datelined "Hazleton, Penn.," related that $1,000 dollars were missing from the brewery's accounts and implicated "Frank Fernsler, a bookkeeper for D. Yuengling and Sons, of this city." Of course, the reporter for the *Times* may have mistaken Hazleton for Pottsville.

23. In Ashland, Ed Zcheck established the first brewery in the area of Centre and 15th streets, but there is no documentation to indicate how long it operated. In 1897 the next brewery would be set up in the Ashland area, the Engel and Schmidt Brewing Company in Fountain Springs. The Ashland Brewing Company, located at the south end of the borough, was noted for its "Augustiner" brand. In Shenandoah, an ex-

ample of the "small" brewery is found. The J. Tunnah Brewery operated from 1878 to 1880. Sales figures from 1879 indicate that the brewery sold 34 barrels of beer that year. As evidence of the large influx of immigrants to Shenandoah in the 1890s, two breweries opened in the borough in that decade. The Columbia Brewing Company opened at 110–114 South Main Street in 1894. In November 1899, the noted Pennsylvania brewer Christian Schmidt opened the Home Brewing Company at 234 North Main St. The Home Brewing Company was incorporated on January 10, 1900. It produced a variety of light and dark beers, porter and ale. The beer was packaged under a separate bottling operation owned by Schmidt.

24. Samuel Wiley, 741–42.

25. Edith Yuengling, 48.

26. *Ibid.*, 47.

27. Bottled beer's arrival in the brewing industry is discussed in several sources, including Stanley Baron, *Brewed in America: A History of Beer and Ale in the United States* (Boston: Little, Brown, 1962), 242–243, and Will Anderson, *The Beer Book: An Illustrated Guide to American Breweriana* (Princeton: The Pyne Press, 1973), 13.

28. Document of D. G. Yuengling and Son, Inc.

29. Donald Miller and William Sharpless, 238.

30. Edith Yuengling, 44.

31. Will Anderson, *The Beer Book*, 52.

32. Mark Lender and James Martin, *Drinking in America: A History* (New York: Free Press, 1982), 96.

33. James Norris, *Advertising and the Transformation of American Society, 1865–1920* (New York: Greenwood, 1990), 123.

34. The advertisement is reproduced in Edith Yuengling's "The Story of the Yuengling Brewery." According to Edith Yuengling, the brewery's Pottsville Porter became particularly known for its medicinal purposes: "The Qualities of this particular product became widely known and many requests came for it from distant places, far beyond the normal range of distribution. These requests were often made on the advice of a doctor. I can remember hearing of such a request not too many years ago from somewhere in Texas" (44).

35. Gary Straub, *Collectible Beer Trays* (Atglen, Pennsylvania: Schiffer, 1995), 44.

36. "The Roaming Keg of Beer: From Pottsville to Chicago Via Wheelbarrow," *Publications of the Historical Society of Schuylkill County*, 7.2 (1952), 68–69. This anonymous essay is a detailed account of Guetling's journey. It labels the odyssey "Pottsville's greatest physical achievement of all time."

37. Edith Yuengling, 44. Sousa, who was well-known for patriotic marches like "The Washington Post" (1889) and "El Capitan" (1896), died in Reading, Pennsylvania, in 1932. His death at the age of 77 came following a rehearsal with Berks County's Ringgold Band, in which the last piece he conducted was his most famous work, "The Stars and Stripes Forever" (1896).

38. "The Brotherly Brewers," *Fortune* (April 1950), p. 1, quoted in Baron, 272.

39. Perry Duis, *The Saloon: Public Drinking in Chicago and Boston, 1880–1920* (Chicago: U of Illinois P, 1983), 25. Duis provides a helpful overview of the tied-house system, 21–43.

40. As brewery ownership became commonplace by the mid-1880s, the word saloon — rooted in the French word "salon"—caught the fancy of the American public and was used as reference to most drinking establishments. The use of words like tavern, inn, alehouse, and taproom seemed to be more in tune with the colonial period and became somewhat antiquated, at least temporarily.

41. Baron, 272–273.

42. One of the earliest and most respected brewing schools in America is the Siebel Institute of Technology in Chicago which was established in 1868, decades after D. G. Yuengling opened his business, by German immigrant Dr. John Ewald Siebel.

43. Information on the Betz brewing career are drawn from a variety of sources, including Will Anderson, *The Beer Book* (Princeton: The Pyne Press, 1973); John P. Arnold and Frank Penman, *History of the Brewing Industry and Brewing Science*; Dale P. Van Wieren, *American Breweries II* (West Point, Pennsylvania: Eastern Coast Brewiana Association, 1995); and *One Hundred Years of Brewing*, 388.

44. Some sources indicate that the Betz family settled in Schuylkill Haven; however, the Betz family may also have a connection to the Schuylkill County community of Saint Clair just north of Pottsville. In his study of the community, *Saint Clair*, Anthony Wallace notes that a John Betz was the landlord of a hotel in the community in the 1840s. Wallace notes that "Betz and his wife were German–born and so were all of their guests except a two-year-old child living their with her father, who, like the other residents, was a miner" (165).

45. John F. Betz and Son, Ltd., shut down during Prohibition but opened as John F. Betz and Son Inc. upon repeal. The company operated until 1939.

46. *One Hundred Years of Brewing*, 395.

47. Betzwood was eventually sold to pioneer silent film maker Siegmund Lubin in 1912. The film producer transformed the estate into a movie studio. For more on Betzwood and its significance as a film studio, see Joseph P. Eckhardt's *The King of the Movies: Film Pioneer Siegmund Lubin* (Madison: Fairleigh Dickinson University Press, 1997).

48. Clausen brewing operations in New York are described in *One Hundred Years of Brewing*, 260 and 379.

49. Edward Davies, *The Anthracite Aristocracy: Leadership and Social Change in the Hard Coal Regions of Northeastern Pennsylvania, 1800–1930* (DeKalb, Illinois: Northern Illinois University Press, 1985), 103.

50. Men in the Yuengling family from subsequent generations would also become members of the Good Intent Fire Company.

51. For additional details on the Yuengling operation in Richmond, Virginia, see Stephen Pytak, "The Other Yuengling," *Pottsville Republican* 18–19, December 1999, 1+.

52. Sales figures are drawn from an appendix in Frederick William Salem's *Beer, Its History and Its Economic Value as a National Beverage* (1880) (New York: Arno, 1972).

53. Maury Kline, *The Life and Legend of Jay Gould* (Baltimore: Johns Hopkins University Press, 1986), 223–24.

54. "A Model Brewery," *New York Times*, June 7, 1885, 4.

55. One of David Jr.'s brewmasters went on to establish his own successful business. Leonhard Michel worked for thirteen years at Yuengling's Manhattan brewery. In 1889, he went on to establish the India Wharf Brewery on Hamilton Avenue in Brooklyn. The large structure had a capacity of 150,000 barrels a year and one of the largest ice plants in that section of New York.

56. *New York Times*, June 7, 1885, 4.

57. *New York Times*, November 12, 1897, 5.

58. *New York Times*, October 14, 1900, 19.

59. *New York Times*, September 28, 1908, 1+.

60. *New York Times*, October 14, 1900, 19.

61. *New York Times*, September 28, 1908, 1+.

62. *Ibid.*

63. Document of D. G. Yuengling and Son, Inc.

64. Horton Pilsener Brewing Company, "A Century and a Half of Making the Best Beer Brewed in America." This document is part of the Yuengling archives. The reference to "Jans Yuengling" in the 1770s in Richmond, Virginia, is addressed in Pytak, "The Other Yuengling."

65. *Miners' Journal*, August 8, 1898.

66. *Ibid.*

67. *Ibid.*

68. *Ibid.*

69. *Ibid.*

70. *New York Times*, January 4, 1899, 7. In an intriguing twist, the *New York Times* originally reported that "Fred" Yuengling, David Jr.'s son, was the Yuengling family member who had passed away on January 2, 1899. Fred Yuengling's "death" was probably anticipated by reporters of the *Times* who had written about his allegedly reckless lifestyle. "The New York Times was in error yesterday in publishing an obituary notice of Frederick D. Yuengling. The man who died in Pottsville, Penn., on Monday was Frederick G. Yuengling, an uncle of Frederick D. Yuengling," stated the correction in the newspaper. Fred Yuengling went on to live for about another decade after reading his own obituary in the *Times*.

71. *Miners' Journal*, January 2, 1899.

72. *Miners' Journal*, January 6, 1899.

73. Edith Yuengling, 49.

74. Document of D. G. Yuengling and Son, Inc.

75. *Pottsville Republican*, January 2, 1899.

76. Edith Yuengling, 49.

77. Frank Julian Warne's account of conditions in the region, *The Slav Invasion and the Mine Workers: A Study in Immigration* (1904) (New York: Jerome Ozer, 1971), provides some insight into Schuylkill County's thriving beer trade. Its breweries produced 230,000 barrels of beer during the first eight months of 1903. Thirty breweries located outside the county also helped quench the thirst of county residents. Each of these companies reported selling about 20,000 barrels. The county issued 1,167 liquor licenses in that year (112–13).

78. Adolf Schalck and Hon. D.C. Henning, eds., *History of Schuylkill County Pennsylvania*, 547.

79. David Yuengling, *Letters to an Unknown Generation* (Hicksville, New York: Exposition Press, 1979), xi.

80. *Ibid.*

81. A helpful study of immigration trends in Pennsylvania is Sarah Florence Elliot's unpublished master's thesis, "Immigration to Pennsylvania, 1860–1920" (Pennsylvania State University, 1923).

82. Biographical information on Reverend Roberts is drawn from Paul McBride's "Peter Roberts and the YMCA Americanization Program, 1907-World War I," *Pennsylvania History* 44.2 (1977), 145–162. In 1907, Roberts left his post in Mahanoy City and accepted a position as

Special Secretary for Immigration Affairs for the YMCA.

83. See Roberts, *Anthracite Coal Communities* (1904) (New York: Arno, 1970); *The Anthracite Coal Industry* (New York: Macmillan, 1901; "The Saloon in the Anthracite Coal Fields," *Charities* XV (1906), 691–93, and "The Sclavs in Anthracite Coal Communities," *Charities* XII (1904), 215–22. According to the editors of *Charities* magazine, there are two spellings for the word "Slav" and Roberts preferred to include a "c" in all his writings. Unless Roberts is directly quoted, the shorter version of the word will be used here.

84. Roberts, *Anthracite Coal Communities*, vi.

85. Michael Barendse, "Slavic Immigrants in the Pennsylvania Anthracite Fields, 1880–1902: A Study of the Contrast Between Social Expectations and Immigrant Behavior" (Unpublished dissertation, Ball State University, 1976), 73.

86. Roberts, "The Sclavs in Anthracite Coal Communities," *Charities* XIII (1904), 215.

87. Roberts, *Anthracite Coal Communities*, 241.

88. *Ibid.*

89. *Ibid.*, 206.

90. *American Issue, Pennsylvania Edition,* December 23, 1910, quoted in Kaylor, 361.

91. Roberts, *Anthracite Coal Communities*, 232.

92. *Ibid.*, 237.

93. *Ibid.*, 232.

94. Roberts, "The Saloon in the Anthracite Coal Fields," 691.

95. Roberts, *Anthracite Coal Communities*, 226. Roberts also describes an occasion in Shenandoah when a brewer who violated alcohol laws was denied a license to operate; however, he was quick to add that brewers carried more political power than temperance reformers.

96. Frank Julian Warne, *The Slav Invasion and the Mine Workers: A Study in Immigration* (New York: Jerome Ozer, 1971), 114. At about the time Warne was covering the anthracite coal strike, he attended the University of Pennsylvania and earned a Ph.D. in Economics. Later, he became secretary of the New York State Immigration Commission and then took a position with the U.S. Bureau of the Census, where he served as a special expert on the foreign-born population.

97. *Ibid.*

98. Roberts, *Anthracite Coal Communities*, 224.

99. *Ibid.*, 225.

100. Estimates of the number of speakeasies in Lackawanna County are striking. The *Pennsylvania Edition*, in December, 1910, cited an article in the *Liquor Dealers Journal* which reported that over 500 speakeasies flourished unmolested in Lackawanna County. See Kaylor, "The Prohibition Movement in Pennsylvania," 360. The term "speakeasy" first became popular in the late 1880s. According to several sources, the term originated in Pennsylvania. Samuel Hudson, a Pittsburgh newspaper reporter, heard the word when he came across a shop where an English woman was selling liquor without a license. The woman warned her customers to "spake asy" when they came to purchase the hooch. Smuggler's dens in Ireland were also referred to as "spake aisies" over a hundred years earlier.

101. Roberts, *Anthracite Coal Communities*, 235.

102. *Ibid.*, 242.

103. "Pottsville Saloons of Days of Yore," *History of Pottsville and Schuylkill County, Pennsylvania*, Joseph Henry Zerbey, ed. (Pottsville: Pottsville Republican, 1933–1935), 187. This articles provides short descriptions of the major saloons in Pottsville's history and their proprietors. Drinking establishments with colorful names like the "Pig and Whistle," "The Varieties," "The Klondike," "The Bee Hive," "The Stars and Stripes," and "The Globe" are noted.

104. *Ibid.*, 191.

105. *Ibid.*, 188.

106. *Ibid.*, 189.

107. *Ibid.*, 190.

108. *Ibid.*, 191.

109. Perry Duis, *The Saloon: Public Drinking in Chicago and Boston, 1880–1920* (1983) (Chicago: University of Illinois Press, 1999), 181–82.

110. Roberts, *Anthracite Coal Communities*, 236.

111. In *Faces Along the Bar*, Madelon Powers describes binge drinking in the late nineteenth century as "a form of protest and rebellion, albeit inchoate and unfocused. Workers asserted their bid for independence and their right to spend their time and money as they pleased, without attempts by employers, wives, or others to restrain or reform them"(54).

112. Roberts, "The Sclavs in Anthracite Coal Communities," 219.

113. Roberts, *Anthracite Coal Communities*, 236.

114. Powers, *Faces Along the Bar: Lore and Order in the Workingman's Saloon, 1870–1920*. Chicago: U of Chicago P, 1998, 67.

115. Roberts, *Anthracite Coal Communities*, 235.

116. *Ibid.*, 294.

117. *Ibid.*, 292.

118. *Ibid.*, 291.

119. Roberts, "The Sclavs in Anthracite Coal Communities," 219.

120. Roberts, *Anthracite Coal Communities,* 242.

121. *Ibid.*, 242.

122. Roberts, "The Sclavs in Anthracite Coal Communities," 218–19.

123. Roberts, "The Saloon in the Anthracite Coal Fields," 692.

124. *New York Herald,* September 30, 1900, quoted in Victor Greene, *The Slavic Community on Strike: Immigrant Labor in Pennsylvania* (Notre Dame, Indiana: Notre Dame), 113–14.

125. Roberts, "The Sclavs in Anthracite Coal Communities," 219.

126. Miller and Sharpless, 203.

127. Roberts, "The Saloon in the Anthracite Coal Fields," 691.

128. Powers, 50.

129. Roberts, "The Saloon in the Anthracite Coal Fields," 691.

130. Roberts, *Anthracite Coal Communities,* 232.

131. Kaylor, 46.

132. Powers, 122.

133. Roberts, *Anthracite Coal Communities,* 205.

134. *Ibid.*, 350.

135. *Ibid.*

136. *Ibid.*, 207.

137. Lew Bryson, *Pennsylvania Breweries* (Mechanicsburg, Pennsylvania: Stackpole Books, 1998), *xiv.*

Chapter 3

1. The Prohibition era has been the subject of extensive analysis. Most scholars are highly critical of the "noble experiment." Significant general studies of the Prohibition era consulted for this chapter include Herbert Asbury, *The Great Illusion: An Informal History of Prohibition* (Garden City, New York: Doubleday, 1950); Jack S. Blocker Jr., ed., *Alcohol, Reform and Society: The Liquor Issue in Social Context* (Westport, Conn.: Greenwood, 1979); Donald Barr Chidsey, *On and Off the Wagon: A Sober Analysis of the Temperance Movement from the Pilgrims through Prohibition* (New York: Cowles Books, 1969); Norman H. Clark, *Deliver Us From Evil: An Interpretation of American Prohibition* (New York: W.W. Norton, 1976); Leigh Colvin, *Prohibition in the United States* (New York: George Doran, 1926); John Kobler, *Ardent Spirits: The Rise and Fall of Prohibition* (New York:

Putnam, 1973); Henry Lee, *How Dry We Were: Prohibition Revisited* (Englewood Cliffs, N. J.: Prentice-Hall, 1963); Charles Merz, *The Dry Decade* (Seattle: University of Washington Press, 1969); and Andrew Sinclair, *Prohibition: The Era of Excess* (Boston: Little, Brown and Company, 1962). A classic study of temperance history focusing on employers and efforts to control drinking among their workers is John Rumbarger, *Profits, Power, and Prohibition: Alcohol Reform and the Industrializing of America, 1800–1930* (Albany: State University of New York Press, 1989).

2. Dick Yuengling Jr., quoted in Carl M. C. Childs, "'Brewed and Aged the Old-Fashioned Way': Prohibition, Near Beer, and the Diversification of the D. G. Yuengling Brewery" (Unpublished master's thesis, James Madison University, 1992), 19. Childs' scholarly study is the most detailed analysis of the Yuengling Brewery during the Prohibition era.

3. The Pottsville Maroons' NFL championship was later revoked by the league for an alleged rule violation. Efforts to reverse the ruling by the league failed in 2003. For more on the Maroons, see William Gudelunas and Stephen Couch, "The Stolen Championship of the Pottsville Maroons: A Case Study in the Emergence of Modern Professional Football," *Journal of Sports History,* 9.1 (Spring 1982), 53–64. There were other third-class cities that had NFL teams during this period, including Green Bay, Wisconsin, and Canton, Ohio.

4. Benjamin Schwarz and Christina Schwarz, "John O'Hara's Protectorate," *Atlantic Monthly* (March 2000), 110. Pottsville's social scene during the Prohibition era and afterwards is the focus of an historical novel by Charles Strange, *Mountain Majesties* (Pottsville, Pennsylvania: J.F. Seiders Printers, 1996). Frank Yuengling and his family are depicted in the novel.

5. Charles Bassett, "The Fictional World of John O'Hara" (Ph.D. dissertation, University of Kansas, 1964), 16.

6. "Liederkrantz Nears Diamond Jubilee," *History of Pottsville and Schuylkill County, Pennsylvania.* Joseph Henry Zerbey, ed. (Pottsville: *Pottsville Republican,* 1933–1935), 162–65.

7. "Pottsville Saloons of Days of Yore," 187–195. Some eating and drinking establishments catered to German customers. The "Red Lion" at 10th and West Market Streets., for example, served "roast goat and sauer kraut lunches and other German dishes."

8. Benjamin Schwarz and Christina Schwarz, 109.

9. *Ibid.*, 110.

10. Chapter VI and Chapter VII of Earl Kaylor's dissertation, "The Prohibition Movement in Pennsylvania, 1865–1920" (Ph.D. diss., Pennsylvania State University, 1963), provide details about the rise of the Women's Christian Temperance Union (WCTU) in Pennsylvania.

11. *Ibid.*, 197–98.

12. Bell, 3–4.

13. Quoted in Kaylor, 217. Kaylor's study is the key source in this chapter regarding action by the state legislature on temperance and prohibition issues.

14. *Ibid.*, 206.

15. Roberts, *Anthracite Coal Communities*, 202.

16. *Ibid.*, 204.

17. *Ibid.*, 203. The Father Mathew Society was named after the famed leader of the temperance movement in Ireland in the nineteenth century, Father Theobald Mathew (1790–1856). Despite the reputation for a fondness for the bottle among the Irish, Father Mathew's campaign made Ireland a temperance stronghold in the 1830s and 1840s. In the late nineteenth century, America's Catholic clergy revived Father Mathew's crusade. The Father Mathew Society joined hands with the WCTU, as well as the Catholic Total Abstinence Union, in its efforts to encourage temperance.

18. *Ibid.*, 204.

19. *Ibid.*

20. Roberts, "The Saloon in the Anthracite Coal Fields," 691.

21. *Ibid.*, 692–93.

22. Leigh Colvin, *Prohibition in the United States* (New York: George Doran, 1926), 204–05.

23. Quoted in Kaylor, 275.

24. Quoted in Kaylor, 276.

25. Kaylor, 278.

26. Roberts, *Anthracite Coal Communities*, 238.

27. Eric Burns, *The Spirits of America: A Social History of Alcohol* (Philadelphia: Temple University Press, 2004), 169.

28. Herman Ronnenberg, *The Politics of Assimilation: The Effects of Prohibition on the German-Americans* (New York: Carlton Press, 1975), 74. Ronnenberg provides the most extensive study of German-Americans in the Prohibition era.

29. Burns, 167.

30. Stanley Baron, *Brewed in America: A History of Beer and Ale in the United States* (Boston: Little, Brown, 1962), 313.

31. Kaylor, 379.

32. *Ibid.*

33. Childs, 23.

34. *Pottsville Republican*, November 1, 1919.

35. *Pottsville Republican*, November 4, 1919.

36. Lew Bryson, *Pennsylvania Breweries* (Mechanicsburg, Pennsylvania: Stackpole Books, 1998), 20.

37. Quoted. in Childs, 33.

38. Will Anderson, *Beer, USA* (Dobbs Ferry, New York: Morgan and Morgan, 1986), 38.

39. Childs, 31.

40. Dale P. Van Wieren, *American Breweries II* (West Point, Pennsylvania: Eastern Coast Breweriana Association, 1995), 350.

41. Many brewers took up the challenge of prohibition with the same integrity. Beer-baron Adolph Coors, according to a family legend, even gave up beer and all other forms of alcohol when Colorado went dry on New Year's Eve, 1915: "Family lore says he never tasted a glass of beer after watching his barrels of foamy brew rejoin Clear Creek on New Year's Eve, 1915. To do so would have broken the law." See Dan Baum, *Citizen Coors: An American Dynasty* (New York: HarperCollins, 2000), 13. Also see Herman Ronnenberg's *The Politics of Assimilation: The Effect of Prohibition on German Americans* (Carlton Press, 1975), 84–85. The conscious efforts by Coors and Frank Yuengling to stay within the law supports Ronnenberg's contention that illegal trafficking in beer "had little ethnic German flavor to it."

42. Harold Wiegand, "Prohibition, A date in history better forgotten," *Philadelphia Inquirer*, November 28, 1983, 11a. For more on the political career of Boies Penrose and his campaign against advocates of temperance and prohibition, see Walter Davenport, *Power and Glory: The Life of Boies Penrose* (1931) (Reprint: New York: AMS, 1969) and Robert Bowden, *Boies Penrose: Symbol of an Era* (1937) (Reprint: Freeport, New York: Books for Libraries, 1971).

43. Herbert Asbury, *The Great Illusion: An Informal History of Prohibition* (Garden City, New York: Doubleday, 1950), 137.

44. Donald Chidsay, *On and Off the Wagon: A Sober Analysis of the Temperance Movement from the Pilgrims through Prohibition* (New York: Cowles, 1969), 85.

45. Baron, 315.

46. Leland Bell, *The Anti-Saloon League in Pennsylvania* (Master's thesis, Pennsylvania State University, 1963), 112.

47. Ibid, 105.

48. *Harrisburg Patriot*, January 28, 1920.

49. Ronnenberg, 87.

50. Burns, 192.

51. Charles Merz, *The Dry Decade* (1930) (Reprint: Seattle: University of Washington Press, 1969), 171.

52. Ronnenberg, 85.

53. Robert Janosov, *Cold and Gold in the Poconos: A History of the Stegmaier Brewing Company, Wilkes-Barre, Pennsylvania* (Nanticoke, Pennsylvania: Tres Canis Publishing, 1997), 35.

54. Quoted in Childs, 40.

55. Patrick Canfield, *Growing Up With Bootleggers, Gamblers, and Pigeons* (Wilmington, Delaware: Interlude Enterprises, 1992), 10.

56. John O'Hara, quoted in Frank MacShane's *The Life of John O'Hara* (New York: Dutton, 1980), 10. Biographies of O'Hara usually devote considerable space to life on Mahantongo Street in the opening decades of the twentieth century. In addition to MacShane's book, other biographical treatments of O'Hara include Finis Farr, *John O'Hara: A Biography* (Boston: Little, Brown, and Company, 1973); Geoffrey Wolff, *The Art of Burning Bridges: A Life of John O'Hara* (New York: Knopf, 2003); and Charles Bassett, *The Fictional World of John O'Hara* (Ph.D. dissertation, University of Kansas, 1964).

57. O'Hara joined a long list of American writers who struggled with alcohol and other addictions. Literary tipplers include Ernest Hemingway, F. Scott Fitzgerald, Jack London, and Thomas Wolfe. A powerful study of the ravages of drink and twentieth-century American writers, including a brief discussion of O'Hara, is Donald Newlove, *Those Drinking Days: Myself and Other Writers* (New York: Horizon, 1981).

58. Newlove, 131.

59. Farr, 65.

60. Bassett, 20.

61. *Ibid.*, 65.

62. For details on the Shenandoah incident, see Chapter One of Francis Norton Gallagher's tales about the community, *The Only Western Town in the East* (Ardmore, Pennsylvania: Dorrance, 1980.)

63. Ronnenberg, 85.

64. *Pottsville Journal*, July 15, 1919.

65. *Pottsville Journal*, July 19, 1919.

66. Childs, 55.

67. For background on the development of the Philadelphia and New York Roseland ballrooms, see Richard Severo, "Roseland Recalls Old Times Tonight," New York *Times*, July 1, 1974, 42. The business venture is also discussed in Childs, 44–48.

68. David G. Yuengling, *Letters to an Unknown Generation* (Hicksville, New York: Exposition Press, 1979), xxi. Frank Yuengling apparently took some time to take a break from business when he was in Philadelphia. The family did have a yacht, which was docked at the

port in the city. The name of the ship, appropriately, was "Mahantongo."

69. Burns, 223.

70. William Wilhelm, "Letter to the Editor," New York *Times*, May 22, 1925.

71. *Ibid.*

72. *Pottsville Republican*, April 6, 1933.

73. *Pottsville Republican*, April 6, 1933.

74. *Pottsville Republican*, April 7, 1933.

75. *Pottsville Republican*, April 7, 1933.

76. George Wilson, "State Liquor Laws Go Back to the '30s," *Philadelphia Inquirer*, September 23, 1983, 19–A.

77. Ronnenberg, 102.

78. First-person accounts from those who experienced the decline of the anthracite coal region are featured in Thomas Dublin, *When the Mines Closed: Stories of Struggles in Hard Times* (Ithaca, New York: Cornell University Press, 1998).

79. Miller and Sharpless, 313.

Chapter 4

1. The F. & M. Schaefer Brewing Company and the development of its brewery in the Lehigh Valley is described in Will Anderson, *The Breweries of Brooklyn: An Informal History of a Great Industry in a Great City* (New York: Will Anderson, 1976).

2. Stanley Baron, *Brewed in America: A History of Beer and Ale in the United States* (Boston: Little, Brown and Company, 1962), 343–44.

3. Ibid, 338. In Wilkes-Barre, for example, Stegmaier's management invested $250,000 in 1937 in an attempt to double its bottling capacity.

4. Carl M. C. Childs, "'Brewed and Aged the Old Fashioned Way': Prohibition, Near Beer, and the Diversification of the D. G. Yuengling Brewery" (Master's thesis, James Madison University, 1992), 71.

5. John Farro, "Letter to the Editor," *Pottsville Republican*, October 16, 2003, 5.

6. Dan Baum, *Citizen Coors: An American Dynasty* (New York: HarperCollins, 2000), 24.

7. Thomas Dublin, *When the Mines Closed: Stories of Struggles in Hard Times* (Ithaca, New York: Cornell University Press), 8.

8. Ibid, 10.

9. Robert Janosov, *Cold and Gold in the Poconos: A History of the Stegmaier Brewing Company, Wilkes-Barre, Pennsylvania* (Nanticoke, Pennsylvania: Tres Canis Publishing, 1997), 39.

10. Walson then decided to drop his appliance business and concentrate on the cable industry, naming it Service Electric Cable TV, Inc.

The company would become a multi-million dollar corporation serving communities in Pennsylvania and New Jersey. Information on the early history of television in Schuylkill County is drawn from the documents of Service Electric Cable Television.

11. For more on Stegmaier's advertising strategies during this period, see Janosov, 39.

12. Dick Yuengling Jr., interview by author, Pottsville, Pennsylvania, February 2002.

13. The vacated Stegmaier Brewery was purchased by the city of Wilkes-Barre for back taxes in 1978. The brewery is highly admired for its architecture. For details on efforts to preserve the history of the Stegmaier Brewery, including preservation of the plant, see the epilogue of Janosov's *Cold and Gold from the Poconos*, 57–60.

14. Will Anderson, *Beer USA*, (Dobbs Ferry, New York: Morgan and Morgan, 1986), 156.

15. As part of the agreement, the Yuengling Brewery reportedly supplied kegs of beer to the production crew as they were shooting the film in Eckley, a small mining village near Hazleton that served as the backdrop for the movie. Whether the Yuengling name appears in the background of *The Molly Maguires'* many bar scenes is open to debate. Dick Yuengling Sr. once insisted that the brewery name and logo were in the movie but added that they were very difficult to spot. His son, however, has said that it was ultimately the name and logo of the Stegmaier brand that made it into the film.

16. Anderson, *Beer, USA*, 161.

17. Christopher Lawton, "Quirky Laws Give Yuengling Edge at Home," *Wall Street Journal*, March 23, 2004, B1.

18. The earliest description of Dick Yuengling Jr. is featured in a letter written by his uncle, David, in 1944: "Richard Yuengling Jr. will have his first birthday the day after tomorrow .... The youngster is growing very big, and for a boy one year old he is quite large. He has begun to walk and does so quite well. He is a good-humored little fellow; very fat and with an unusual amount of curley [sic] hair."

19. Founded as a "family boarding school" in 1851, the Hill School in Pottstown has been recognized as one of the best secondary schools in the United States. The school accepted only young men for most of its history until becoming coeducational in 1998.

20. John Corr, "Born to Brew," *Philadelphia Inquirer*, January 14, 1993, D3.

21. *Ibid.*

22. David G. Yuengling, *Letters to an Unknown Generation* (Hicksville, New York: Exposition Press, 1979), 19–20. David G. Yuengling

was highly educated. He attended Georgetown University's School of Foreign Service and used his training in the Pacific theatre during World War II. He then earned a Master of Arts degree in history from the University of Pennsylvania and taught courses at the Admiral Billiard Academy in New London, Connecticut. A prolific writer, his extensive body of letters is on reserve in the archives of the Historical Society of Pennsylvania. *Letters to an Unknown Generation* provides a small sample of his correspondence.

23. Michael Capuzzo, "Light-Headed in Pottsville," *Philadelphia Inquirer*, July 28, 1986, 10E.

24. Philip Van Munching, *Beer Blast: The Inside Story of the Brewing Industry's Bizarre Battle for Your Money* (New York: Random House, 1997), 30.

25. Ibid, 32.

26. Susan Hanna and Michael O'Malley, "America's Oldest Brewery: A Pictorial History," *Pennsylvania Heritage* (1980), 28.

27. Significantly, an entry on the Boston Beer Company in the classic study *One Hundred Years of Brewing* is found immediately before the entry describing the Yuengling Brewery. Part of the brewery's mission was to substitute "malt liquors for distilled spirits as a popular drink. See *One Hundred Years of Brewing* (1903). (New York: Arno, 1974), 197.

28. Lew Bryson, *Pennsylvania Breweries* (Mechanicsburg, Pennsylvania: Stackpole Books, 1998), 21.

Chapter 5

1. Dave Carroll, "5th-generation Yuengling Runs Brewery," *Pottsville Republican*, July 24, 1985, 17.

2. Quotations from Dick Yuengling are taken from several personal and phone interviews by the author. Information and comments are also drawn from several profiles of the brewery president that have appeared in a wide variety of local, state, and national publications. Articles that provide insight into his management style include Peter Binzen, "A small specialty brew with strong brand loyalty," *The Philadelphia Inquirer*, November 24, 2003, D-1; John Corr, "Born to Brew," *The Philadelphia Inquirer*, January 14, 1993, D6ff; Marj Charlier, "Yuengling's Success Defies Convention," *Wall Street Journal*, August 26, 1993, B1; Peter Reid, "Forever Yuengling" *Modern Brewery Age*, January 18, 1999; Julie Androshick, "Mr. Go-it-Alone," *Forbes*, December 30, 1996; and Len Barcousky, "All the right brews," *Pittsburgh Post-Gazette*, July 18, 1999, C-1. For details about Yuengling's

life outside the brewery and his relationship to the Pottsville community, see Joshua Sophy, "Dick Yuengling, Schuylkill life a fit," *Pottsville Republican*, May 25, 2002, 1+.

3. Will Anderson, *Beer, USA* (Dobbs Ferry, New York: Morgan and Morgan, 1986), 110.

4. The commonwealth's beer renaissance is covered extensively in Lew Bryson, *Pennsylvania Breweries* (Mechanicsburg, Pa.: Stackpole Books, 1998). The book, which includes a chapter on the Yuengling Brewery, offers insightful overviews of dozens of micros and provides helpful information about brewery tours. Bryson also utilizes his expertise to offer picks about the best beers each brewery offers. Bryson's pick for the Yuengling Brewery is "a do-it-yourself black and tan mixed from Porter and Lord Chesterfield Ale."

5. Philip Van Munching, *Beer Blast: The Inside Story of the Brewing Industry's Bizarre Battles for Your Money* (New York: Random House, 1997), 149. Van Munching's book provides considerable insight into the marketing of beer during the "microboom" and is the key source of information on the Samuel Adams brand.

6. *Ibid.*, 153.

7. *Ibid.*, 203.

8. *Ibid.*, 153. In his discussion of Koch's marketing strategy and his battle against imported brands, Van Munching points out that "the micros were able to trade on home-grown appeal …. Was it any surprise that some folks would rally around Koch's admonitions to throw out the foreigners?"

9. Harold Bauld, "Good for What Ales You," *Boston* magazine, June 1986. Quoted in Van Munching, 162.

10. Michael Capuzzo, "Light-Headed in Pottsville," *Philadelphia Inquirer*, July 28, 1986, 10Eff.

11. Van Munching, 130.

12. Van Munching, 152.

13. Charlier, B1.

14. Van Munching, 151.

15. Charlier, B1.

16. Tom Gogola, "Bar Necessity: Is Long-lost Yuengling Beer — once a Local Cult Favorite — returning to New York?" *New York*, 32.23, 14.

17. Lew Bryson, *Pennsylvania Breweries*, 22. The Yuengling Brewery tour is also the focus of a chapter in Therese Boyd, *The Best Places You've Never Seen: Pennsylvania's Small Museums-A Traveler's Guide* (University Park: The Pennsylvania State University Press, 2003), 15–19.

18. Traditional Amber Lager played such a significant role in the Yuengling Brewery's growth in the 1990s that the *Pottsville Republican*

published several articles about the brand on August 16, 1997, to mark the tenth anniversary of its return to the market.

19. Yuengling's expansion under the fifth-generation president has been covered in dozens of articles in the *Pottsville Republican*, and these newspaper reports have been helpful in the development of this chapter. Reporters writing about the brewery during this period include Dave Carroll, Patricia Hippler, Steve Pytak, Kimm Montone, Kathleen Roberts, Dan Roman, Michael Sanchez, Joshua Sophy, and James Rowbottom.

20. Reid, "Forever Yuengling," 10.

21. Andoschick, "Mr. Go-it-alone."

22. These organizations, which are considered "neoprohibitionist" in some circles, include Mothers Against Drunk Driving (MADD) and Students Against Drunk Driving (SADD).

23. For insight into contract brewing, particularly the Samuel Adams brand, see Van Munching, 159–164.

24. The Stroh Brewery of Detroit acquired Schaefer's Allentown facility in 1981. In 1999, Stroh sold the brewery to Pabst, which closed it in September of 2001. A few months later, the Stroh Brewery was purchased by Guinness North American for $29.8 million, for the production of its popular, vodka-based drink, Smirnoff Ice.

25. Patricia Hippler, "Yuengling Announces Plans for New $50 Million Brewery," *Pottsville Republican*, May 8, 1998, 1ff.

26. Michael Sanchez, "Familiar Yuengling eagle already visible at new site," *Pottsville Republican*, May 19, 1999, 1ff.

27. Some brewers aggressively promote their brands on college campuses. Anheuser-Busch, for example, has been known to send "Bud Girls" to campus parties to promote the brand name.

28. David Kinney (Associated Press), "Oldest U.S. Brewery, Enjoying New Prosperity, Spurns Big Rivals' Offers," *Los Angeles Times*, January 14, 1997, 14.

29. Information on the Molson case is taken from a document from the U.S. Department of Commerce Patent and Trademark Office, Trademark Trial and Appeal Board, Molson Breweries v. D. G. Yuengling & Son, Inc.

30. "Yuengling is still 'Oldest,'" *Pottsville Republican*, November 13, 1998, 4.

31. James Rowbottom, "Yuengling workers toast retiring brewmaster," *Pottsville Republican*, January 23, 1999, 1ff. The Yuengling management and staff were saddened in October 2001 when Brewmaster Norbert died at Abington Memorial Hospital, Abington, Pennsylvania.

32. "Richard L. Yuengling Sr." Obituary,

Pottsville Republican, March 27, 1999, 2. A few years prior to Dick Sr.'s death, the Yuengling family and the Pottsville community also mourned the passing of his wife, Marjorie H. "Marge" Yuengling, in 1996 at the age of 75.

33. Christopher Lawton, "Quirky Laws Give Yuengling Edge at Home," *Wall Street Journal*, March 23, 2004, B1.

Epilogue

1. For more on the current state of the coal industry in Schuylkill County, see Ford Turner, "For Hard Coal, Hard Times," Harrisburg *Patriot-News*, March 28, 2004, 1ff.

2. Rory Schuler, "A History Steeped in Booze," *Pottsville Free Press*, November 25, 2003, 1ff.

3. Stephen Pytak, "NPR radio spotlights Yuengling," *Pottsville Republican*, June 1, 2000, 1ff.

4. Patricia Hippler, "Daughters' commitment led to investment." *Pottsville Republican*, May 9, 1998, 1ff.

Selected Bibliography

Anderson, Sonja, and Will Anderson. *Beers, Breweries & Breweriana: An Informal Sketch of United States Beer Packaging and Advertising*. Carmel, N. Y.: Sonja and Will Anderson, 1969.

Anderson, Will. *The Beer Book: An Illustrated Guide to American Breweriana*. Princeton: The Pyne Press, 1973.

____. *The Beer Poster Book*. Harrison, Pa.: Cameron House, 1977.

____. *Beer, USA*. Dobbs Ferry, New York: Morgan and Morgan, 1986.

____. *The Breweries of Brooklyn: An Informal History of a Great Industry in a Great City*. New York: Will Anderson, 1976.

Androshick, Julie. "Mr. Go-it-alone." *Forbes*, 30 December 1996: 129–30.

Arnold, John, and Frank Penman. *History of the Brewing Industry and Brewing Science in America*. Chicago: United States Brewers Association, 1933.

Asbury, Herbert. *The Great Illusion: An Informal History of Prohibition*. Garden City, New York: Doubleday, 1950.

Baker, Donna. *Vintage Anheuser-Busch: An Unofficial Collectors Guide*. Atglen, Pa.: Schiffer Publishing, 1999.

Bamforth, Charles. *Beer: Tap Into the Art and Science of Brewing*. 2nd ed. New York: Oxford University Press, 2003.

Banham, Russ. *Coors: A Rocky Mountain Legend*. Lyme, Conn.: Greenwich Publishing Group, Inc., 1998.

Barcousky, Len. "All the right brews." *Pittsburgh Post-Gazette*, 18 July 1999: C-1.

____. "A tour today is a trip through the past." *Pittsburgh Post-Gazette*, 18 July 1999: C-1.

Barendse, Michael. "Slavic Immigrants in the Pennsylvania Anthracite Fields, 1880–1902: A Study of the Contrast Between Social Expectations and Immigrant Behavior." Ph.D. thesis. Muncie, Ind.: Ball State University, 1976.

Baron, Stanley. *Brewed in America: A History of Beer and Ale in the United States*. Boston: Little, Brown and Company, 1962.

Barrows, Susanna, and Robin Room. *Drinking: Behavior and Belief in Modern History*. Berkeley: University of California Press, 1991.

Bassett, Charles. "The Fictional World of John O'Hara." Ph.D. thesis: Lawrence: University of Kansas, 1964.

Baum, Dan. *Citizen Coors: An American Dynasty*. New York: HarperCollins, 2000.

Baumgartner, Nancy. "For small brewer, a time for cheers." *Philadelphia Inquirer*, 27 February 1995: 1Eff.

Bell, Leland. "The Anti-Saloon League in Pennsylvania." Master's thesis: University Park: Pennsylvania State University, 1963.

Berthoff, Roland. "The Social Order of the Anthracite Region, 1825–1902." *Pennsylvania Magazine of History and Biography* 89 (1965): 261–91.

Bimba, Anthony. *The Molly Maguires* (1932). New York: International Publishers, 1950.

Binder, Frederick. "Anthracite Enters the American Home." *Pennsylvania Magazine of History and Biography* 82.1 (1958): 82–99.

Binzen, Peter. "A small specialty brew with

strong brand loyalty." *Philadelphia Inquirer*, 24 November 2003: D-1.

Blocker, Jack, ed. *Alcohol, Reform and Society: The Liquor Issue in Social Context.* Westport, Conn.: Greenwood, 1979.

Bowden, Robert. *Boies Penrose: Symbol of an Era.* 1937. Freeport, NY: Books for Libraries, 1971.

Boyd, Therese. *The Best Places You've Never Seen: Pennsylvania's Small Museums: A Traveler's Guide.* State College, Pa.: Penn State Press, 2003.

Broehl, Wayne. *The Molly Maguires.* Cambridge: Harvard University Press, 1964.

Brown, Mary Louise. "The Stork and Anheuser-Busch Imagery, 1913–1933." *Gateway Heritage* 9.2 (1988): 18–23.

Browning, Darrell. "A family tradition." *Small Business News* (Philadelphia), July 1997.

Bryson, Lew. *Pennsylvania Breweries.* Mechanicsburg, Pa.: Stackpole Books, 1998.

Bull, Donald. *Beer Advertising: Knives, Letter Openers, Ice Picks, Cigar Cutters, and More.* Atglen, Pa.: Schiffer Publishing, 2000.

Burns, Eric. *The Spirits of America: A Social History of Alcohol.* Philadelphia: Temple University Press, 2004.

Calkins, Raymond. *Substitutes for the Saloon.* Boston: Houghton Mifflin, 1901.

Canfield, Patrick M. *Growing Up With Bootleggers, Gamblers, and Pigeons.* Wilmington, Del.: Interlude Enterprises, 1992.

Capuzzo, Michael. "Light-Headed in Pottsville." *Philadelphia Inquirer*, 28 July 1986: 10Eff.

Carroll, Dave. "5th-generation Yuengling Runs Brewery." *Pottsville Republican*, 24 July 1985: 17.

Chalfant, Harry Malcolm. *Father Penn and John Barleycorn.* Harrisburg, Pa.: The Evangelical Press, 1920.

Charlier, Marj. "Yuengling's Success Defies Convention." *Wall Street Journal*, 26 August 1993: B1.

Chidsey, Donald Barr. *On and Off the Wagon: A Sober Analysis of the Temperance Movement from the Pilgrims Through Prohibition.* New York: Cowles, 1969.

Childs, Carl M. C. "'Brewed and Aged the Old-Fashioned Way': Prohibition, Near Beer, and the Diversification of the D. G. Yuengling Brewery." Master's thesis: Harrisonburg, Va.: James Madison University, 1992.

Cissna, William. "A Tradition Brewing." *Pennsylvania Heritage* XI (Fall 1985): 26–31.

Ciulla, Joanne. *The Working Life: The Promise and Betrayal of Modern Work.* New York: Random, 2000.

Clark, Norman. *Deliver Us From Evil: An Interpretation of American Prohibition.* New York: Norton, 1976.

Cochran, Thomas. *The Pabst Brewing Company: The History of an American Business.* New York: New York University Press, 1948.

Cohn, Jeffrey. "Pottsville Population Dips More Slowly." *Pottsville Republican / Evening Herald* 14 March 2001: 1ff.

Coleman, James Walter. *The Molly Maguire Riots: Industrial Conflict in the Pennsylvania Coal Region.* Richmond: Garrett and Massie, 1936.

Colvin, Leigh. *Prohibition in the United States.* New York: George Doran, 1926.

Corr, John. "Born to Brew." *Philadelphia Inquirer*, 14 January 1993: D6ff.

Davenport, Walter. *Power and Glory: The Life of Boies Penrose* (1931). New York: AMS, 1969.

Davies, Edward. *The Anthracite Aristocracy: Leadership and Social Change in the Hard Coal Regions of Northeastern Pennsylvania, 1800–1930.* DeKalb: Northern Illinois University Press, 1985.

Dochter, Rich, and Rich Wagner. "Brewerytown, U.S.A." *Pennsylvania Heritage* 17.3 (1991): 24–31.

Downard, William. *The Cincinnati Brewing Industry: A Social and Economic History.* Cincinnati: Ohio University Press, 1973.

_____. *Dictionary of the History of the American Brewing and Distilling Industries.* Westport, Conn.: Greenwood, 1980.

Dublin, Thomas. *When the Mines Closed: Stories of Struggles in Hard Times.* Ithaca, N. Y.: Cornell University Press, 1998.

Duis, Perry. *The Saloon: Public Drinking in Chicago and Boston, 1880–1920* (1983). Chicago: University of Illinois Press, 1999.

Eckhardt, Joseph. *The King of the Movies: Film Pioneer Siegmund Lubin*. Madison: Fairleigh Dickinson University Press, 1997

Elliot, Sarah Florence. "Immigration to Pennsylvania, 1860–1920." Master's thesis. University Press: Pennsylvania State University, 1923.

Ensslen, Klaus. "German-American Working-Class Saloons in Chicago: Their Social Function in an Ethnic and Class-Specific Cultural Context." *German Workers' Culture in the United States 1850 to 1920*. Helmut Keil, ed. Washington: Smithsonian Institution Press, 1988: 157–180.

Farr, Finis. *John O'Hara: A Biography*. Boston: Little, Brown and Company, 1973.

Farro, John. "Letter to the Editor." *Pottsville Republican*, 16 October 2003: 5.

Filippelli, Ronald. "Pottsville: Boomtown." *Historical Review of Berks County* 35.4 (1970): 126ff.

Foote, Andrea. "Hearth and heritage." *Beverage World* 121.1719, 15 October 2002: 38ff.

"Frank D. Yuengling Dies; President Of Brewery Since 1914." *Pottsville Republican*, 29 January 1963: 1ff.

Gallagher, F. N. *The Only Western Town in the East*. Ardmore, Pa.: Dorrance, 1980.

Gillespie, Angus. *Folklorist of the Coal Fields: George Korson's Life and Work*. State College, Pennsylvania: The Pennsylvania State University Press, 1980.

Gogola, Tom. "Bar Necessity: Is Long-lost Yuengling Beer — once a Local Cult Favorite — returning to New York?" *New York* 32.23: 14.

Greene, Victor. *The Slavic Community on Strike: Immigrant Labor in Pennsylvania*. Notre Dame, Ind.: University of Notre Dame Press, 1968.

Gudelunas, William. "Nativism and the Demise of Schuylkill County Whiggery: Anti-Slavery or Anti-Catholicism." *Pennsylvania History* (1978): 225–36.

_____, and Stephen Couch. "The Stolen Championship of the Pottsville Maroons: A Case Study in the Emergence of Modern Professional Football." *Journal of Sports History* 9.1 (Spring 1982): 53–64.

_____, and William Shade. *Before the Molly Maguires: The Emergence of the Ethno-Religious Factor in the Politics of the Lower Anthracite Region, 1844–1872*. New York: Arno, 1976.

Hanna, Susan, and Michael J. O'Malley. "America's Oldest Brewery: A Pictorial History." *Pennsylvania Heritage* (1980): 25–30.

Haydock, Helen, and Herb Haydock. *World of Beer Memorabilia*. Paducah, Ky.: Collector Books, 1997.

Hernon, Peter, and Terry Ganey. *Under the Influence: The Unauthorized Story of the Anheuser-Busch Dynasty*. New York: Simon and Schuster, 1994.

Hippler, Patricia. "Yuengling Announces Plans for New $50 Million Brewery." *Pottsville Republican*, 8 May 1998: 1ff.

_____. "Daughters' commitment led to investment." *Pottsville Republican*, 9 May 1998: 1ff.

Holihan, Timothy. *Over the Barrel: The Brewing History and Beer Culture of Cincinnati, 1800 to the Present*. Vol. 1. Saint Joseph, Miss.: Sudhaus Press, 2000.

Holt, Stephen. *Foreigners in Their Own Land*. University Park: The Pennsylvania State University Press, 2002.

Hornung, Clarence Pearson. *The American Eagle in Art and Design: 321 Examples*. New York: Dover, 1981.

Isaacson, Philip. *The American Eagle*. Boston: Little, Brown, and Company, 1975.

"It's still 'America's Oldest'." *Pottsville Republican*, 11 November 1998: 1ff.

Jackson, Michael. *The World Guide to Beer*. Englewood Cliffs, N. J.: Prentice-Hall, 1977.

Janosov, Robert. *Cold and Gold from the Poconos: A History of the Stegmaier Brewing Company, Wilkes-Barre, Pennsylvania*. Nanticoke, Pa.: Tres Canis Publishing, 1997.

Kann, Kenneth. "Working Class Culture and the Labor Movement in Nineteenth Century Chicago." Ph.D. thesis. Berkeley: University of California, 1977.

Kashatus, William. *Diamonds in the Coalfields: 21 Remarkable Baseball Players, Managers, and Umpires from Northeast*

Pennsylvania. Jefferson, NC: McFarland, 2002.

Kaylor, Earl. "The Prohibition Movement in Pennsylvania, 1865–1920." Ph.D. thesis. University Park: Pennsylvania State University, 1963.

Keil, Helmut, ed. *German Workers' Culture in the United States 1850 to 1920.* Washington: Smithsonian Institution Press, 1988.

Keller, Christian. "Germans in Civil War-era Pennsylvania: Ethnic Identity and the Problem of Americanization." Ph.D. thesis. University Park: Pennsylvania State University, 2001.

Kenny, Kevin. *Making Sense of the Molly Maguires.* New York: Oxford, 1998.

____. "Nativism, Labor, and Slavery: The Political Odyssey of Benjamin Bannan, 1850–1860." *Pennsylvania Magazine of History and Biography* 118.4 (October 1994): 325–361.

Kinney, David. "Oldest U.S. Brewery, Enjoying New Prosperity, Spurns Big Rivals' Offers." *Los Angeles Times*, 14 January 1997: 14.

Kislingbury, Roger. *Saloons — Bars — Cigar Stores: Historical Interior Photographs.* Pasadena, Calif.: Waldo and VanWinkle, 1999.

Klein, Maury. *The Life and Legend of Jay Gould.* Baltimore: Johns Hopkins University Press, 1986.

Kobler, John. *Ardent Spirits: The Rise and Fall of Prohibition.* New York: Putnam, 1973.

Korson, George. *Black Rock: Mining Folklore and the Pennsylvania Dutch.* Baltimore: Johns Hopkins University Press, 1960.

Kostka, William. *The Pre-prohibition History of Adolph Coors Company 1873–1933.* Golden, Co.: Adolph Coors Co., 1973.

Krebs, Roland. *Making Friends Is Our Business: 100 Years of Anheuser-Busch.* Saint Louis: Anheuser-Busch, Inc., 1953.

Lawton, Christopher. "Quirky Laws Give Yuengling Edge at Home." *Wall Street Journal*, 23 March 2004: B1.

Lee, Henry. *How Dry We Were: Prohibition Revisited.* Englewood Cliffs, N.J.: Prentice-Hall, 1963.

Lender, Mark, and James Martin. *Drinking in America: A History.* New York: Free Press, 1982.

"Liederkrantz Nears Diamond Jubilee." *History of Pottsville and Schuylkill County, Pennsylvania.* Joseph Henry Zerbey, ed. Pottsville: *Pottsville Republican*, 1933–1935: 162–65.

Lukas, Paul. "Ale in the Family: Family-run breweries — the few that remain — offer visitors a trip back in time." *Money* 29.3 (March 2000): 189–190.

Lynch, Charles, and John Loose. "A History of Brewing in Lancaster County, Legal and Otherwise." *Journal of the Lancaster County Historical Society* 70.1 (1966): 1–99.

MacShane, Frank. *The Life of John O'Hara.* New York: Dutton, 1980.

Martin, Asa Earl. "The Temperance Movement in Pennsylvania Prior to the Civil War." *Pennsylvania Magazine of History and Biography* 49 (1925): 195–230.

McBride, Paul. "Peter Roberts and the YMCA Americanization Program, 1907 — World War I." *Pennsylvania History* 44.2 (1977): 145–162.

McWilliams, Peter. *Ain't Nobody's Business If You Do: The Absurdity of Consensual Crimes in a Free Society.* Los Angeles: Prelude, 1993.

Merz, Charles. *The Dry Decade* (1930). Seattle: University of Washington Press, 1969.

Miller, Carl. *Breweries of Cleveland.* Cleveland: Schnitzelbank, 1998.

Miller, Donald, and Richard Sharpless. *The Kingdom of Coal: Work, Enterprise, and Ethnic Communities in the Mine Fields.* Philadelphia: University of Pennsylvania Press, 1985.

[Munsell and Co.]. *History of Schuylkill County, Pa. with Illustrations and Biographical Sketches of Some of its Prominent Men and Pioneers.* New York: W.W. Munsell Co, 1881.

Newlove, Donald. *Those Drinking Days: Myself and Other Writers.* New York: Horizon, 1981.

Newspaper Commemorating the 160th Anniversary of the Yuengling Brewery. Pottsville, Pa.: *Pottsville Republican*, 1989.

Nolan, J. Bennett. *The Schuylkill.* New Brunswick, N.J.: Rutgers University Press, 1951.

Nolt, Stephen. *Foreigners in Their Own Land: Pennsylvania Germans in the Early Republic.* University Park: Pennsylvania State University, 2002.

Norris, James. *Advertising and the Transformation of American Society, 1865–1920.* New York: Greenwood, 1990.

Nowak, Carl. *New Fields for Brewers and Others Active in the Fermentation and Allied Industries.* Saint Louis: C.A. Nowak, 1917.

O'Brien, Bill. "A golden anniversary: 50 years ago today the golden beverage returned to legal status." (Shenandoah) *Evening Herald* 7 April 1983: 10ff.

One Hundred Years of Brewing: A complete History of the Progress made in the Art, Science and Industry of Brewing in the New World, particularly during the Nineteenth Century (1903). New York: Arno, 1974.

Palladino, Grace. *Another Civil War: Labor, Capital, and the State in the Anthracite Regions of Pennsylvania, 1840–68.* Urbana: University of Illinois Press, 1990.

Park, Peter. "The Supply Side of Drinking: Alcohol Production and Consumption in the United States before Prohibition." *Contemporary Drug Problems* 12 (1985): 473–509.

Plavachan, Ronald Jan. *A History of Anheuser-Busch 1852–1933.* New York: Arno, 1976.

Pluta, Joseph E. *Regional Change in the U.S. Brewing Industry.* Austin: Bureau of Business Research, University of Texas at Austin, 1983.

Poet, Jonathan. "Nation's Oldest Brewer Sees Vat Possibilities." *Washington Post,* 6 January 2002: AO2.

"Pottsville Saloons of Days of Yore." *History of Pottsville and Schuylkill County, Pennsylvania.* Joseph Henry Zerbey, ed. Pottsville: *Pottsville Republican,* 1933–1935: 187–95.

Powers, Madelon. "Decay from Within: The Inevitable Doom of the American Saloon." *Drinking: Behavior and Belief in Modern History.* Susanna Barrows and Robin Room, eds. Berkeley: University of California Press, 1991: 112–131.

_____. *Faces Along the Bar: Lore and Order in the Workingman's Saloon, 1870–1920.* Chicago: University of Chicago Press, 1998.

Pytak, Stephen. "The Other Yuengling." *Pottsville Republican,* 18–19 December 1999: 1ff.

Reid, Peter V.K. "Forever Yuengling: America's Oldest Brewery is Building One of America's Newest Breweries, Right in Its Hometown of Pottsville, PA." *Modern Brewery Age,* 25 January 1999: 8–11.

"The Roaming Keg of Beer: From Pottsville to Chicago Via Wheelbarrow." *Publications of the Historical Society of Schuylkill County* 7.2 (1958): 65–69.

Roberts, James. "Drink and Industrial Work Discipline in 19th Century Germany." *Journal of Social History* 15 (Fall 1981): 25–38.

Roberts, Peter. *Anthracite Coal Communities.* (1904). New York: Arno, 1970.

_____. *The Anthracite Coal Industry: A Study of the Economic Conditions and Relations of the Cooperative Forces in the Development of the Anthracite Coal Industry of Pennsylvania.* New York: Macmillan, 1901.

_____. *Immigrant Races in North America.* New York: The Young Men's Christian Association Press, 1910.

_____. *The New Immigration: A Study of the Industrial and Social Life of Southeastern Europeans in America.* New York: Macmillan, 1912.

_____. "The Saloon in the Anthracite Coal Fields." *Charities* XV (1906): 691–93.

_____. "The Sclavs in Anthracite Coal Communities." *Charities* XIII (1904): 215–22.

Roberts, Richard. "John O'Hara: The Child Becomes the Man." *Pennsylvania Heritage* 19.2, (1993): 4–9.

Ronnenberg, Herman W. *The Politics of Assimilation: The Effect of Prohibition on the German Americans.* New York: Carlton Press, 1975.

Rorabaugh, W. J. *The Alcoholic Republic.* New York: Oxford University Press, 1979.

Rowbottom, James. "Brewery still biggest draw." *Pottsville Republican,* 5 January 1998: 1ff.

_____. "For Norbert, It Was in the Blood." *Pottsville Republican,* 23 January 1999: 1ff.

____. "Yuengling workers toast retiring brewmaster." *Pottsville Republican*, 23 January 1999: 1ff.

Rudin, Max. "Beer and America." *American Heritage* 53.3 (2002): 28–38.

Rumbarger, John. *Profits, Power, and Prohibition: Alcohol Reform and the Industrializing of America, 1800–1930*. Albany: State University of New York Press, 1989.

Salem, Frederick William. *Beer, Its History and Its Economic Value as a National Beverage* 1880. New York: Arno, 1972.

Sanchez, Michael. "Familiar Yuengling Eagle Already Visible at New Site." *Pottsville Republican / Evening Herald*, 19 May 1999: 1ff.

Schalck, Adolf and Hon. D.C. Henning, eds. *History of Schuylkill County, Pennsylvania: ... including a Genealogical and Biographical Record of Many Families and Persons in the County*. Madison, Wis.: State Historical Association, 1907.

Schuler, Rory. "A History Steeped in Booze." *Pottsville Free Press*, 25 November 2003: 1ff.

Schuylkill County: Scenes and Profiles, 1810 Through 1960s. Schuylkill Haven, Pa.: Pennsylvania State University, Schuylkill Campus, 1992.

Schwarz, Benjamin, and Christina Schwarz. "John O'Hara's Protectorate." *Atlantic Monthly*, (March 2000): 108–12.

Severo, Richard. "Roseland Recalls Old Times Tonight." *New York Times*, 1 July 1974: 42.

Siebel, John, and Anton Schwartz. *History of the Brewing Industry and Brewing Science in America*. Chicago: G.L. Peterson, 1933.

Sinclair, Andrew. *Prohibition: The Era of Excess*. Boston: Little, Brown and Co., 1962.

Smith, Gregg. *Beer in America: The Early Years: 1587–1840*. Boulder, Colo.: Siris, 1998.

Sophy, Joshua. "Dick Yuengling, Schuylkill life a fit." *Pottsville Republican*, 25 May 2002: 1+.

Stivers, Richard. *Hair of the Dog: Irish Drinking and Its American Stereotype* (1976). New York: Continuum, 2000.

Strange, Charles. *Mountain Majesties: A Historical Novel Set in Schuylkill County, Pennsylvania in the Decade of 1927–1937*. Pottsville, Pa.: J.F. Seiders Printers, 1996.

Straub, Gary. *Collectible Beer Trays*. Atglen, Pa.: Schiffer, 1995.

Sweet, William Warren. *The Story of Religion in America*. New York: Harper and Bros., 1950.

Thompson, Peter. *Rum Punch and Revolution: Taverngoing & Public Life in Eighteenth-Century Philadelphia*. Philadelphia: University of Pennsylvania Press, 1999.

Turner, Ford. "For Hard Coal, Hard Times." *Harrisburg Patriot-News*, 28 March 2004: 1ff.

Turner, George Kibbe. "Beer and the City Liquor Problem." *McClure's* 33 (1909): 528–543.

Tyrrell, Ian. *Sobering Up: From Temperance to Prohibition in Antebellum America, 1800–1860*. Westport, Conn.: Greenwood, 1979.

Van Munching, Philip. *Beer Blast: The Inside Story of the Brewing Industry's Bizarre Battles for Your Money*. New York: Random House, 1997.

Van Wieren, Dale P. *American Breweries II*. West Point, Pa.: Eastern Coast Brew[er]iana Association, 1995.

Wagner, Rich. "Lauer's Brewery, Circa 1874." *Zymurgy*, Summer (1983): 24–27.

Wallace, Anthony. *St. Clair: A Nineteenth Century Coal Town's Experience with a Disaster-Prone Industry*. New York: Knopf, 1987.

Ward, Leo, and Mark Major. *Images of America: Pottsville*. Charleston, SC: Arcadia, 1995.

Warne, Frank Julian. *The Slav Invasion and the Mine Workers: A Study in Immigration* (1904). New York: J.S. Ozer, 1971.

Weeks, Morris. *Beer and Brewing in America*. New York: United States Brewers Foundation, 1949.

Wiegand, Harold J. "Prohibition: A Date in History Better Forgotten." *Philadelphia Inquirer*, 28 November 1983: 11–A.

Wiley, Samuel. *Biographical and Portrait Cyclopedia of Schuylkill County, Pennsylvania*. Philadelphia: Rush West and Co., 1893.

Wilhelm, William. "Letter to the Editor." *New York Times*, 22 May 1925: 18.

Wilson, George. "State Liquor Laws Go Back to the '30s." *Philadelphia Inquirer*, 23 September 1983: 19–A.

Wines, Frederic, and John Koren. *The Liquor Problem in Its Legislative Aspects*. 2nd ed. Boston: Houghton Mifflin, 1898.

Wokeck, Marianne. *Trade in Strangers: The Beginnings of Mass Migration to North America*. University Park: Pennsylvania University Press, 1999.

Wolff, Geoffrey. *The Art of Burning Bridges: A Life of John O'Hara*. New York: Knopf, 2003.

Yearley, C. K., Jr. *Enterprise and Anthracite: Economics and Democracy in Schuylkill County, 1820–1875*. Baltimore: Johns Hopkins Press, 1961.

Yuengling, David. *Letters to an Unknown Generation*. Hicksville, NY: Exposition Press, 1979.

Yuengling, Edith. "The Story of the Yuengling Brewery" (1957). *Publications of the Historical Society of Schuylkill County* 9.1 (1989): 38–53.

"Yuengling is still 'Oldest.'" *Pottsville Republican*, 13 November 1998: 4.

Zerbey, Joseph Henry, ed. *History of Pottsville and Schuylkill County, Pennsylvania*. Pottsville: *Pottsville Republican*, 1933–1935.

Index

*Numbers in **boldface** refer to illustrations.*

217